INEQUALITY IN RURAL EUROPE

CORN PUBLICATION SERIES 18

Inequality in rural Europe

(Late Middle Ages – 18th century)

Edited by
GUIDO ALFANI and ERIK THOEN

BREPOLS

All authors publishing in the CORN Series have been invited by the editors. All articles are intensively discussed at preparatory meetings, reviewed by the book editors and double blind peer reviewed by external reviewers.

D/2020/0095/242
ISBN 978-972-503-59052-3
E-ISBN 978-972-503-59053-0
DOI 10.1484/M.CORN-EB.5.120837

ISSN 1780-3225
E-ISSN 2565-9413

Printed in the EU on acid-free paper.

CONTENTS

LIST OF CONTRIBUTORS

Guido ALFANI	Department of Social and Political Sciences, Bocconi University, Milan, Italy
Pinar CEYLAN	Department of Economics & Department of History, Ghent University, Belgium
Davide CRISTOFERI	Department of History, Ghent University, Belgium
Daniel CURTIS	Erasmus University of Rotterdam, Department of History, The Netherlands
Matteo DI TULLIO	Department of Social and Political Sciences, Bocconi University, Milan, Italy
Andreia FIDALGO	Departamento de Arte, Humanidades, Universidade do Algarve and CIES-IUL, Portugal
Thijs LAMBRECHT	Department of History, Ghent University, Belgium
Esteban NICOLINI	Department of Economics, Universidad Carlos III de Madrid, Spain
Fernando RAMOS-PALENCIA	Universidad Pablo de Olavide, Sevilla, España
Wouter RYCKBOSCH	Department of History, Vrije Universiteit Brussels, Belgium
Erik THOEN	Department of History, Ghent University, Belgium

LIST OF FIGURES

LIST OF TABLES

GUIDO ALFANI, ERIK THOEN

1 Economic inequality in rural Europe: an introduction

Studies of inequality in preindustrial European societies have multiplied in recent years. This is partly the consequence of novel and exciting research questions that can be answered only on the basis of historical evidence, and partly of the high social relevance that inequality studies have acquired. Regarding the second point, it is quite clear that the Great Recession that started in 2008, and the related events, contributed to heighten the perception of inequality across society as well as to make it a hot topic of political debate. The first point (the new, exciting research questions) is obviously connected to the second, if one thinks of the huge impact that Thomas Piketty's book, *Capital in the Twenty-First Century*, has had on public debates (Piketty 2014). Piketty's study was mostly concerned with the industrial and post-industrial era, but it soon became clear that pressing questions about the historical trends of both income and wealth inequality, as well as about the factors that induce the growth or decline of inequality over time, could be answered only by taking into account preindustrial times as well. Very soon, the quickly-expanding literature on modern inequality merged with the few works that, before Piketty, had been investigating the connection between economic growth and increased inequality in preindustrial Europe (Van Zanden 1995; Alfani 2010a; 2015) as well as with a growing number of new studies aimed at providing more abundant and more reliable information about inequality in medieval and early modern times. Restricting the picture to Europe, such works covered (in country alphabetical order) Britain (Lindert 2000; Broadberry et al. 2015; Allen 2019), Finland (Bengtsson et al. 2018), Germany (Alfani, Gierok and Schaff 2020; Wegge 2018), Italy (Alfani 2010a; 2015; 2017; Alfani and Ammannati 2017; Alfani and Di Tullio 2019), the Low Countries (Hanus 2013; Ryckbosch 2016; Alfani and Ryckbosch 2016), Poland (Malinowski and Van Zanden 2016), Portugal (Reis 2017), Spain (Santiago-Caballero 2011; Fernández and Santiago-Caballero 2013; Nicolini and Ramos Palencia 2016a; 2016b; García-Montero 2015), and Sweden (Bengtsson et al. 2017).

Many of the above-mentioned studies tried to move beyond the cities and to cover rural inequality as well. It is clear, however, that in relative terms the urban distribution of income and wealth remains much better known compared

Guido Alfani • Bocconi University, Dondena Centre and IGIER

Erik Thoen • Ghent University

Inequality in rural Europe (Late Middle Ages – 18th century), ed. by Guido Alfani and Erik Thoen, CORN, 18 (Turnhout, 2020), pp. 13–24.

 DOI 10.1484/M.CORN-EB.5.122501

to the rural. This book intends to reduce this gap in knowledge, bringing rural inequality to the fore of current research. Maybe a bit paradoxically, in some sense this is a return to the past – as distribution of assets in rural areas attracted a lot of research in the 1960s and the 1970s. In part, this reflected a broader interest in the history of the rural areas, based on the 'democratic' argument that in preindustrial societies the vast majority of the population lived outside cities and these rural dwellers were mostly peasants (think for example of the many seminal studies from the French *Annales* school, some of which also focused on inequality, like the work of Le Roy Ladurie 1966). Often these also reflected political beliefs and a scholarly focus on the historical development of social classes – and on changes in the relative ability of each class to control the means of production (chief among them, in rural societies, was obviously the land). National historical schools focusing on class distribution of wealth tended to be influenced by Marxism and were to be found across Europe, for example in Germany (for a synthesis, see Sreenivasan 2013). In England, this line of research resulted in the well-known 'Brenner's debate' (Brenner 1976; Aston et al. 1987). In Italy, which as it is well known used to be the western European country with the strongest communist party, the Marxist school of economic history was particularly strong as well – and interestingly, it was also particularly focused on studying the distribution of land across time (compare for example Porisini 1963; Rotelli 1966. For a brief synthesis of this literature, Alfani 2014: 63-65). Unfortunately, this Italian school (as well as its equivalents in other countries) tended to aggregate data per class, often adopting somewhat questionable definitions of 'class', hence imposing an a priori criterium to the wealth distributions they reconstructed. Consequently, the published results from the European Marxist historical schools are often not usable, or are only partly useful, for studies of household distributions of wealth (Cf. Alfani 2017 for further discussion). In some countries, local research traditions developed whose scholarly interests and scientific approach led to produce information that is more in line with today's prevailing approaches. This is the case, for example, of the German Historical School of economics, active from the late nineteenth to the early twentieth century (see Alfani, Gierok and Schaff 2020 for details). These are, however, exceptions: most of the information currently available to our scientific objectives are the output of very recent research, as clearly shown, for different parts of the continent, by the chapters collected in this book.

But what are our scientific objectives? First and foremost to produce reliable and comparable information about household-level distribution of income and wealth. In contrast to many older studies, the preferred unit of analysis today is the household (note that very rarely would it be possible to focus on individual-level distributions, given the intrinsic characteristics of medieval and early modern historical sources). Beyond being coherent with the kind of information available for modern-day societies, this approach also gives us extra flexibility: as household-level (or individual-level) information about income or economic assets is precisely what we need to estimate the vast majority of indicators of inequality or social polarization. Extra information related to each household (for example, about the sex of the household head, her/his occupation, or even her/his 'class') only gives us extra flexibility in analysing the data. Based on this, European teams are currently pursuing a range of different research avenues – but all of them have something in common: a renewed interest in distribution. This was not only Marx's concern, but a crucial research topic for all classical economists, beginning with Adam Smith (see Alfani 2020). After many decades of relative neglect, this is again a need highly felt across the social sciences. As Tomas Piketty argued, "[we should place the] study of distribution and of the long-run back at the center of economic thinking" (Piketty 2015: 68). The studies collected by this book intend to provide much-needed fuel to sustain these renewed debates – to which they add their own pressing research questions, as briefly discussed in the following.

* * *

What is the contribution to current debates of the chapters in this book dealing with inequality in rural areas? The reasons to focus on economic inequality in rural areas go much beyond the relative lack of good-quality information which has been discussed above. Indeed, the point could be made that without a decent knowledge of inequality levels in the countryside, it would be impossible to get even a glimpse of the overall inequality of a region, let alone a whole state. Additionally, looking at the rural areas is crucial when trying to identify the underlying causes of inequality trends in the long run of history – an aspect which has been the object of particularly intense debate in recent years.

Related to the first point, there are two aspects to consider. First, which were the trends followed by inequality in rural areas? And secondly, how large were the urban-rural wealth differentials (measured for example as the ratio of the average household wealth of urban and rural dwellers)? Inequality in rural areas is highly relevant to current debates because many explanations of long-term distributive changes tend to look at the impact of growing urbanization, and sometimes at the interaction between city and country. But first, we need to know about the situation in the rural areas *per se*. A general finding, which comes from a relatively large number of studies and consequently can be considered one of few well-established 'stylized facts' about preindustrial inequality, is that rural communities tended to be less unequal than cities. This finding had already been reported, for Tuscany in 1427, by David Herlihy (1968; 1978), a pioneer in the study of medieval inequality. Although Herlihy did not provide us with precise measures of wealth concentration, like the Gini index (which varies from the level 0, or perfect equality, to 1, or perfect inequality: all the wealth is owned by a single household), in his study of the village of Santa Maria Impruneta in the Florentine *contado* he underlined the fact that the share of wealth owned by the poorest 50% of the population was more than double in the countryside compared to the city of Florence (6% versus 2.7%) (Herlihy 1968, 259). These tentative conclusions were recently confirmed by Alfani and Ammannati (2017: 1085). For the Florentine *contado*, they found that around 1450 the Gini index of wealth inequality for rural communities ranged from 0.429 to 0.523 in villages, versus the 0.600 found in the city of Arezzo, or the 0.683 of Prato. These authors reported similar differences for other parts of Tuscany, like the territories of Pistoia and Livorno. Again for Tuscany in the same period, Davide Cristoferi in his contribution to this book reports a Gini of 0.57 for the Tuscan village of San Giovanni in Petroio.

Findings for Tuscany in the fifteenth century have been confirmed for other Italian regions and periods, from Piedmont in the northwest (Alfani 2015) to Apulia in the southeast (Alfani and Sardone 2015). Alfani and Di Tullio's chapter in this book provides further support, based on data for the Republic of Venice in north-eastern Italy. For example, in the province of Padua, around 1600 the Gini index of wealth inequality was 0.728 in the rural areas and 0.788 in the cities. Around 1700, the difference in inequality levels remained significant (0.747 in rural areas versus 0.799 in cities). One century later, the distance between the two had reduced only marginally (0.799 versus 0.747). Outside Italy, the finding that preindustrial rural villages were, at least from the fourteenth century onwards, more egalitarian than cities has recently been confirmed for Germany (Alfani, Gierok and Schaff 2020), Sweden (Bengtsson et al. 2017), and Portugal (Reis 2017). Also for Portugal, Andreia Fidalgo in her contribution to this book reports income inequality around 0.65 Gini points for some rural communities in the Algarve region during the eighteenth century, considerably lower than that reported for cities like Guarda (0.74) or Porto (0.7) (although the information underlying these estimates is not perfectly comparable). Particularly abundant information about the relative inequality levels between city and country has been provided by Esteban Nicolini and Fernando Ramos Palencia (2016a) for Castille (Spain) around 1750. They provide further details in their contribution to this book, confirming the pattern reported above. For example, in the province of Palencia the concentration of land (which in a mostly agrarian context can be taken as a rough proxy for overall wealth) was 0.990 for the city, while for the settlements below 1,000 inhabitants it ranged from 0.400 to 0.823. For this part of Europe, it is also possible to get some information about income inequality. This was 0.607 in the city of Palencia, while in the villages with less than 1,000 inhabitants it ranged from 0.289 to 0.600. Some information about relative income inequality in city and country is available also for the northern Low Countries. Jan Luiten Van Zanden (1995: 653) reported a Gini index of 0.35 in the countryside of Holland in 1561, growing to 0.38 in 1732. In the cities, at both dates the Gini index was much higher (0.52 and 0.59 respectively).

Holland is also one of the very few European areas for which we can get a glimpse of long-term changes in the levels of economic inequality in the countryside. Although this Dutch trend is based on two dates only (see above), the impression we get is one of growing income inequality during the early modern period. In a very tentative way, the same trend has been proposed for the southern Low Countries as well (Alfani and Ryckbosch 2016: Appendix D, Figure D7). Wouter Ryckbosch, in his contribution to this book, provides further information about inequality in land ownership (taken as a proxy of wealth inequality) and in land use (taken as a proxy of income inequality) in sixteenth-century Flanders. For the area immediately south of Flanders, northern Hainault, Thijs Lambrecht delivers new data documenting an increasing inequality from the late fifteenth to the mid-sixteenth century. For Portugal, Jaime Reis (2017: 309) reported rural income inequality growth between 1565 and 1700, possibly followed by decline until 1770. For other parts of Europe, more solid information exists for wealth inequality. A range of regional studies has reported a protracted tendency for growing rural wealth inequality in early modern times. For example, in the Sabaudian State in north-western Italy (the region roughly corresponding to nowadays Piedmont) the Gini index for rural areas grew from 0.586 in 1500, to 0.655 in 1600, 0.695 in 1700 and 0.781 in 1800 (Alfani 2015). The same trend has been reported for the rural areas of the Republic of Venice in north-eastern Italy and of the Florentine State in central Italy (Alfani and Ryckbosch 2016; Alfani and Ammannati 2017). In their contribution to this book, Alfani and Di Tullio compare directly the trends of these Italian pre-unification states (see their Figure 4.4) and provide additional details. A partly different case is that of Germany: while the overall tendency for growing inequality in rural areas in early modern times is confirmed, a phase of temporary decline in rural (and urban) inequality has also been reported, triggered by the exceptional conditions created by the Thirty Year's War (1618-1648) in association with the terrible plague of 1627-1629 (Alfani, Gierok and Schaff 2020).

Almost all recent studies dealing with inequality, including those published in this book, begin their analyses no earlier than the late fourteenth century. In order to find better explanations for the inequality trends reported for that century (which were heavily influenced by the Black Death: see below) studies about the previous period of growth, often labelled 'Great Reclamation Period', would have been very useful. Unfortunately, the resources for that period are very scarce – but they do exist, at least for some regions, often dating back to the second half of the thirteenth century. However, these sources often require different competences and scientific approaches compared to the documentation available for later periods. Here too, ample space remains for future research.

Catastrophe-induced reduction in inequality has been the object of considerable recent research (Alfani and Murphy 2017; Scheidel 2017). However, it should be noticed that in European history, from the Middle Ages until the end of the early modern period, the only catastrophe that seems to have been capable of producing long-lasting egalitarian consequences is the Black Death that affected the continent during 1347-1352. Indeed, the fact that the last great plagues in the seventeenth century, the worst of which affected Southern

Europe on a scale not very dissimilar from the Black Death (compare Alfani and Murphy 2017), *did not* produce the same consequences is something as worthy of specific research as the distributive consequences of the Black Death (Alfani and Di Tullio 2017; Alfani 2020). Germany was the notable exception at the time of the seventeenth-century plagues, probably due to the combination of an exceptionally severe epidemic with the most destructive war in the history of early modern Europe. Daniel Curtis' contribution to this book provides further discussion and evidence supporting the argument that we need to be very careful about making a-priori assumptions about the ultimate distributive consequences of epidemics and other large-scale catastrophes like, for example, floods that have received considerable attention in the last few years (Curtis 2016; van Bavel, Curtis and Soens 2018). For the purposes of this introduction, it will suffice to add that in the particularly rare instances when we have information about rural inequality before and after the Black Death, almost invariably we find significant inequality decline. This is the case, for example, of Tuscany which is probably the world region for which we have the best historical sources to study distributive dynamics in the aftermath of that terrible pandemic (Alfani and Ammannati 2017).

The distributive consequences of large-scale catastrophes feature quite prominently in current debates about the causes of inequality change in preindustrial times. Before focusing on these debates, however, we need to briefly cover a final aspect: the large urban-rural wealth differentials that characterized early modern Europe. While the existence of such differentials is a well-known feature of European (and non-European) preindustrial societies, recent attempts at estimating inequality at a regional level have led to the necessity of measuring such differentials more systematically than was common in the past – essentially because they are a source of inequality *between* city and country, itself an important component of overall regional- or state-level inequality. Such differentials were quite steep. For example, in the Florentine state rural households were found to be between 20 and 30% as wealthy as urban households throughout the period 1450-1750 (Alfani and Ryckbosch 2016: Appendix D). In the same period, rural households in the Republic of Venice were found to be about 20% as wealthy as urban households (Alfani and Di Tullio 2019: 188).

The fact that overall, inequality in rural areas was found to grow almost everywhere from at least the end of the fifteenth century, and that a large urban-rural wealth differential existed, has a number of consequences for the current debates about the causes of inequality change – and provides further motivation to expand the still-inadequate amount of information we have available for rural areas by means of new archival research. Consider for example those explanations that look at growing urbanization rates as the cause of widespread inequality growth, both per se (due to 'Kuznetsian' dynamics) and because urbanization growth can be taken as indicative of economic growth. Kuznetsian dynamics were recalled, in a very effective way, by Van Zanden in his seminal article of 1995: "[As i]n early modern Europe urban incomes were without doubt higher than those in the countryside", then "The gradual urbanization that typified ... [early modern Europe] probably contributed to a rise in income inequality through the mechanism described by Kuznets" (Van Zanden 1995: 656), that is simply by the transfer of population (or workforce) from the country to the city. This line of reasoning, introduced for income, can obviously be applied to wealth as well, given the existence of the enrooted urban-rural wealth differentials documented above.

Urbanization-based Kuznetsian dynamics, however, seem to be inadequate as a general explanation for preindustrial inequality trends, for two reasons. First, because empirically we find that changes in urbanization rates do not predict changes in inequality, either of income or of wealth (see Alfani and Di Tullio 2019; Alfani 2020 for a detailed discussion). Second, and more importantly for this book, because they could not easily explain the fact that rural areas were themselves experiencing growing inequality. To be precise, these rural dynamics could not be explained by growing urbanization, unless by imposing pretty strong assumptions about the nature of migration from rural areas to cities (generally speaking, this would require assuming that only the middling rural groups migrated to the cities, leaving the poorest and the richest to reside in the rural areas). Interestingly, this line of reasoning points directly towards a gaping hole in our knowledge of preindustrial inequality: how the many forms of migration that, as we now know, were a constant of European preindustrial societies, affected inequality dynamics and contributed to shape the observed trends (note that before the so-called Demographic Transition of the nineteenth century and the associated reduction in mortality, cities could not have existed without a constant influx of rural population). Unfortunately, studying directly these processes requires micro-level data over time and across large territories (at the very minimum, a city and the surrounding countryside) that are extremely difficult to find for any European region (the rare example so far is the district of Ivrea in northwestern Italy: Alfani 2009; 2010a; 2010b). Consequently, we remain in the dark about these potentially crucial processes, and any new study able to explore them would be particularly useful to advance our knowledge.

As mentioned above, urbanization levels are often used as a rough proxy for relative levels of economic development. From this point of view, they are an alternative measure compared to others, like estimates of per-capita GDP. The availability of the latter has been steadily growing over the last few years, as well as their quality (although for the earlier periods they remain highly hypothetical). However, the currently-available estimates of per-capita GDP do not prove better than urbanization rates at predicting changes in preindustrial inequality. Consequently, the case has been made that based on the available information, economic growth could not be taken as a general explanation for inequality growth in preindustrial Europe (see Alfani 2020 for further discussion). Recently, Bas Van Bavel (2016) also argued for a connection between economic growth and inequality growth, although making less strong assumptions and without embracing the 'optimistic' positions typical of a large part of this literature. For Van Bavel, inequality started to rise in association with growing prosperity coming from the development of market economies, but soon enough this tended to be followed by a phase of "increasing social polarization, institutional sclerosis, markets that become increasingly skewed towards the interest of market elites, and economic growth stagnating" (Van Bavel 2016: 251). While this position undoubtedly has greater potential for explaining rising inequality in the absence of economic growth (a nasty combination which has now been reported for many European areas in different historical periods), some doubts remain about its generalizability beyond the specific cases selected by Van Bavel.

Recent research has explored many other potential explanations for inequality growth in preindustrial societies. Proletarianization has attracted considerable attention (for example, Ryckbosch, 2016; Alfani and Ryckbosch 2016). The concept of proletarianization is connected to the Marxist tradition of economic history mentioned above, and refers to the process leading many European small-owners to lose the ownership of the means of production and to start selling their labour for wages. However, in European history proletarianization tended to come in waves triggered by large-scale crises (Tilly 1984), hence it does not seem very well-suited to explain the monotonically-growing trends in inequality usually found across Europe (see the chapter by Alfani and Di Tullio for additional discussion of proletarianization). More recently, the focus has shifted towards institutions and political systems, often reframing earlier Marxist analyses from a 'new institutional' perspective. Walter Scheidel (2017) for example has pointed at the highly uneven distribution of political power (and of coercive force) as the ultimate origin of a perennial tendency towards inequality growth (except for 'egalitarian' phases following large-scale, even civilization-destroying catastrophes). Other scholars have tried to illuminate how institutional developments typical of specific periods and areas were able to continuously fuel the growth of inequality. For early modern Europe, it has been argued that the rise of the fiscal-military state had particularly important consequences, given that it was associated with large increases in the per-capita fiscal pressure (independently from whether the economy of a given country was growing or stagnating) in the context of overall regressive fiscal systems (Thoen and Soens 2008; Alfani 2015; Alfani and Ryckbosch 2016; Alfani and Di Tullio 2019). In the presence of a regressive fiscal system, post-tax inequality is automatically higher than pre-tax inequality, and increases in per-capita taxation only increased the power of the State to produce more inequality over time – mostly to the advantage of the ruling elites. This was especially true when a public system of poor relief was absent or very limited, as was the case in most areas in preindustrial times. Importantly, across Europe one major source of fiscal regressiveness was the disadvantaged situation (in terms of heavier taxation per unit of income or wealth) suffered by rural dwellers compared to urban dwellers. Alfani and Di Tullio's chapter in this book discusses in this light the example of the Republic of Venice, while Ceylan's chapter offers interesting details about the re-distributive (and surplus-extracting) character of the Ottoman institutional framework(s) in the sixteenth century. Finally, Nicolini and Ramos Palencia's contribution underlines the many elements of regressiveness characterizing taxation in the Crown of Castile – although in the mid-eighteenth century, a valiant (but ultimately doomed) attempt at establishing a regime of proportional taxation was made, in the form of the Ensenada Cadastre. Interestingly, a few years later the aim of reducing the overall burdens weighing on the peasants was pursued in Portugal as well, by means of the encompassing economic reforms introduced by the Marquis of Pombal in the 1760s and 1770s, as detailed in Fidalgo's chapter. Unfortunately for the peasants, local elites proved quite effective in preventing the actual application of the reforms – although there is also evidence that they were at least partially successful.

The overview presented so far is not meant to be an exhaustive account, but simply to give an idea of the scope of current research on preindustrial rural inequality. And surely, the points that have been mentioned above do not cover all the interesting aspects that are currently being developed, including by scholars contributing to this volume. So for example, Curtis' chapter reminds us that the catastrophes' redistributive consequences went much beyond their impact on wealth, income, or wages – but also affected access to the commons and the ways to manage them, or the balance of power between the sexes. Cristoferi underlines the importance of agrarian contracts, especially when, as in the case of the *mezzadria* widespread in many Italian areas, they led to significant divergence between formal ownership of land and actual economic use of the land. Hence changes in time in the diffusion of the *mezzadria* had distributional consequences of their own that would surely be worthy of additional study. A similar point (about the importance of leasehold) is made by Ryckbosch about Flanders in the sixteenth century, elaborating on previous research by Thoen and Soens (2015). In Flanders, changes in the mix of peasant land ownership and leasehold seem to have been a major factor in defining changes in inequality levels across the region. For the same area, however, Lambrechts shows in his chapter that differences in inequality between the rural commercially-oriented coastal region on the one hand, and the inland areas with a majority of 'commercial' peasants on the other hand, was less pronounced around 1500 than assumed by earlier research. Finally, the role played by institutional design – especially by the structures of rights and privileges of different social-economic categories, by the way in which the fiscal systems was designed and organized, and by the interaction between different levels of government – features quite prominently in many of the contributions collected in this book: but none more than in Ceylan's chapter on the Ottoman Empire during the sixteenth century, which raises a number of relevant research questions about the comparative distributive consequences of the varying institutional frameworks prevalent in different parts of Europe, or of the world. But this is not, again, an exhaustive compendium, and to do justice to our authors' work, we cannot but invite the reader to move on to the next chapter.

Bibliography

Alfani, G. (2009), 'Prima della curva di Kuznets: dinamiche della ricchezza tra Medioevo ed Età Moderna' in: G. Afani, M. Barbot (eds) *Ricchezza, valore, proprietà in Età preindustriale. 1400-1850*, Venezia 2009, pp. 143-167.

Alfani, G. (2010a) 'The effects of plague on distribution of property: Ivrea, Northern Italy 1630', *Population Studies*, 64, pp. 61-75.

Alfani, G. (2010b) 'Wealth inequalities and population dynamics in early modern Northern Italy', *Journal of Interdisciplinary History*, 40, pp. 513-549.

Alfani, G. (2014) 'Back to the peasants: new insights into the economic, social, and demographic history of northern Italian rural populations during the Early Modern period', *History Compass*, 12, 1, pp. 62-71.

Alfani, G. (2015), 'Economic inequality in northwestern Italy: A long-term view (fourteenth to eighteenth centuries)', *The Journal of Economic History*, 75, 4, pp. 1058-1096.

Alfani, G. (2017), 'The rich in historical perspective: evidence for preindustrial Europe (ca. 1300-1800)', *Cliometrica*, 11, 3, pp. 321-348.

Alfani, G. (2020), 'Economic inequality in preindustrial times: Europe and beyond', *Journal of Economic Literature*, forthcoming.

Alfani, G. and F. Ammannati (2017), 'Long-term trends in economic inequality: the case of the Florentine State, *c.* 1300-1800', *Economic History Review*, 70, 4, pp. 1072-1102.

Alfani, G. and M. Di Tullio (2019), *The Lion's Share. Inequality and the Rise of the Fiscal State in Preindustrial Europe*, Cambridge.

Alfani, G., V. Gierok and F. Schaff (2020), 'Economic inequality in preindustrial Germany: a long-run view (fourteenth to nineteenth centuries)', Stone Center Working Paper Series no. 03.

Alfani, G. and T. Murphy (2017), 'Plague and lethal epidemics in the pre-industrial world', *Journal of Economic History*, 77, 1, pp. 314-343.

Alfani, G. and W. Ryckbosch (2016), 'Growing apart in early modern Europe? A comparison of inequality trends in Italy and the Low Countries, 1500-1800', *Explorations in Economic History*, 62, pp. 143-153.

Alfani, G. and S. Sardone (2015), 'Long-term trends in economic inequality in southern Italy. The Kingdom of Naples and Sicily, 16th-18th centuries: first results', paper given at the Economic History Association Annual Meeting, Nashville.

Allen, R. C. (2019), 'Class structure and inequality during the industrial revolution: lessons from England's social tables, 1688-1867', *Economic History Review*, 72, 1, pp. 88-125.

Aston, T. H. et al. (eds) (1987). *The Brenner Debate: Agrarian class structure and economic development in pre-industrial Europe*, Cambridge.

Bavel, B. van (2016) *The invisible hand? How market economies have emerged and declined since AD 500*, Oxford.

Bavel, B. van, D. R. Curtis and T. Soens (2018), 'Economic inequality and institutional adaptation in response to flood hazards: a historical analysis', *Ecology and Society*, 23, 4, art. 30.

Bengtsson, E., A. Missiaia, M. Olsson and P. Svensson (2017), 'Wealth inequality in Sweden, 1750-1900', *Economic History Review*, 71, 3, pp. 772-779.

Bengtsson, E., A. Missiaia, I. Nummela and M. Olsson (2018), 'Unequal poverty and equal industrialisation: Finnish wealth, 1750-1900', *Scandinavian Economic History Review*, online-first version.

Brenner, R. (1976), 'Agrarian class structure and economic development in pre-industrial Europe', Past & Present, 70, 1, pp. 30-75.

Broadberry, S., B. M. S. Campbell, A. Klein, M. Overton and B. Van Leeuwen (2015), *British Economic Growth 1270-1870*, Cambridge.

Curtis, D. R. (2016) 'Danger and displacement in the Dollard: the 1509 flooding of the Dollard Sea (Groningen) and its impact on long-term inequality in the distribution of property', *Environment and History*, 22, pp. 103-135.

Fernández, Eva, and Carlos Santiago-Caballero (2013) 'Income inequality in Madrid, 1500-1850'. Paper given at the Economic History Society Annual Conference, York.

García-Montero, H. (2015) 'Long-term trends in wealth inequality in Catalonia, 1400-1800: Initial Results', *Dondena Working Paper* n. 79.

Hanus, J. (2013) 'Real inequality in the early modern Low Countries: the city of 's-Hertogenbosch, 1500-1660', *Economic History Review*, 66, 3, pp. 733-756.

Herlihy, D. (1968) 'Santa Maria Impruneta: a rural commune in the late middle ages', in N. Rubinstein (ed.) *Florentine studies: politics and society in Renaissance Florence*, London, pp. 242-276.

Herlihy, D. J. (1978) 'The distribution of wealth in a renaissance community: Florence 1427', in P. Abrams and E. A. Wrigley (eds), *Towns in Societies: Essays in Economic History and Historical Sociology*, Cambridge, pp. 131-157.

Le Roy Ladurie, E. (1966) *Les Paysans de Languedoc*, Paris.

Lindert, P. H. (2000) 'Three centuries of inequality in Britain and America', in A. B. Atkinson and F. Bourguignon (eds), *Handbook of Income Distribution*, London, pp. 167-216.

Malinowski, M. and J. L. Van Zanden (2017) 'Income and its distribution in preindustrial Poland', *Cliometrica*, 11, 3, pp. 375-404.

Nicolini, E. A. and F. Ramos Palencia (2016a) 'Decomposing income inequality in a backward pre-industrial economy: Old Castile (Spain) in the Middle of the 18th Century', *Economic History Review*, 69, 3, pp. 747-772.

Nicolini, E. A. and F. Ramos Palencia (2016b) 'Comparing income and wealth inequality in pre-industrial economies: lessons from 18th-century Spain', EHES Working Papers no. 95.

Piketty, T. (2014), *Capital in the Twenty-First Century*, Cambridge MA.

Piketty, T. (2015) 'Putting distribution back at the center of economics: reflections on capital in the twenty-first century', *Journal of Economic Perspectives*, 29, 1, pp. 67-88.

Porisini, G. (1963) *La proprietà terriera nel Comune di Ravenna dalla metà del secolo XVI ai giorni nostri*, Milan.

Reis, J. (2017), 'Deviant behaviour? Inequality in Portugal 1565-1770', *Cliometrica*, 11, 3, pp. 297-319.

Rotelli, C. (1966) *La distribuzione della proprietà terriera e delle colture a Imola nel XVII e XVIII secolo*, Milan.

Ryckbosch, W. (2016), 'Economic inequality and growth before the industrial revolution: the case of the Low Countries (fourteenth to nineteenth centuries)', *European Review of Economic History*, 20, pp. 1-22.

Santiago-Caballero, C. (2011), 'Income inequality in central Spain, 1690-1800', *Explorations in Economic History*, 48, 1, pp. 83-96.

Scheidel, W. (2017) *The Great Leveller: Violence and the Global History of Inequality from the Stone Age to the Present*, Oxford.

Sreenivasan, G. P. (2013), 'Beyond the village: recent approaches to the social history of the earlymodern German peasantry', *History Compass*, 11, 1, pp. 48-49.

Thoen, E. and T. Soens, (2008), 'The social and economic impact of central governement taxation on the Flemish countryside (end 13th-18th centuries)', in *La fiscalità nell'economia europea secc. XIII-XVII*, Fondazione Istituto Internazionale di Storia « F. Datini », Prato, Firenze University Press, pp. 957-971.

Thoen, E. and T. Soens (2015), 'The family or the farm: a Sophie's choice? The late medieval crisis in Flanders', in: J. Drendel, (ed.) *Crisis in the later Middle Ages: beyond the Postan-Duby paradigm*. Series: The Medieval Countryside 13, Brepols Publishers, Turnhout, pp. 195-224.

Tilly, C. (1984), 'Demographic origins of the European proletariat', in Levine, D. (ed.), *Proletarianization and Family History*, Orlando, pp. 1-85.

van Zanden, J. L. (1995), 'Tracing the beginning of the Kuznets Curve: Western Europe during the Early Modern Period', *Economic History Review*, 48, 4, pp. 643-664.

ESTEBAN NICOLINI,
FERNANDO RAMOS-PALENCIA

2 Inequality in Spain during the Early Modern Period, 1500-1800. Notes and results*

[T]here is nothing more pernicious than the extreme wealth of some and the extreme poverty of others, in which our republic is unbalanced.

Martín González de Cellórigo. *Memorial de la política necesaria, y útil restauración de la República de España, y estados della, y del desempeño universal destos reinos.* Valladolid: J. de Bustillo, 1600, p. 15-revés.

I have said virtue, wealth, and generosity, because a great man who is vicious will be a great example of vice, and a rich man who is not generous will be merely a miserly beggar; for the possessor of wealth is not made happy by possessing it, but by spending it, and not by spending as he pleases, but by knowing how to spend it well.

Miguel de Cervantes. *The History of Don Quixote,* Volume II. Chapter VI: Of what took place between Don Quixote and his niece and housekeeper; one of the most important chapters in the whole history. https://www.gutenberg.org/files/5946/5946-h/5946-h.htm#ch6b

I. Historical background

The marriage between Isabel of Castile and Fernando of Aragon in 1469 is traditionally considered to be the birth of present-day Spain. Unfortunately,

* The authors acknowledge financial support from the *Ministerio de Economía y Competitividad* and *FEDER* through grant HAR2016-77794-R.

Esteban Nicolini • University Carlos III of Madrid

Fernando Ramos-Palencia • University Pablo de Olavide of Seville

Inequality in rural Europe (Late Middle Ages – 18th century), ed. by Guido ALFANI and Erik THOEN, CORN, 18 (Turnhout, 2020), pp. 25–43.

 DOI 10.1484/M.CORN-EB.5.121946

the legacy of the Spanish *Trastámara* royal house was very brief. The premature deaths of both their son Juan in 1497 and their elder daughter Isabel in 1498 caused that the crown passed to their daughter Juana and her spouse Philip of Habsburg (future Felipe I of Castile). However, due to the unexpected death of Felipe (1506) and Juana's madness, the crown fell on their son Carlos (1500-1558), grandson of Isabel and Fernando. Being just sixteen years old in 1516, Carlos became king of Spain (Carlos I) and three years later he became Holy Roman Emperor (Charles V) and head of the House of Habsburg. Under Emperor Charles V, a patchwork of several diverse territories were united, although functioning autonomously under the same dynasty.[1] There was no common administrative structure nor a common fiscal policy; there was only a common foreign policy. In short, present-day Spain entered the 16th century concomitant with two unexpected events: (i) the accidental birth of an empire that reflected no particular ideology; and (ii) the discovery of America, which displaced Europe's centre of gravity from the Mediterranean to the Atlantic.

Between 1550 and 1650, the Hispanic Monarchy[2] (under the Habsburg dynasty) faced the European powers of England, France, the Netherlands, and Turkey. In Asia, America, and Africa, Spanish ships were harassed by English and Dutch ships; in the Mediterranean, they had to contend with pirate ships and the Ottoman Empire. Although since the 16th century the arrival of silver (and/or gold) from America engrossed the public revenues, it also 'infected' the Castilian Crown with the so-called *Dutch disease*.[3] In addition, given increased expenditures due to continuous warfare, American gold and silver failed to prevent the Hispanic Monarchy from going bankrupt in 1557, 1575, 1596, 1607, 1627, and 1647. From the end of the 16th century and throughout most of the 17th century, the Castilian Crown suffered a major financial crisis

---

1 The dominions inherited included a (i) unified Spain (crowns of Castile, Aragon and Navarre) with its southern Italian kingdoms of Naples, Sicily, and Sardinia and reaching overseas to Spanish America; and (ii), the Burgundian Netherlands and the Austrian hereditary lands. As Holy Roman Emperor, Charles V extended his dominions from the German States to northern Italy.

2 The Hispanic Monarchy controlled territories that included present-day Spain, Spanish America until 1820s (present-day South America except Brazil, present-day Central America, part of the Caribbean Islands, present-day Mexico, Florida and the Southwestern and Pacific Coastal regions in the USA), overseas territories in Asia (e.g. Philippines, Formosa and Guam) and Oceania from 1565 until 1890s, Portugal and overseas territories between 1580 and 1640, the kingdoms of Naples, Sicily and Sardinia between 1516 and 1713 (treaty of Utrecht), the Duchy of Milan between 1556 and 1707, the Spanish Netherlands that were involved in a long war in the Netherlands independence from Spanish Habsburg (Eighty Years' War, 1568-1648), and, the former French region of Franche-Comté until 1678 (Peace of Nijmegen). The political and economic axis of the Hispanic Monarchy under the Habsburgs was in Madrid and Seville, both cities in the former Crown of Castile.

3 The 'Dutch disease' is the decline of some economic sectors of an economy because of the increase in prices resulting from the abundance of an internationally tradable product or natural resources. See for more details Drelichman, 2005.

caused by declining returns in the agricultural sector and a steady increase of fiscal pressure. Castilian revenues did not match their 1560-1580 levels until well into the 18th century. During the Thirty Years' War (1618-1648), Spain supported the Catholics against the Protestants in Germany, the Catholic League against the Huguenots in France, and the Austrians against the Turks. In the 1640s, Portugal (added to the Hispanic Monarchy in 1580) formed a successful alliance with France and England for achieving independence and Catalonia led a revolt that turned into warfare waged by the rich against the poor (Elliott, 1963). The deficits caused by these ventures were paid with funds amassed in the Americas (used, in turn, to repay loans from Flanders and Genoa) and by increasing the tax burden. The increasing fiscal demands of the Hispanic Monarchy – channeled through an inefficient and fragmented tax system – "created enormous asymmetries among its different polities" (Yun-Casalilla, 2012: 28). Fiscal pressure generated political conflicts between the Crown and the territories that had their own institutions and fiscal regimes. After the Treaty of Westphalia (1648) the monarchy's loss of world political status was confirmed and the Spanish model for economic growth was no longer based on the role of Castile; instead, it came to be characterised by the coastal Mediterranean's supremacy and, to a lesser extent, that of the North east coast of Spain (Grafe, 2012).

The 18th century did not begin well for the Hispanic Monarchy. The death of Carlos II without issue led to the War of Spanish Succession (1702-1714): an international conflict for the throne of Spain that resulted in a bloody civil war between supporters of the Bourbons (Felipe V) and the Habsburgs (Archduke Charles), the latter supported by England and the Netherlands. Castile, the Basque provinces, and Navarre supported Felipe V, while the Crown of Aragon mainly opted for Archduke Charles. After the Spanish War of Succession, the Bourbons implemented a range of institutional and economic reforms aimed at centralizing power and restoring the Spanish monarchy's political and economic clout. The Bourbon regime: (i) abolished the institutions and tax system in the former Crown of Aragon (Aragon, Balearic Islands, Catalonia and Valencia), via the Decree-Law of *Nueva Planta*, because that territory had not supported the Bourbon claim; (ii) maintained the privileges (e.g., fiscal exemption) in the Basque Provinces and Navarre for their support of Felipe V; and (iii) reformed the former Crown of Castile's institutions and fiscal regime. Although the rest of the 18th century was overall positive for Spain, its main economic indicators lagged behind those of other European regions (Álvarez-Nogal and Prados de la Escosura, 2007, 2013). One reason for that lag was demographic evolution. Spain showed less increase in population size compared to England, France, Germany, and Italy. Reher (1990) mentions that less than a third of the Spanish population lived in urban environments at the end of the 18th century. The regions with the highest urban concentration were located in the coastal areas of the Mediterranean (Andalusia, the Balearic Islands, and Valencia-Murcia), while the country's interior areas (the historical territories of the Crown of Castile) had the lowest urbanisation rates. Vilar (1999: 27-62) paints the following picture: Madrid and the Seville–Cádiz–Jerez axis were, in the mid-18th century, two islands amid two areas of rural misery in the former Crown of Castile. As described by Herr (1960/1988: 28), there was an imaginary line running from Salamanca to Albacete. Above this line, farmers and day labourers lived in small and heavily indebted farms (in Galicia and León, day labourers accounted for scarcely 5% of the population); below this line were large areas of privately owned land, and more than 70% of the population consisted of day labourers with low wages and high seasonal unemployment. So the Spanish agricultural sector in this period was characterised by low productivity and high production costs, which entailed low wages for workers as well as high prices for agricultural products. Furthermore, land ownership was static and seldom changed except to increase its concentration in the hands of privileged sectors. Such strongly polarised distribution, when combined with livestock interests promoted by the *Mesta* lobby, limited not only the expansion of arable land but also technological progress.

In terms of craft production, the Crown of Castile was characterised by widely distributed looms, flour mills, ironworks, and similar enterprises. Grupo 75 (1977: 169) uses Ensenada Cadastre data and estimates that the secondary sector contributed 12.3% to national income, a substantially lower share than that contributed by either the tertiary sector (29.5%) or the primary sector (58.2%). The low percentage of return on manufacturing products is not surprising when one considers that more than 85% of the Ensenada Cadastre's household heads were either unskilled workers or engaged in rural activities. Catalonia was the first Spanish region to industrialise and the only one that experienced significant pre-industrial growth (Marfany, 2012). Catalan economic expansion started near the end of the 17th century with its integration into Atlantic trading circuits and its resulting access to the American colonial market through Lisbon, Cádiz, and Gibraltar; that expansion was further aided by Catalonia's expanding commercial relations with England and the Netherlands, areas that accounted for more than half of its imports and to which liquor and textile products were exported. This industrial expansion led to a Catalan diaspora that was facilitated by the reduced enforcement of intranational tariffs during the 18th century and was motivated by the search for new markets in the Iberian Peninsula. Finally, a 1778 decree allowing for free trade with America – which effectively ended the monopoly of the *Casa de Contratación de Indias* – lent an international dimension to expanding Catalan industry.

II. Review: what is known about economic inequality in pre-industrial Spain

As is the case with other pre-industrial societies, it is difficult to study inequality in Spain because there are no documentary sources that incorporate long-term data series; in particular, there are no direct measures of income or wealth.[4] Hence the most common research method involves using data extracted from fiscal sources to construct 'social tables', which group income recipients into occupational categories to which income can later be imputed (Milanovic et al., 2011). Another approach is to use indirect data, thereby constructing such measures of inequality as the ratio of land rent to wages (Williamson, 2002).

For instance, Álvarez-Nogal and Prados de la Escosura (2007, 2013) evaluate the ratio of land rent to wages and show that economic inequality in Spain was cyclical during the Early Modern Age: periodically rising and falling in response, for the most part, to war, disease, and other calamities. These authors also argue that the observed fluctuations in inequality were *not* driven by the *Kuznets hypothesis*.[5] Referring to the Books of Estimates (*Llibres d'estimes*),[6] García-Montero (2015) similarly rules out a 'super Kuznets curve' as an explanation for the wealth inequality in rural Catalonia between 1400 and 1800. Instead, García-Montero claims that the growth of inequality roughly paralleled per capita grown in gross domestic product (GDP) ever since about the middle of the 17th century. Yet the trend of inequality in previous periods was not related to economic growth: even during the second half of the 16th century, economic growth was associated with a reduction of wealth inequality.

Other regional studies include Santiago-Caballero (2011), who estimates income concentration – using grain production as a proxy of income – during the last third of the 18th century in central Spain (Guadalajara). He posits that inequality decreased because the redistribution of communal lands following the 1766 Esquilache riots allowed many small landholders to produce more than subsistence levels and, by extension, to take advantage of trade opportunities and high grain prices. Using annual income data for Castile (Palencia province) derived from the Ensenada Cadastre (*c.* 1750), Nicolini and Ramos-Palencia (2016a) analyse the contribution of different production factors to income inequality. According to that paper, the main cause of income inequality was land; this production factor was responsible for 52% of inequality whereas livestock accounted for 15%. These results correspond with other studies of income structures in European pre-industrial societies, where the distribution

4 On the differences between *income* inequality and *wealth* inequality in pre-industrial societies, see Nicolini and Ramos-Palencia (2016b).

5 In 1955 Kuznets suggested that – mainly in rich countries as the USA and the UK – inequality is first increasing and then decreasing in the course of a growth process. Since then, this hypothesis was the main tool used by inequality economists in order to describe the relationship between growth (and/or development) and inequality. However, Milanovic (2016) shows "the Kuznets curve gradually fell out of favour because its prediction of low inequality in very rich societies could not be squared with the sustained increase in income inequality that started in the late 1970s in practically all developed nations".

6 The Books of Estimates served as a registry of wealth and property because they assessed immovable property and sometimes movable property as well. The seven Catalan rural locations used by García-Montero (2015) are – in alphabetical order – Almoster, Castellvell, Cervera, Manresa, Resus, Tárrega, and Vergos.

of nonhuman wealth is usually seen to be the main determinant of economic inequality. Along these lines, Oto-Peralías and Romero-Ávila (2017) suggest that the Christian Reconquest (722-1492) in the former Kingdom of Granada generated a land ownership pattern that led to persistent wealth inequality.

Nicolini and Ramos-Palencia (2016a) remark that, despite the importance of land ownership, labour income was also a significant contributor in accounting for 18.5% of inequality. This finding is relevant to any analysis of the relation between labour income and human capital; for example, Álvarez and Ramos-Palencia (2018) show that human capital could easily have contributed to the inequality of pre-industrial income (and hence of household income) during the mid-18th century in northern and central Spain (provinces of Palencia and Guadalajara). They find a positive and statistically significant association between skills and average earnings. In theory, wage differences associated with human capital should be greater in urban areas than in rural areas and should differ according to the sector of activity. In this context, numeracy skills led to statistically significant differences in agriculture and literacy in the tertiary sector but not in manufacturing. The highest level of professional qualification was better paid in the primary and tertiary sectors than in the secondary sector; this outcome is consistent with the low technological development of Castile manufacturers, which focused primarily on coarse textiles. García-Montero (2016) uses anthropometric measures as indicators of biological and nutritional well-being and establishes a significant correlation between economic inequality and height disparity in central Spain (province of Toledo) during the 18th century.

With respect to the economic transition that occurred between the 18th and 19th centuries, Brea-Martínez and Pujadas-Mora (2018) analyse the effect of industrialisation on economic inequality in the Barcelona area between 1715 and 1860; for this purpose the authors use the Barcelona Cathedral marriage registers, which recorded the payment of a proportional tax depending on the social status of the parties. These authors claim that a process of *proletarianization* – in Marxist terms, when middle class become absorbed into the working class – was responsible for increased inequality between economic sectors and within the secondary sector of textiles. Álvarez-Nogal and Prados de la Escosura (2013) and Prados de la Escosura and Santiago-Caballero (2018) point out that the Napoleonic Wars in Spain (1808-1814) were the cause of a generalised destruction that coincided with greater volatility in real wages and a temporary increase in the inequality of total income. When that conflict ended, nominal wages increased more than did land leases; hence income inequality declined.

III. Efficiency vs. fairness in the Castilian tax system: legitimised institutional inequality

The Habsburg dynasty built an international composite monarchy around the Castilian tax regime. At the same time, the Habsburgs used Genoese bankers to access the international credit markets. The consequences of this relationship proved detrimental to Spain – mainly for the Castilian economy – because of the transfer of public expenditures out of the Crown of Castile and its subordination to the Genoese financial system (Comín and Yun-Casalilla, 2012: 233-266). Addressing the topic of inequality in this context requires a series of preliminary clarifications (cf. Domínguez Ortiz, 1951). Firstly, of the empire's territories, the greatest tax burden fell on the Crown of Castile.[7] The empire's other territories (i.e., the Crown of Aragon, the Basque provinces, Navarre, the Italian territories, and Flanders) paid no more than was strictly necessary. In fact, Castile supplied much of the financial resources needed to crown Charles V as emperor and to underwrite the new status quo in Europe. Over time, it became clear that Castile – with only 4-5 million inhabitants – did not have the resources necessary to reign effectively over this patchwork of territories. Moreover, the complexity of the Castilian tax system did not help matters. This system included: (i) regular taxes (on ecclesiastical and noble income, on income from the American trade monopolies, and on, inter alia, mail, tobacco, salt, sealed paper, and currency); (ii) taxes on municipal income (called *rentas de propios* and *arbitrios*); (iii) indirect taxes on imported and exported products; and (iv) other taxes (e.g., on liquor, soap, tallow candles, snow, and sugar). Also, special taxes, known as *servicios ordinarios* and *extraordinarios*, could be assessed depending on the monarchy's financial needs. Within this tax scheme, the most significant item was usually the wide range of indirect taxes, the *rentas provinciales*,[8] from which the clergy and the nobility were exempt. Moral Ruiz (1990: 24-25) indicates there were about 15 major taxes within the *rentas provinciales*, of which some came to be subdivided into 46 denominations. The main taxes were the *alcabala* (10% on sales or exchanges) and the *cientos* (an additional 4% on the *alcabala*) and the *millones* (charged on the retail sales of basic consumer items: wine, oil, vinegar, meat, soap, candles, etc.). According to the enlightened minister

7 On this subject there is no consensus among historiographers. Domínguez Ortiz (1960) emphasizes the tiny contribution of the Crown of Aragon, but Vilar (1987) discounts that interpretation because Catalonia played no part in the empire's foreign policy. During the 16th century, Catalonia's per capita tax contribution was higher than that of Castile: although Castile's population was 20 times larger than Catalonia's, it contributed only 5 times more absolute tax than did Catalonia.

8 Following González Enciso (2017: 99), the *Rentas Provinciales* were a group of indirect taxes on consumer and mercantile transactions since the late seventeenth century and paid in the provinces of the former Crown of Castile. Briefly, they comprised the *alcabalas* (sales taxes), the *millones* (consumer tax), the *servicios* (an indirect poll tax) plus many sundries. In this fiscal system, the most important taxes were the alcabalas and the millones. The *alcabalas* was a tax on all sales, including successive sales of the same good; it also taxed exchanges and swaps. Thus, all goods that entered or exited any given location were subject to special surveillance, as were the movements of retail merchants and the places where products were stored. The *millones* (established in 1590) taxed consumption, notably wine, vinegar, oil, meat, sugar, chocolate, raisins, fish, paper, and tallow candles.

López de Lerena's "Report on the nature of public income in Spain, the number of employees and the salaries they enjoy" (1789-1790/1990: 60), the *rentas provinciales* accounted for nearly 123 million *reales* per year. To collect them, 3,150 individuals were employed; their salaries amounted to some 10 million *reales* (about 7% of the total collected). Moral Ruiz (1990: 35) shows that the provincial revenues accounted for approximately 15% of the state's ordinary income before 1785 (excluding American revenues); after that year's Floridablanca–Lerena reform, they amounted to more than 20% of the total tax revenue. The tax exemption enjoyed by the nobility motivated many to pursue ennoblement, but the Crown's financial needs during the 17th century – and the considerable taxes on personal fortunes – progressively discouraged such pursuit. During the 18th century, nobles received rent from their land and from feudal charges yet obtained most of their income from (i) monopolies on the use of ovens, mills, wineries, inns, roads, bridges, and boat tolls; and (ii) interest on *juros* (private loans to the Crown that dated back to 1489). For this reason, the Spanish nobility during that century intensified their pursuit of revenue by assuming ecclesiastical positions and civil offices (e.g., mayors, notaries). In sum, the *rentas provinciales* were applied not only to basic necessities (e.g., meat, wine, vinegar, oil, soap, etc.) but also to contracts (ranging from the sale of property and real estate to small daily market sales) and the within-province trade of products. Note also that these taxes fluctuated over time and varied between the different provinces of the Castilian Crown. Additionally, collecting the *rentas provinciales* was problematic, because they were not collected directly by the State Treasury (Comín and Yun-Casalilla, 2012: 243-248).

Following the Spanish War of Succession and the subsequent dynastic change, the *Nueva Planta* decrees (1707-1716) sought to eliminate tax discrimination between the Crowns of Castile and Aragon by requiring direct contributions based on property and labour income; this scheme was given the names *única contribución*, *catastro*, *talla*, and *equivalente* in (respectively) the Kingdom of Aragon, the Principality of Catalonia, the Kingdom of Mallorca, and the Kingdom of Valencia – the historical territories of the Crown of Aragon.[9] Territories that supported the Bourbons during the war were

9 The reforms intended by the *Nueva Planta* decrees were doomed to failure because there were no reliable statistics or inventories for establishing either the income of taxpayers or the property wealth of the old Crown of Aragon; so in practice, essentially fixed amounts were assessed from 1720 to 1845. Ferrer Alós (2002: 34-35) states that only in Catalonia did the *catastro* play a part in taxation. Besides the *catastro*, assessments were made on inheritance rights and "troop accommodation" rights as well as on income from tobacco, salt, sealed paper, and customs; 1769 saw the introduction of an indirect tax on the consumption of imported products (e.g., sugar, cocoa, cinnamon, wool, silk, hats) and also on foreign trade more generally. In 1765, the state's income from the *catastro* (resp., indirect taxes) accounted for about 45% (resp., 35%) of its revenue. Gelabert (1999: 235) indicates that, until the 1730s, an average of 26.8 *reales* per person was paid in Castile and 43 *reales* in Catalonia. By 1790, the amount had increased to 220.5 *reales* in Castile but to only 124.3 *reales* in Catalonia.

exempt from making these contributions. Instead, they remitted an annual lump sum: a 'subsidy' paid by Navarre and a 'donation' paid by the Basque provinces. In the mid-18th century, reforms driven by the Marquis of Ensenada failed to rid Castile's tax system of its complexity, notwithstanding this new tax regime's similarity to the single tax implemented in the former Crown of Aragon. Although further reform attempts emerged in 1770 (a return to the Ensenada Cadastre) and in 1785 (the Floridablanca–Lerena reform), they were unsuccessful due to conflicts between centralised and 'parallel' taxation: seigniorial, ecclesiastical, and municipal. Thus, fiscal discrimination between the historical territories of the Crowns of Castile and Aragon continued until the so-called liberal reform of 1845; the special fiscal regime of Navarre and the Basque provinces lasted until 1876.

Thus it is clear that, during the 16th and 17th centuries in Spain, an unfair fiscal system prevailed: the less affluent classes – artisans and peasants – paid proportionally more than did the nobility and clergy (who also enjoyed tax exemptions and other privileges). This system was also regressive in that it was heavily reliant on indirect taxes from food and basic necessities. In addition, the ownership of property was limited in Castile by the institution of *Mayorazgo*, whereby all movable and immovable property was bequeathed to the eldest son. Such property could not be confiscated to satisfy creditors; it could be appropriated only in cases where payment was suspended. It was likewise nearly impossible for either ecclesiastical properties or municipal properties managed by the local oligarchy to be sold. In fact, the Church's wealth could be increased only by new donations from the faithful or by land appropriated in response to non-payment of interest on *censos* (mortgages).

During this period, fiscal burdens were not equitably distributed within the former Crown of Castile. The same tax laws applied to all Castilian territory; however, not all provinces, cities, and towns paid the same. This arbitrary distribution of fiscal pressure encouraged migration from rural areas to nearby towns and other rural areas, where the tax burden was lower. In his Agrarian Law Report of 1795, Jovellanos – one of the most important enlightened ministers of the time – observed that Spanish tax laws were hampering economic growth and were a burden on the less affluent. Thus, in the second half of the 18th century, earning enough to buy a kilogram of bread required a spinner, a bricklayer, a miner, or a blacksmith to work six hours; in contrast, a senior state or ecclesiastical official could earn the same amount in just ten minutes (Pontón, 2016: 282).

IV. Inequality as evidenced by the Ensenada Cadastre: perhaps the world's first income tax

Economic inequality prior to 1800 can only be studied indirectly, since pre-20th-century regular income taxes were rare. It is therefore common to resort to fiscal sources, social tables, and proxy variables to estimate income and/or wealth.

A fortunate exception was the Ensenada Cadastre, conducted in the former Crown of Castile. We have already indicated that, at the beginning of the 18th century, the Hispanic Monarchy was a backward economy as compared with its Northern European rivals and was also severely weakened politically after the War of Succession and the Treaty of Utrecht. Even so, Spain's continued possession of American colonies maintained its position as a world power. It even defeated the British Empire in Cartagena de Indias (1741), which secured the Spanish-American colonies for another 70 years, and helped the North American colonies gain their independence from the British. In this context, the Marquis de La Ensenada – who was the secretary of Finance, War, Navy, and America between 1743 and 1754 – proposed (without success) an improvement to the former Crown of Castile's fiscal regime by replacing its complex tax system with a scheme of 'single contributions' proportional to the individual income of each taxpayer. The proposal included taxing the Church and the nobility, which was unprecedented.[10] This new tax regime required the government to record the income and wealth of all Castilian households (approximately 7 million inhabitants). It is fair to say that the Ensenada Cadastre was the 18th-century version of the microdata on which today's regular income tax is based.

The Ensenada Cadastre includes the General Answers (*Respuestas Generales*), which describe the demographic and socioeconomic features of each city, town, and village. However, it also contains the Private Answers (*Respuestas Particulares*), or the individual statements from the head of the family about his profession, place of residence, age, marital status, household composition, and all sources of income. We used data collected from the *Respuestas Particulares* to compute the annual income of all household heads from different locations in five provinces (Palencia, Guadalajara, Madrid, Jaén, and Granada); see Figure 1. 'Annual income' includes: labour income; income from land, urban real estate, and nonland properties; income originated in livestock production; and interest derived from any financial asset or mortgage.[11]

In table 2.1, the towns have been placed in descending order according to their Gini index (tenth column), showing quite a wide range of variation: Úbeda city, a typical pre-industrial agro-city in southern Spain, has the calculated maximum of 0.661 while Valberzoso (Palencia province) has the minimum of 0.289. Information contained in the table (2.1) reveals

10 These reforms did not succeed because the Marquis de Ensenada was removed from office. His opposition consisted of three pressure groups: (i) the Anglophile sector, which influenced the monarchy; (ii) the merchants, who controlled the American trade routes and the transfer of silver to Europe; and (iii) traditional Castilian institutions. This third group included the privileged estates of the clergy and the nobility, the urban oligarchies, and the rich landowners, farmers, and livestock owners of the various Castilian provinces.

11 See Nicolini and Ramos-Palencia (2016a) and Álvarez and Ramos-Palencia (2018) for exhaustive analyses of the methodology used in the Ensenada Cadastre.

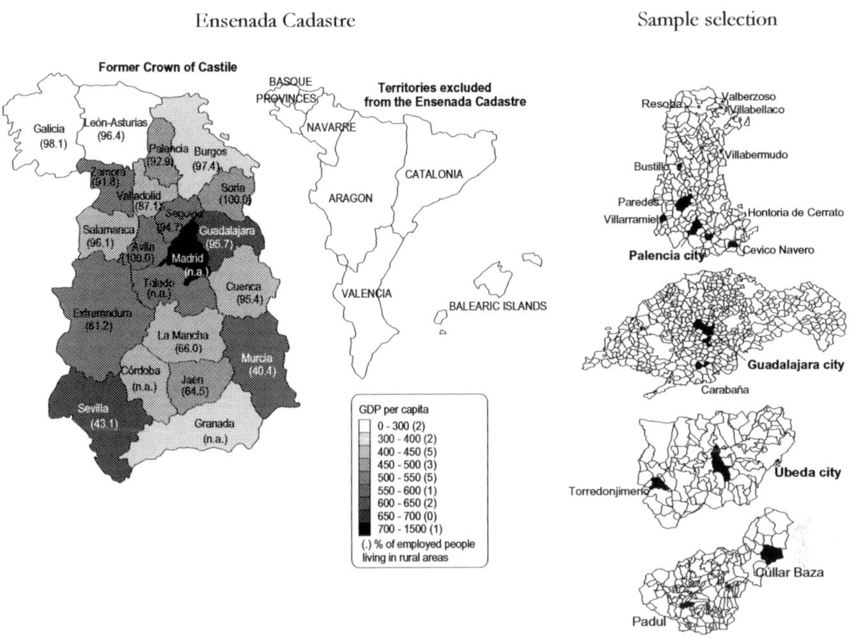

Figure 2.1. Territory covered by the Ensenada Cadastre and sample selection (per capita GDP, in *reales*, and % of employed population living in rural areas)

Notes: The map on the figure's left-hand side shows the current borders of the 22 provinces comprised by Castile in 1750 (the former province of Toro is included in Zamora); numbers in parentheses are the percentages of employed people living in rural locations. Urban areas are defined as cities or towns with more than 1,250 household heads (approximately 5,000 inhabitants). The colour of the provinces corresponds to an interval of per capita GDP. See Álvarez and Ramos-Palencia (2018: 110) for additional details. The maps on the figure's right-hand side show the current borders of the provinces of Palencia, Guadalajara-Madrid, Jaén and Granada with the places included in the sample.

several interesting patterns about income inequality in a relatively retarded pre-industrial economy of the eighteenth century. The first pattern is the confirmation that inequality tends to be higher in cities and large towns than in small rural localities; the three cities with more than one thousand households (Úbeda, Palencia and Guadalajara) are ranked within the five highest Gini indices. With the exception of Villarramiel, all the towns with a Gini index below 0.55 have small population concentrations with fewer than 150 households. The second pattern is that there is a clear correlation between land ownership inequality (measured as the Land distribution income) and the Gini coefficient: even though inequality is greater in cities, the distribution of income accruing from land ownership (which is, of course, related to land distribution inequality) is a very good predictor of overall income inequality. The third pattern is a negative correlation between the Gini coefficient and the incomes of the 25th and the 50th percentile (as can be seen in figure 2) while the income of the 95th percentile is not consistently higher in those localities

Table 2.1. Comparative household income inequality in towns and rural areas, *c.* 1750

Town/village	Province	Households	Population*	Land distribution index**	Household income in *reales* (percentile)				Gini index
					25th	50th	95th	95th ÷ 25th	
Úbeda city	Jaén	2,563	10,252	0.939	254.5	400.5	2509.0	9.86	0.661
Cúllar Baza	Granada	678	2,712	0.908	263.0	404.0	2426.0	9.22	0.621
Guadalajara city	Guadalajara	1,301	5,204	0.932	254.5	540.0	3300.0	12.97	0.613
Padul	Granada	258	1,032	0.837	480.0	513.0	4941.0	10.29	0.608
Palencia city	Palencia	2,259	9,036	0.990	360.0	456.0	3300.0	9.17	0.607
Paredes Nava	Palencia	722	2,888	0.892	480.0	573.3	3857.5	8.04	0.600
Carabaña	Madrid	182	728	0.797	260.0	508.8	3285.0	12.63	0.563
Torredonjimeno	Jaén	841	3,364	0.941	204.0	409.0	1678.0	8.23	0.551
Bustillo	Palencia	34	136	0.740	389.0	727.0	4311.0	11.08	0.544
Villabellaco	Palencia	32	128	0.597	325.3	764.8	3234.5	9.94	0.444
Villabermudo	Palencia	77	308	0.568	488.0	738.5	2410.5	4.94	0.409
Villarramiel	Palencia	377	1,508	0.606	515.5	812.5	2720.0	5.28	0.407
Hontoria	Palencia	69	276	0.522	585.0	850.0	2223.5	3.80	0.355
Resoba	Palencia	63	252	0.423	551.0	796.5	1966.5	3.57	0.336
Cevico Navero	Palencia	132	528	0.823	819.5	984.5	2395.5	2.92	0.304
Valberzoso	Palencia	30	120	0.400	536.0	866.8	1902.0	3.55	0.289

* These figures are approximate, given that 'population' is obtained by multiplying the number of household heads by 4. Members of the clergy are not included. ** This index is an approximation (via the Gini index) of annual yields from the land properties held by household heads.

Source: Author calculations based on data from the Ensenada Cadastre.

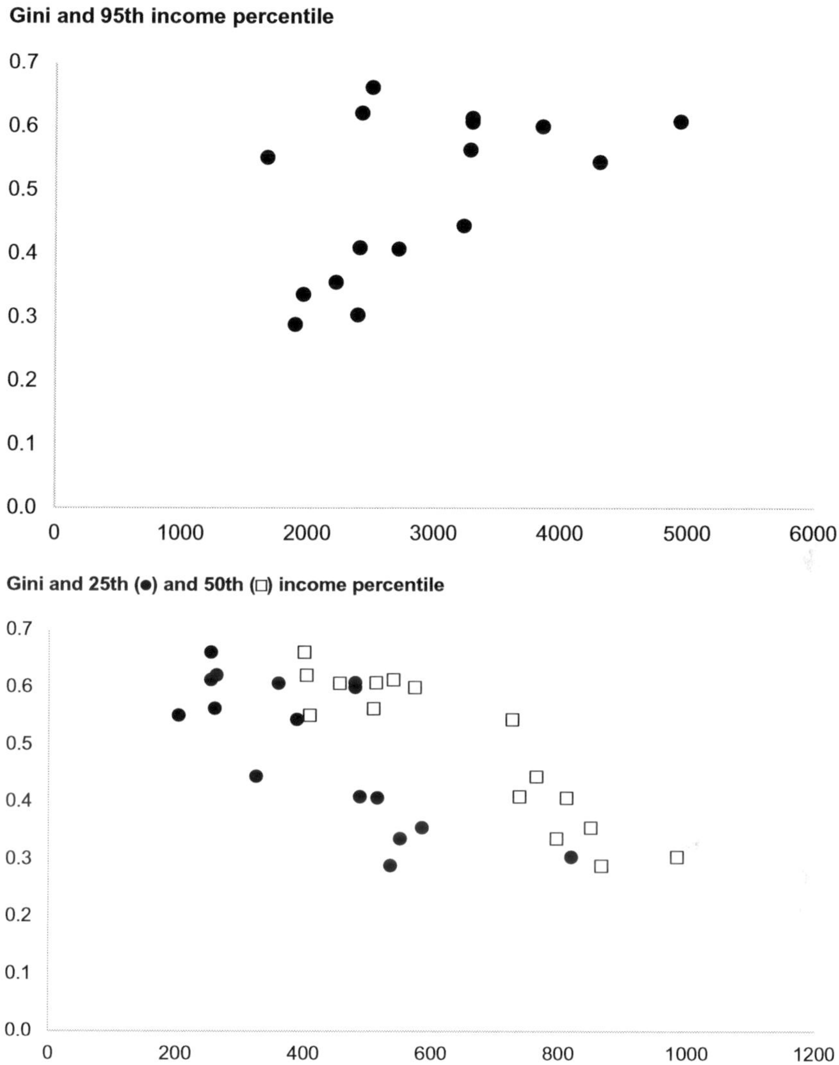

Figure 2.2. Gini indices and percentile ratios, Spain *c.* 1750

Source: Author calculations based on data from the Ensenada Cadastre.

with highest inequality. This suggests that those places with higher inequality are characterized by lower incomes in the bottom part of the distribution rather than higher incomes in the top. Given that the Ensenada Cadastre is a particularly good source to gather information on incomes at both tails of the distribution (compared with other sources from pre-industrial economies) this finding opens potentially interesting avenues for research on poverty in both rural and urban environments in eighteenth century Spain.

We remark that, according to all indications, there should have been increases in the rental of land and in agricultural product prices throughout the 18th century since land ownership was so highly concentrated (see the column labeled 'Land distribution index' in Table 2.1). In addition, one should bear in mind that there was no land market per se because most rural properties could not be sold. As described by Anes (1970: 430-431) and other historians, the period between 1754 and 1789 was notable for constantly increasing agricultural prices and land rents, trends that favoured large landowners. Consequently, this period witnessed several episodes of agricultural product accumulation that stimulated speculation and subsistence crises. García Sanz (1985: 652) stresses that most conflict in rural areas resulted from evictions – often due to increased land value– and the institutional privileges of the livestock lobby, the *Mesta*.

All these factors must surely have promoted increasing inequality. As we have already said, data obtained from the Ensenada Cadastre translate into Gini indices ranging from 0.289 to 0.661. What are the implications of these values? Grigoli and Robles (2017) estimate a critical threshold above which current inequality could affect future economic growth in the present-day economies. Their findings suggest that, above the critical point of a Gini index of 0.27, less egalitarian income distributions produce lower subsequent economic growth. Similarly, Acemoglu and Robinson (2000) demonstrated that increases in 19th-century inequality could have limited the economic growth resulting from industrialisation. With regard to pre-industrial societies, Milanovic et al. (2011) proposed that inequality be studied by incorporating the notion of a 'frontier' of inequality possibilities. Here the implication is that, in every society, there is a maximum feasible level of inequality that can be sustained in the long term which is smaller than the theoretical maximum because it requires that every individual or household perceives at least the minimum of subsistence. If this is the case, some pre-industrial societies, even when relatively low levels of inequality can be close to the feasible maximum, pushing a large portion of the society very close to the level of subsistence and creating the conditions for social unrest. In this context, it is of considerable interest to assess the extent to which an increase in inequality could lead to social conflict, wars, and/or revolutions. The data provided by Milanovic et al. reveal that The Netherlands had a Gini index of 0.611 in 1732, England and Wales had an index of 0.459 in 1759, and pre-Revolutionary France had an index of 0.559 in 1788. Scheidel (2017) argues that a society's unequal income and wealth tend to become even more unequal absent a sufficiently large social shock. This author identifies four main 'levelers' of inequality: political revolution, wars involving massive mobilisation, deadly pandemics, and the collapse of state.

In 18th-century Spain there were no revolutions per se although there were major episodes of social conflict, of which the most significant event was probably the Esquilache riots in 1766.[12] Vilar (1972) mentions minor

12 A study of social conflict in 18th-century Spain exceeds the scope of this text. For summaries, see Domínguez Ortiz (1976), Fernández Díaz (1985), and Martínez-Ruiz and Romero-Samper (1990).

revolts caused by increases in the prices of basic necessities (e.g., bread, oil, bacon).[13] These riots were serious enough to cause several fatalities in Madrid, Zaragoza (Aragon), and Guipúzcoa (a Basque province). Within our sample of locations there were actions – mainly demonstrations and revolts – involving assault and substantial physical violence in Palencia (Gini index = 0.607) and Quesada (40 km from Úbeda, whose Gini index was 0.661). Other conflicts that occurred during the 18th century included (among the most documented) those associated with high food costs in the regions of Baza (1723),[14] Granada (1748), Salamanca (1762-1767), and Barcelona (1789). There were also labour conflicts throughout the 18th century at the royal factory in Guadalajara city (González Enciso, 1980); the Gini index for our sample locale in that city was 0.613. Fernández (1985) identifies participants in the Esquilache riots, the 1789 bread riots (*Rebomboris del Pa*) in Barcelona, and the numerous revolts in Valencia and the Basque Country (the *machinadas*) as including not only the rebellious urban masses but also poor people belonging to guilds as well as tramps and peasants who had emigrated to the cities.

It is tempting to hypothesize that inequality was both a symptom and consequence in all these episodes of social conflict that occurred in rural and urban environments. Underlying this evolution of inequality were a number of complex phenomena (Van Zanden, 1995), such as: (i) structural change induced by the size and growth of urban areas (Castells-Quintana, 2018) and by the expansion of manufacturing and commerce; (ii) a proletarianization of employment due to reduced real wages; (iii) the concentration of capital in urban pressure groups; and (iv) changes in human capital, wage payments, and premium skill (Álvarez and Ramos-Palencia, 2018).

V. Conclusions

Between 1500 and 1800, the current territory of Spain was basically an agricultural society that moved very slowly toward urbanisation. At the same time, it was a society whose unequal nature was institutionally legitimised by three factors: (i) its various territories had historically been under different tax regimes; (ii) both the Church and the nobility enjoyed special fiscal privileges; and (iii) within each territory there were differences – among places – of which their significance reflected the impact of municipal, seigniorial, and

13 The 1766 riots were not prevented by the 1765 decree – in response to a bread shortage – that wheat circulates freely and that prices be reduced. Free circulation favoured the import of wheat from as far away as Naples and Sicily. The price of wheat continued to rise nonetheless because the supply was controlled by large owners, who (along with speculators) actually supported the Esquilache riots because their profit margins had been reduced.

14 According to the Municipal Historic Archive of Cúllar (Libro Capitular from 1723 and cuaderno de cuentas del pósito de 1712-33, legajo 12, vol. III), in 1723 a group of farmers and locals in Cúllar-Baza travelled to Madrid with 34 carriages to acquire 500 *fanegas* of wheat. Recall that, based on our sample, Cúllar-Baza had a Gini index of 0.621.

ecclesiastical taxation. This institutionalised inequality – together with an unequal distribution of land and very low incomes in the bottom distribution of income in large towns and middle-size cities – was largely responsible for high economic inequality, which led in turn to numerous episodes of social conflict. These episodes were closely related to the skewed distribution of landownership and were more frequent in areas with the greatest number of inhabitants.

Bibliography

Acemoglu, D. and J. Robinson (2000) 'Why did the west extend the franchise? Democracy, inequality, and growth in historical perspective', *The Quarterly Journal of Economics* 115 (4), pp. 1167-1199.

Álvarez, B. and F. Ramos-Palencia (2018) 'Human capital and earnings in eighteenth-century Castile', *Explorations in Economic History* 67 (1), pp. 105-133.

Álvarez-Nogal, C. and L. Prados de la Escosura (2007) 'The decline of Spain (1500-1850): conjectural estimates', *European Review of Economic History* 11 (3), pp. 319-366.

Álvarez-Nogal, C. and L. Prados de la Escosura (2013) 'The rise and fall of Spain (1270-1850)', *Economic History Review* 66 (1), pp. 1-37.

Anes, G. (1970) *Las crisis agrarias en la España Moderna*, Madrid.

Brea-Martínez, G. and J. M. Pujadas-Mora (2018) 'Transformación y desigualdad económica en la industrialización en el área de Barcelona, 1715-1860', *Revista de Historia Económica* 36 (2), pp. 241-273.

Castells-Quintana, D. (2018) 'Beyond Kuznets: Inequality and the size and distribution of cities', *Journal of Regional Sciences* 58 (3), pp. 564-580.

Comín, F. and B. Yun-Casalilla, B. (2012), 'Spain: from composite monarchy to nation-state, 1492-1914', in B. Yun-Casalilla and P. O'Brien (eds) *The Rise of Fiscal States: A Global History, 1500-1914*, Cambridge University Press.

Domínguez Ortiz, A. (1951) 'La desigualdad contributiva en Castilla durante el siglo XVIII', *Anuario de historia del derecho español*. Madrid: BOE, año 1951-1952, pp. 1222-1272.

Domínguez Ortiz, A. (1960) *Política y hacienda de Felipe IV*, Madrid.

Domínguez Ortiz, A. (1976) *Sociedad y Estado en el siglo XVIII español*, Barcelona.

Drelichman, M. (2005) 'The curse of Moctezuma: American silver and the Dutch Disease', *Explorations in Economic History* 42 (3), pp. 349-380.

Elliott, J. H. (1963) *The revolt of the Catalans: A study in the decline of Spain (1598-1640)*, Cambridge: Cambridge University Press.

Fernández Díaz, R. (1985) *España en el siglo XVIII*, Barcelona.

Ferrer Alós, Ll. (2002) '¿Modernización fiscal? La implantación del Catastro en Cataluña', *Revista CT/Catastro* 46 (diciembre), pp. 27-35.

García Sanz, Á. (1985) 'El interior peninsular en el siglo XVIII: un crecimiento moderado y tradicional' in R. Fernández Díaz (ed.) *España en el siglo XVIII*, Barcelona.

García-Montero, H. (2015) 'Long-term trends in wealth inequality in catalonia, 1400-1800: initial results', Working Papers 079, Carlo F. Dondena Centre for Research on Social Dynamics (DONDENA), Università Commerciale Luigi Bocconi.

García-Montero, H. (2016) 'The nutritional status of manufacturing workers and craftsmen in Central Spain in the eighteenth century', *Revista de Historia Industrial* 25 (64), pp. 51-75.

Gelabert, J. (1999) 'Castile, 1504-1808' in R. Bonney (ed.) *The rise of the fiscal state in Europe, c. 1250-1815*, Oxford.

González Enciso, A. (1980) *Estado e industria en el siglo XVIII: la fábrica de Guadalajara*, Madrid.

González Enciso, A. (2017) *War, power and the economy. Mercantilism and state formation in 18th-century Europe*, 1st Edition, Routledge.

Grafe, R. (2012) *Distant tyranny: markets, power, and backwardness in Spain, 1650-1800*, Princeton.

Grigoli, F. and A. Robles (2017) 'Inequality overhang', *IMF Working Papers* No. 17/76.

Grupo 75 (1977) *La Economía del Antiguo Régimen. La 'Renta Nacional' de la Corona de Castilla*, Madrid.

Herr, R. (1960/1988) *España y la Revolución del siglo XVIII*, Madrid.

Herr, R. (1974) *An Historical essay on Modern Spain*, California: https://libro.uca.edu/herr/essay.htm

Kuznets, S (1955) 'Economic growth and income inequality', *American Economic Review*, 45 (1), pp. 1-28.

López de Lerena, P. (1789-1790/1990): *Memoria sobre las rentas públicas y balanza comercial de España (1789-1790)*, Madrid.

Marfany, J. (2012): *Land, proto-industry and population in Catalonia, c. 1680-1829. An alternative transition to capitalism?*, Abingdon.

Martínez-Ruiz, E. and M. Romero-Samper (1990) 'Conflictos y conflictividad social en la España del siglo XVIII', in *Coloquio Internacional Carlos III y su Siglo: Actas*, Vol. 1, 1990, pp. 387-423, Madrid.

Milanovic, B (2016) *Global inequality: A new approach for the age of globalization*, Harvard University Press.

Milanovic, B., P. H. Lindert, and J. G. Williamson (2011) 'Pre-industrial Inequality', *The Economic Journal* 121 (551), pp. 255-272.

Moral Ruiz, J. (1990) 'Estudio preliminar' in López de Lerena, [1789-1790]): *Memoria sobre las rentas públicas y balanza comercial de España (1789-1790)*, Madrid, pp. 7-48.

Nicolini, E. and F. Ramos-Palencia (2016a) 'Decomposing income inequality in a backward pre-industrial economy: Old Castile (Spain) in the middle of the eighteenth century', *The Economic History Review* 69 (3), pp. 747-772.

Nicolini, E. and F. Ramos-Palencia (2016b) 'Comparing income and wealth inequality in pre-industrial economies: Lessons from 18th-century Spain', Working Papers 0095, *European Historical Economics Society* (EHES).

Oto-Peralías, D. and D. Romero-Ávila (2017) 'Historical frontiers and the rise of inequality: the case of the frontier of Granada', *Journal of the European Economic Association* 15 (1), pp. 54-98.

Pontón, G. (2016) *La lucha por la desigualdad: una historia del mundo occidental en el siglo XVIII*, Barcelona.

Prados de la Escosura, L. and C. Santiago-Caballero (2018) 'The Napoleonic Wars: A Watershed in Spanish History?', Working Papers 0130, *European Historical Economics Society* (EHES).

Reher, D. S. (1990) *Town and country in pre-industrial Spain. Cuenca 1550-1870*, Cambridge.

Santiago-Caballero, C. (2011) 'Income inequality in central Spain, 1690-1800', *Explorations in Economic History* 48 (1), pp. 83-96.

Scheidel, W. (2017) *The great leveler. violence and the history of inequality from the stone age to the twenty-first century*, Princeton.

Vilar, P. (1972) 'El motín de Esquilache y las crisis del Antiguo Régimen', *Revista de Occidente* no. 108, pp. 199-249.

Vilar, P. (1987) *Cataluña en la España Moderna*, Barcelona.

Vilar, P. (1999) *Hidalgos, Amotinados y Guerrilleros*. Barcelona.

Williamson, J. G. (2002) 'Land, labor, and globalization in the Third World, 1870-1940', *The Journal of Economic History* 62 (1), pp. 55-85.

Yun-Casalilla, B. (2012) 'Introduction: the rise of the fiscal state in Eurasia from a global, comparative and a transnational perspective', in B. Yun-Casalilla and P. O'Brien (2012) (eds) *The rise of fiscal studies: a global history 1500-1914*, Cambridge (UK): Cambridge University Press, pp. 1-35.

van Zanden, J. L. (1995) 'Tracing the beginning of the Kuznets Curve: Western Europe during the Early Modern Period', *Economic History Review* XLVIII (4), pp. 643-664.

ANDREIA FIDALGO

3 Landownership and social inequality: the Algarve example in the 60s and 70s of the eighteenth century*

I. Introduction

The study of pre-industrial economies has become increasingly relevant in historiography, with current debates focusing on analysing medieval and early modern economies as a way of understanding the developmental differences between the north and the south of Europe, which increased during the industrial period. As pre-industrial economies were centred in agriculture this has consequentially generated an interest in topics such as property rights, the institutions that managed and regulated it, and the structure and distribution of landownership.

In this context, many of the studies developed have emphasised 'inequality' as a key element for the understanding of the economic development in rural areas in pre-industrial periods, as social inequality is closely related to unequal property ownership distribution. Using as an example the economies of the New World, authors like Engerman and Sokoloff (2002: 41-88) sought to demonstrate that societies with greater inequality in wealth distribution and with dominant social elites were focused on creating institutions with the main goal of maintaining these elites' benefits and privileges and not economic development. On the other hand, societies with a more equal wealth distribution and egalitarian social structure tended to create a more efficient institutional structure, capable of promoting economic development.

By emphasising wealth distribution inequality, mainly stemming from property ownership, this theory also focuses on social stratification. It proposes the idea that questions relating to property and property rights must be analysed primarily from the perspective of social history (Congost & Santos, 2010: 15-38) and that social actors had a crucial role in the implementation of an institutional structure that allowed them to guarantee their own rights.

* The results presented in this chapter were obtained via research developed within the scope of the doctorate funded by scholarship granted by the *Fundação para a Ciência e a Tecnologia* (PD/BD/105850/2014). My thanks to Liliana Arcanjo (liliana.arcanjo@gmail.com) for the English translation.

Andreia Fidalgo • University of Algarve and CIES-IUL

Inequality in rural Europe (Late Middle Ages – 18th century), ed. by Guido Alfani and Erik Thoen, CORN, 18 (Turnhout, 2020), pp. 45–64.

 DOI 10.1484/M.CORN-EB.5.121947

Studies like that of Santos e Serrão (2013: 475-494), for example, analysing Alentejo (Portugal) at the end of the eighteenth century as a case study, demonstrate how institutional changes to property law implemented by the political power were appropriated and subverted by social agency in order to serve the interests of agricultural landowners, showing the importance of analysing social variables. Moreover, recent investigations have further shown that, in order to understand the socioeconomic effects of institutional changes made to property law in different societies, it's fundamental to understand the concrete social appropriation and application of new institutional rules and regulations (Congost, Gelman & Santos eds, 2017).

Research focused on a local or regional scale has also attempted to analyse social stratification, landownership, and property rights in relation to agricultural development. Lana-Berasain (2013: 26-50), for example, analyses the case of southern Navarra (Spain) between 1600 and 1935, pointing towards unequal land and wealth distribution as one of the aspects that, along with others such as geographical and environmental features, allow to explain the failure of institutional changes to property law and the limitations in economic development.

Analysing the case of Guadalajara, between 1690 and 1800, Santiago-Caballero (2013: 160-179) exposes that unequal property distribution, associated with a strong manorialism-type of system, is a crucial factor in explaining differences in levels of productivity. Santiago-Caballero points out that disproportionate land distribution was largely associated in Spain to the dominant role of large landowners. This meant they had privileges and access to the most productive land and greater flexibility when investing capital, to the detriment of small landowners whose scope of action was more limited.

The above examples demonstrate that the analysis of case studies with a local or regional focus can be a useful tool in reflecting on the relationship between social stratification and landownership, and the economic development of rural areas. It would seem that this type of analysis could offer a similar contribution, when applied to the region of the Algarve. The Algarve is the southernmost region of Portugal, spanning a territory of approximately 4997 km^2, which, for reasons of tradition, held the title of 'Kingdom' until 1910. With the Atlantic Ocean in the south and west, the Guadiana River in the east and the Serra de Monchique and the Serra do Caldeirão mountain ranges in the north, the Algarve is a well delimited region. From the late sixteenth century to the eighteenth century this region remained largely forgotten by the Portuguese Crown. Only in the 60s and 70s of the eighteenth century, amidst a concerted enlightened reformism led by the Marquis of Pombal (Secretary of State of King José I), would the region become a focus of royal interest as the subject of several economic reforms. It is apparent that the Algarve could provide an interesting case study, considering the social and economic situation of the region at the time, and the terms and difficulty of implementation of the reformist plan. Such a case study would allow for a test of the hypothesis relating social inequality and landownership distribution to their impact on the implementation of institutional reform and economic development.

II. The economic 'Restoration' of the Kingdom of the Algarve

In the 1760s and 1770s, the Algarve would become the subject of a reformist project, with the ultimate goal being the economic recovery of the region. The project followed in the wake of a series of other economic measures enacted in the reformist policy of the Marquis, aimed to fortify Portugal, after an economic crisis in the 60s caused by the reduction of the gold-mining production in Brazil. Despite the region's potential, with its Mediterranean agriculture and vast coastal area with bountiful fishing, when the Portuguese Crown turned its interest to the Algarve it found a mostly rural and economically depressed territory. The situation was the result of a continuous process of deterioration of the main economic activities, particularly agriculture and fisheries. This process became accentuated by end of the sixteenth century (Magalhães, 1993), when the region lost its strategic function providing support to the Portuguese strongholds in the north of Africa and with it royal interest.

The attempt at 'Restoring the Kingdom of the Algarve' – referred to as such in documentary sources – consisted of a comprehensive legislative package, implemented mostly from 1773 onward, created with full consideration of the degradation that affected the region since the sixteenth century. The Pombaline measures put in place were mostly economic and looked to overturn the state of economic stagnation in the region, while also contributing to centralizing a government that sought to be absolute.

Among the main economic measures, due to the importance ascribed to them, emphasis must be given to the ones directly related to the Algarve's greatest source of wealth: fishing. In the Provision of 13th January 1773, the fishing tax was reduced to two *dizimas* (a customs tax over goods), but the tax paid for fish exported fresh outside the Kingdom was doubled. Pombal's goal was clear: regulate fishing, increase the production and exportation of dried and salted fish, by forbidding the exportation of fresh fish, while simultaneously revitalising the salt extraction industry. Two days after, in 15th January, the *Companhia Geral das Reais Pescarias do Reino do Algarve* (General Company of Royal Fishing of the Kingdom of the Algarve) was constituted. The last of the Pombaline monopolist companies, it guaranteed governmental control and intervention over the fish considered privileged or royal – corvina and tuna, the most lucrative – and left the remainder to free trade.

The culmination of the interventions focused on fishing was the edification *ex-nihilo* of Vila Real de Santo António, with its strategic localisation on the left bank of the Guadiana River, facing the neighbouring kingdom of Spain. Inaugurated in 13th of May 1776, this *industrial village* held combined economic and political functions. Conceived for the regulation of fishing and its transformation, the village would guarantee Portuguese dominion over the fishing of sardine, until then controlled by Catalan fishermen installed in the beach of Monte Gordo (Correia, 1997).

There were other important fiscal measures that did not focus directly on fishing but on the region's agriculture. A charter issued on 18th January 1773 exempted grains, flours and vegetables of the entry tax into the Kingdom of the Algarve. Even more relevant is the law of 4th February 1773, which ended the 'heinous distinction' between the kingdoms of Portugal and of the Algarve, eliminating the multitude of taxes and tolls paid by products that left the region into the remainder of Portugal, allowing the institution of an internal free trade policy. Added to all these political interventions were also measures aimed at problems related to landownership, the impact and significance of which have not been widely studied. It's precisely this that we are interested in exploring in this article, in correlation with the society of the time.

II.1 Reformist legislation regarding the ownership of land

While the bulk of the Pombaline intervention in the Algarve took place in the decade of 1770, the region had begun to warrant the attention of the Crown in the previous decade; then it was directed at the underdevelopment of agriculture, which was associated with problems related to landownership and the contracts for its exploitation, namely the usurious *foros* and *censos* (both types of property usage annuities) charged in the Kingdom of the Algarve. As Pombal himself would witness, "the agriculture was in large part reduced to terms of impossibility", as the land had almost all been bought from the 'needy' and become the possession of a reduced wealthy elite, that would then burdened it with "such *foros* and so onerous that they exceeded the land's production".[1]

By the Provision of 8th January 1765, the recently appointed ombudsman of the District of the Kingdom of the Algarve, Judge José António de Oliveira Damásio, was mandated to ensure the enforcement of the *foros*, interest, and *censos* stipulated in the law of 23th May 1668, which had reduced them to an annual rate of 5%. Subsequently, a charter from 15th September 1766 would create a committee, presided by the same Judge, to evaluate the usurious *foros* and *censos* in the Kingdom of the Algarve, with the goal to assess the legitimacy of the same.[2] The objective was clear: to alleviate charges levied on farmers and end the abuse of illegal executions, which would lead to greater availability of funds to invest in agricultural activities.

However, the measures did not have the desired effects immediately. New legislation would be issued in the 70s with the same intent. The first measure was undertaken in 1772, in a letter of law issued on 13th March, which declared

1 National Library of Portugal, BNP, Colecção Pombalina, PBA 695.

2 National Archives of *Torre do Tombo*, ANTT, Ministério do Reino, mç.608.

null all the contracts taken on the Serra de Tavira, absolving the inhabitants of all rents which had until then been 'extorted' from them. The justification for this letter of law is clear: in 1645, the councilmen of the Municipality of Tavira had, on offer of 'bribery', illicitly donated all the vast territory of the Serra de Tavira to Manuel Godinho de Castelo Branco, chief-captain of the city. His heirs would later sell the property, in 1756, to Manuel Vaz Velho, for an insignificant sum. Instituted as 'lord and possessor of a vast territory', Velho would fully enjoy all its 'privileges, rights and annual rents' and torment the inhabitants through 'abuse and oppression'. The dispositions of the letter of law are equally clear on this matter: with consideration for the 1200 homes in all the Serra, with between five to six thousand inhabitants,[3] subject to the 'abuse and oppression' of Manuel Vaz Velho, the donation by the Municipality of Tavira to Manuel Godinho de Castelo was declared null, subsequently nullifying any sale made by his heirs. The inhabitants of the Serra de Tavira would henceforth retain 'full control and possession' of the buildings they inhabited and the land they worked, which constituted a very significant change regarding property rights.

The most significant charter, given it was aimed at the whole region, would be issued a few months after this one, on 16th January 1773. This new charter intended to regulate the *censos* and *foros* of usurious character, established throughout the Kingdom of the Algarve, with the goal to deter the 'greed of the interested' and end illicit contracts and acquisitions. According to the preface of the charter, neither the charters of 23rd May of 1698, in which a regulatory rate for interest and *censos a retro* was established, nor of 15th September 1766, in which a committee was established in the Algarve to investigate the *foros* and *censos*, were being abided.

Therefore, to avoid the exploitation that tormented the farmers, this new charter suspended all *censos* and *foros* in the region until they were examined by the referred committee. The landowners were required to present their land titles within thirty days, under penalty of having their collections suspended and the charged *censos* and *foros* extinct. From then on the *censos* and *foros* applied were regulated by law. In case the contracts were considered null or usurious, the direct landowners would be required to return the values illegally charged.

II.2 Types of agrarian contracts

To best understand these charters and the terminology used by them, it's important to recall the types of contracts of access to land exploitation that

3 It is worth to note the exaggeration contained in the letter of law, regarding the number of inhabitants of the Serra de Tavira. In 1756, the number of houses in the rural parishes of the council of Tavira would not have been over 916 and the number of inhabitants over 3029, over an extension of territory that not only included the mountain range but also the *barrocal* (in between the mountain range and the coast) and the coast.

were utilized in the Old Regime in Portugal. The most frequent types were essentially two: *emphyteusis* and leasing. As pointed out by Rui Santos, there were also cases of full property rights, where landowners retained full rights to their properties and opted to exploit them directly. However, this was not as common as *emphyteusis* or leasing (Santos, 2012: 286-287).

Emphyteusis contracts were long term, established over the span of at least three life times (from 1757) or in perpetuity, which is to say, 'without term'. These contracts consisted of the division of property in two domains: the 'eminent domain', which belonged to the original landowner, and the 'useful domain', acquired by the *foreiro* (taker). The latter was obligated to pay an annual *foro* to the original landowner, in exchange for the transfer of part of the property, with rights to not only exploit it but also sell it, establish an *emphyteusis* contract of their own or lease it, so long as they obtained consent from the original landowner. This type of contract was largely responsible for the multiplication and overlapping of rights over a singular property, as it allowed the *foreiro* ample property rights (Serrão, 2017), as well as social recognition as a landowner.

In the second type of contract, leasing, the transferable property rights were more restricted. The tenant had the right to cultivate the land, graze their cattle on it and use available infrastructure, without modifying them. Leasing contracts were short term, generally between three and six years, but could be renewed successively if the original landowner was happy with the performance of the tenant (Santos, 2013: 287).

Considering the specific forms of property, resulting from the models of access to the exploitation of land in the 1700s, the contrast between the north and south of Portugal becomes apparent: in the north *emphyteusis* was prevalent, as well as in Lisbon; south of the Tagus river, in Alentejo, mostly made up of *herdades* (estate-like farms), leasing was the leading model (Costa, Lains & Miranda, 2011: 222). Regarding the Algarve, composed mostly of small and medium properties, a preliminary incursion into the notary archives in the region points to a likely prevalence of the *emphyteusis* contract model.

With *emphyteusis* and leasing being the most common types of contract when it came to land exploitation, the charters of 15th September 1766 and 16th January 1773 directed at the Algarve seem to suggest the main concern was not these but other types of contracts, best described as investment capital or credit contracts: reservative *censos* and consignative *censos*.

The reservative *censos* was a contract in which an individual (the *censuísta*) granted another (the *censuário*) full domain over a property, reserving the right to receive over the same an annuity – in money or in produce – that should be paid by the *censuário* until it met the evaluated value of the property. In practise, this *censos* constituted a form of land acquisition without the possibility of immediate payment, which instead deferred over time. Despite being similar to *emphyteusis*, this model differed by not allowing the division of the domain, as both eminent and useful domain belonged to the *censuário* (Rodrigues, 2015b).

Regarding the consignative *censos*, this was a contract in which an individual (the *censuísta*) exchanged a sum of money with another individual (the *censuário*), 'consigned' to one of the latter's properties, under the condition that an annual *censos* be paid. In practise, these were capital investment – or credit – contracts, often disguised as sale contracts, effectively avoiding any usury laws (Rodrigues, 2015a). Unlike the reservative *censos*, the consignative *censos* did not generate the transfer of the property, as the *censuário* kept possession and full usage of it; they were sale contracts in exchange for an annuity, in which the property was not transferred but effectively served only as a guarantee. By charter in 13th December 1614, further reinforced by the charter of 23rd May 1698, the rates of this type of *censos* were fixed at 5% for *censos perpétuos a retro*[4] – the most common – 10% for a one lifetime *censos* and 8.3% for a two lifetimes *censos*.

The terminology used in the legislation created in the 60s and 70s to solve the landownership problems of the Algarve is not always clear: it uses the terms *censos*, *foros* and 'pensions' interchangeably, which presents an obstacle to understanding which type of 'illicit' contracts they were trying to quash. However, there are indications in the very legislation and contemporary documentary sources that allow us to present a hypothesis. Both the provision of 8th January 1765, as well as the charter of 15th September 1766, which established the committee for the investigation of *foros* and *censos* in the Kingdom of the Algarve, indicated the necessity for compliance with the dispositions contained in the charter of 23rd of May 1698. This was especially important regarding the *foros*/*censos perpétuos a retro*, with a legal fixed rate of 5%, but in practise being charged at rates of 10% or more in the region.

The legislation was swiftly questioned: a representation of the ombudsmen of several chapters of *Santa Casa da Misericórdia* (religious charity), of the prelates and other 'powerful' figures of the Kingdom of the Algarve enquired whether the new laws were only applicable to the consignative *censos* or also the reservative *censos*. The then ombudsman of the District of the Kingdom of the Algarve, Judge José António de Oliveira Damásio, would seek to clarify that the charter of 23rd May of 1698, while not specifying the type of *censos* or *foros* which it referred to, stipulated that the rate should be complied with unequivocally. He would then go on to present examples of the type of *censos* practised in the region, demonstrating that consignative *censos* were frequently charged at an annual rate of 10%, which was against the referred law, thus making them illegal. The ombudsman also pointed out that the *censos* referred to as 'reservative' in the region, were not, in fact, truly 'reservative', and therefore also illegal.[5] A law from 16th January 1773 clarified

4 *Censos perpétuos a retro* were *censos* with no term (perpetual), where there was a special clause that allowed the *censuário* to terminate the contract, if the full amount exchanged between parties was returned.

5 National Archives of *Torre do Tombo*, ANTT, Ministério do Reino, mç. 608.

that the 'truly reservative *censos*' were those in which an individual yielded his property, reserving the right to receive a certain portion of the produce or money from its production or annual income, without a specific amount being established, albeit no more than a rate of 5%. In the so called 'reservative' censos practised in the region the establishment of *censos perpétuos a retro* was common, with rates of 10% or more, which made them illegal and usurious.

There seems to have also existed some doubt regarding the applicability of the new legislation to the *emphyteusis foros* – a question generated, it would seem, by the ambiguous nature of the terminology used at the time, in which *censos* and *foros* were often used interchangeably. It would only be during the reign of Queen Maria I, on 15th July 1779, that a charter issued to declare, amplify and partly revoke the previous charters issued in 1773, would clarify the confusion between '*foros* and *censos* and *emphyteusis foros*'. Such confusion should not persist, as, in the latter, "there is freedom to increase above the rate of 5%, without usury, the annuity over the transferred land", further clarifying that the previous charters should not be considered when it concerned *emphyteusis* contracts.

To sum up, despite the ambiguity caused, even at the time, by the legal definitions used, the reformist legislation directed toward landowning matters seems to reveal a concern with usurious *censos* contracts, be they consignative or reservative. Given the precarious economic situation and underutilization of the region's resources, the land had been progressively acquired, for very small sums, by a restricted group of lords – described by the very legislation as 'powerful' – who would then immediately make them 'available again' to the farmers, through the charge of often prohibitive *censos*. Therefore, most of the land was held by a handful of landowning lords, who used illegal contracts to extract from them the greatest amount of profit. The goal of the Pombaline legislation aimed at the region was clear: to end these illicit contracts and relieve the tax burden on the farmers that exploited the land in the stead of the original landowners, who could subsequently bring greater investment and exploitation of the agricultural resources. This was aligned with the larger goal behind the entire 'Restoration' project for the Kingdom of the Algarve: to take advantage of the region's potential and contribute to its economic growth.

III. Landownership and social stratification

All this Pombaline legislation seems to suggest the existence of a landowning imbalance in the region and, consequently, a larger social inequality problem in the fabric of the regional society, in which only a small but dominant group of landowners thrived. The provision of 8th January 1765 referred specifically to the illegal *censos* and interest charged by 'powerful' and 'rich' people who took advantage of other's 'poverty'; the charter of 15th September 1766 employs similar terms, referencing the 'tyranny' practised by the 'powerful'.

In the 70s, the charter of 16th January 1773 intended to "deal with the greed of the interested in usurious *censos* and *foros*", indicating that there was still a dominant group of landowners that perpetuated these activities. The letter of law of 13th March 1772 further exposed this problem by revealing that a vast territory, corresponding to the Serra de Tavira, was under the domain of a single Lord, Manuel Vaz Velho, who 'tormented' its inhabitants with high rents.

In the mostly ruralised society that characterized the Algarve at the time, where social stratification was largely associated with landownership,[6] we'll now reflect on the general distribution of land in the 60s and 70s and identify the possible imbalances that might have motivated the Marquis of Pombal to issue the referred legislation.

First and foremost, it's important to revisit the studies of Joaquim Romero Magalhães about the Algarve, during the early modern age. This historian defines Algarve's society at the time as 'a crystallized society', emphasising the stagnation of several groups and the difficulty in social mobility (Magalhães, 2012). This was a society in which the greater nobility had little expression and in which a dominant group, 'the noble people of governance of the land', stood out. This group not only occupied the administrative roles in the councils but was also one of the wealthiest in the region; a wealth obtained mostly through dominion over landownership. In the context of social stratification associated to landownership, this historian describes a region where small rural property is predominant and medium rural property also has a considerable presence (Magalhães, 1993: 185). Additionally, he describes a group, the merchants and businessmen, which gradually acquired property as a means of 'social promotion' and to get closer to the landowning lords (Magalhães, 1993: 163). Equally relevant in the landowning front, especially in Faro, where the Dioceses' headquarters were located, was the presence of the high clergy: rich men, from great families of 'the noble people of governance of the land', with "the largest fortune in the Algarve – rents, *dizimos*, properties, *foros* – being at the hands of the collective cathedral chapter" (Magalhães, 1993: 355).

In conclusion, the studies of Romero Magalhães point towards the predominance of small to medium property, unevenly distributed, with the prevalence of a strong manorialist-type of regime still. Landownership was essentially in the hands of the local elite (the same that held governmental and military offices or high ecclesiastic functions), to which the rich merchants and businessmen were progressively added. It was this scenario that would've motivated Pombal to issue legislation specifically directed at landownership for the Algarve.

To better understand if, in the specific period in analysis, eighteenth century's 60s and 70s, the social patterns present in property distribution

---

6 As referred by Rui Santos (2013: 283), in a rural society, the extent of property rights held by an individual over the land constituted a key parameter in their position in the social stratification, and was probably one of the elements most closely related to social status.

corresponded to the ones Romero Magalhães identified for a larger chronology, we resorted to a particularly interesting and revealing documentary source: the books of *décimas*, of the municipalities of Faro and Tavira.[7] The *décima* was a tax created in 1641, as a response to the increase in the defensive needs experienced by Portugal, arising from the Portuguese Restoration War. It corresponded to 10% of all income[8] and affected the entire population, making it an invaluable documentary source when analysing income distribution and inequality during this period. The *décima* allows us to isolate specifically the income resultant from landownership and analyse the distribution of said property. Furthermore, we can categorize it as small, medium or large property and also identify the landowners and their respective social background.

III.1 Property dimension

While the *décima* doesn't supply precise direct data about the dimensions of the properties, it does provide data regarding the owner's income. However, in the absence of documentary sources that specifically describe the property's dimensions, basing the analysis on the income value is quite an accurate measure, as evidenced by Serrão (2000: 44-45). On the other hand, this same historian alerted to the difficulty in establishing the income criteria for the classifications of small, medium and large properties. In order to determine these tiers, he made use of the information set in a law of 3rd August 1770, for the regulation of the majorats, which defined as 'significant' a property income of over two hundred thousand *réis* for the provinces of Extremadura and Alentejo, and of one hundred thousand *réis* for the remaining provinces. Consequently, Serrão determines for the region of Lisbon, at the end of the Old Regime, five tiers: 'small property', with an income lower than twenty five thousand *réis*, 'small-medium property', with an income between twenty five and fifty thousand *réis*, 'medium property', between fifty and one hundred thousand *réis*, 'medium-large property', between one hundred and two hundred thousand *réis*, and finally, 'large property', with an income of over two hundred thousand *réis* (Serrão, 2000: 50).

7 Considering the scarcity of documentary sources and its various inherent chronological lapses, we were able to consult the following: the book of *décimas* of rustic properties, of 1773-1774, of the ecclesiastic residents of the parishes of Sé and São Pedro, in Faro; the book of *décimas* of rustic properties, of 1779-1781, of the ecclesiastic and secular residents of the parishes of Sé and São Pedro, in Faro; and the book of *décimas* of rustic and urban properties, of 1779, of the ecclesiastic and secular residents of the parishes of Santa Maria and Santiago, in Tavira. Municipal Historic Archive of Tavira, Fundo: Corregedoria da Comarca de Tavira, PT/AMTVR/CCT/B/002; Municipal Historic Archive of Faro, Fundo: Câmara Municipal de Faro, PT/MFAR/CMFAR/F-A/005/0003 [1779-1781] and PT/MFAR/CMFAR/F-A/006/0001 [1773-1774].

8 The *décima* varied between 10% during war time and 4.5% in time of peace. For the time period being analysed it was fixed at 10%.

Table 3.1. Property dimension in the urban parishes in Faro

Dimension	Income (in *réis*)	No. of properties	%
Small	< 15.000	478	86,4%
Medium	15.000 – 25.000	30	13,4%
	25.000 – 50.000	34	
	50.000 – 100.000	10	
Large	> 100.000	1	0,2%
		553	**100%**

Source: Municipal Historic Archive of Faro, Fundo: Câmara Municipal de Faro, PT/MFAR/CMFAR/F-A/005/0003

Taking into consideration that, in the case of the Algarve, a 'significant' income was stipulated at half of the one in the former example, meaning one hundred thousand *réis*, we chose to adapt this scale using the following tiers: 'small property' is determined as property with income lower than fifteen thousand *réis*, 'small-medium property', with income between fifteen and twenty-five thousand *réis*, 'medium property', between twenty five and fifty thousand *réis*, 'medium-large property', between fifty and one hundred thousand *réis* and 'large property', with an income over one hundred thousand *réis*.

Basing our analysis on the landholdings of landowners resident in the urban parishes of Faro (see Table 3.1) we can see an evident prevalence of small property: in a sample of 553 listed properties, 478 did not possess income over fifteen thousand *réis*. In the medium property bracket we register only 74 properties: 30 in the small-medium tier, 34 in the medium and only 10 in the medium-large tier. Only one property is registered with an income superior to one hundred thousand *réis*.

Small property is the predominant trend, corresponding to 86.4% of the total properties registered, with 13.4% corresponding to medium property. This made for an obvious contrast with the closest region, Alentejo, which was dominated by large property (Santos, 2004: 23-52), and it is more similar to the region of Lisbon, where small and medium property prevailed (Serrão, 2000).

III.2 Relation of number of properties with the number of landowners

Considering the predominance of small property and the total number of properties, 553, it's interesting to try to establish the relation to the total number of landowners, 292. For the data collected for the landowners residing in Faro (see Table 3.2), we see that half of them owned or received some type of revenue from a single property and 22% of them from two. The percentage gradually decreases as the number of properties owned increases, with only 2% of landowners owning or receiving revenue from six properties and 1% from seven or more. An interesting indicator of inequality in property distribution

Table 3.2. Relation between the number of properties and the number of landowners (Faro, a°1779)

No of Properties	No of landowners	(%)
1	168	58%
2	64	22%
3	28	10%
4	17	6%
5	6	2%
6	5	2%
≥ 7	4	1%
	292	100,0%
No of Properties	No of landowners	(%)

Source: Municipal Historic Archive of Faro, Fundo: Câmara Municipal de Faro, PT/MFAR/CMFAR/F-A/005/0003

is the fact you can find in these last two very reduced pools of individuals the owners of some of the largest properties in the council of Faro, as shown next (see Table 3.3).

III.3 Inequality in property income

The relationship between the number of properties and the number of landowners points to the potential imbalance in property distribution but it's not, on its own, a clear enough indicator of inequality. A good method to evaluate inequality is the Gini coefficient: a measure of statistical dispersion, used to determine the degree of concentration of distribution; it can vary between 0 and 1, with 0 representing maximal equality, with perfectly egalitarian distribution and 1 maximal inequality, where all wealth would be concentrated in a single individual.

Using the income associated with the properties of the individuals listed in the books of *décimas* of Faro and Tavira, for the year of 1779, we can calculate for Faro a coefficient of 0.65 and for Tavira of 0.64. These are indicators of high inequality in the concentration of landholding income and are not far from the ones calculated by José Vicente Serrão for the parishes in the region of Lisbon, during the same period, which varied between 0.47 and 0.72 (Serrão, 2000: 74). Furthermore, if we take into account other Gini coefficients calculated for various Portuguese localities during the Old Regime (which took into account all types of income, not only those resultant from landholdings) the values are very similar. This isn't surprising, given the economy relied mainly on agricultural and landholding ventures for income generation. For example, in 1690, for Avis (Alentejo) the estimated Gini coefficient was 0.69, for Arraiolos (Alentejo), in 1700, 0.66 (Faísca &

Lopes, 2015), for Guarda (Beira Alta), in 1766, 0.74 and for Porto, in 1770, 0.70 (Reis, 2016).

III.4 Social groups of the largest landowners

Using Faro in 1779 as an example, among the 292 listed individuals, with an average annual income of 16.040 *réis*, we're able to identify the largest secular landowners residing in the urban parishes of Faro, as well as the number of properties each of them possessed or from which they received some type of revenue (see Table 3.3).

The great majority of these large landowners had three or more properties; one, Manuel de Figueiredo Mascarenhas, receiving income from as many as eighteen different properties. Considering the total universe of landowners, the top eight individuals alone accumulated 32% of all revenue ensuing from landholdings. As far as social class goes, from what we were able to ascertain, the men of local nobility stand out, often officers in local military companies. But, above all, the businessmen in the city of Faro, the main centre of commercial activity in the region at the time, were the most predominant.

In Tavira in 1779, of the 1224 listed landowners with an average annual income of 13.950 *réis*, we were also able to pinpoint the largest landowners resident in urban parishes (see Table 3.4). However, in this case, the rustic and urban properties appear listed together, making it impossible to tell them apart. For this very reason, we cannot grant the top eight landowners the same significance in revenue accumulation as in Faro: the top eight landowners amassed only 14% of all landholding related income.

Of particular note are Judge João Leal da Gama e Ataíde, by far the largest landowner in the council of Tavira and Manuel Vaz Velho, the same mentioned in the letter of law of 13th March 1772, by which the vast property comprising of the Serra de Tavira was removed from him, who despite this still appears on this list as one of the largest landowners.

Returning to Faro, and taking into consideration this was where the headquarters of the Dioceses of the Algarve were situated, it's equally interesting to turn our attention to tax paid by ecclesiastic residents (see Table 3.5). Of the 39 individuals listed, in 1773, at the top of the list we invariably find the men that held high functions in the Dioceses, especially the canons. Between them, the top eight ecclesiastic members held over half (56%) of the total revenue resulting from landholdings of the universe analysed. This data helps corroborate the idea that landownership in the region was also distributed among the high diocesan clergy and reinforces the previously mentioned notion that this group was composed by wealthy men, with deep roots in the great families that made up the Algarve's elite.

The case studies presented allow us to corroborate the studies of Romero Magalhães regarding the regional society of the Algarve. Small property was predominant and medium property held some significance. In Faro, as well as Tavira, the large landowners were either members of the local nobility or

Table 3.3. Largest secular landowners residing in Faro in 1779

	Name	Income (in réis)	No. of properties	Social status/position
1	António José Medina	377.000	2	Legal representative of a Majorat
2	Manuel de Figueiredo Mascarenhas	293.540	18	Nobleman of the Royal House; Professed Knight of the Order of Christ; Chief-Captain
3	João Domingues Sanches	182.700	8	Businessman; Consul for the nation of Spain
4	Urbano Xavier Mendes	149.950	6	Doctor
5	Fernando José Seabra Neto	147.350	9	Nobleman; Field Master
6	João Keating	129.720	6	Businessman
7	Guilherme Pites	125.320	3	Businessman (?)
8	Lourenço da Costa Dias (heirs)	93.900	5	Businessman; Company Captain

Source: Municipal Historic Archive of Faro, Fundo: Câmara Municipal de Faro, PT/MFAR/CMFAR/F-A/005/0003

Table 3.4. The Largest secular landowners residing in Tavira in 1779

	Name	Income (in *réis*)	Social status/position
1	João Leal da Gama e Ataíde	594.910	Judge; Professed Knight of the Order of Christ; *Familiar* of the Holy Office
2	Manuel Marques Neves	417.700	Businessman, Company Captain
3	José Vitorino Guerreiro	357.180	Chief-Captain of Cacela.
4	António Xavier de Oliveira	254.500	Company Captain (?)
5	Pedro André da Franca Telles Côrte-Real	240.420	Majorat
6	Manuel Nunes	181.450	Businessman; Company Captain
7	Ricardo Antunes Araújo Brandão	168.950	Businessman (?)
8	Manuel Vaz Velho	167.100	Businessman; Customs Treasurer for Tavira; Professed Knight of the Order of Christ

Source: Municipal Historic Archive of Tavira, Fundo: Corregedoria da Comarca de Tavira, PT/AMTVR/CCT/B/002

Table 3.5. Largest ecclesiastic landowners residing in Faro

	Name	Income (in *réis*)	Social status/position
1	António José de Brito	122.200	Diocesan Canon
2	António José de Sousa Rosado	111.440	Diocesan Choirsmaster
3	Samuel Pitts Parcar	101.500	Diocesan Canon
4	Pedro Pestana	94.820	Diocesan Canon
5	José da Costa (heirs)	86.260	Diocesan Canon
6	Manuel José Pereira	57.710	Priest
7	Theodoro Pestana da Silva (Dr.)	49.970	Minister of the Ecclesiastical Consistory
8	Francisco Garfias Torres	49.350	Diocesan Canon

Source: Municipal Historic Archive of Faro, Fundo: Câmara Municipal de Faro, PT/MFAR/CMFAR/F-A/006/0001

prosperous businessmen. Together they formed the local elite, the same that occupied and rotated among themselves the local governmental and military offices. And finally, we had the high clergymen from the Dioceses in the Algarve.

It would seem that by the end of the Old Regime, the Algarve was beset by social inequality, where the imbalance in the distribution of landownership was apparent and the prevalent system was one where the lord exploited the farmer, through contracts that did not respect the law. This is precisely what the Pombaline legislation reveals, opposing the interests of the 'powerful', by defending the rights of the farmers exploited by the original landowners through the application of heavy *foros* and *censos*, and trying to ameliorate the situation. However, taking into consideration that the legislation ran against the very deeply rooted interests of the local elite, the question remains of whether these laws had the desired effect or if these powerful interests were able to overrule them.

IV. Implementation of landownership legislation

The Pombaline legislation on landownership and illegal contracts in the Algarve seems to have faced difficulties from the very start. The pioneer provision issue on 8th January 1765 appears to have had the effect of making the "powerful people, in a show of violent hatred and tyrannical revenge", not only continue to charge the same usurious *foros* and *censos* but create new ones. As a consequence of this, the charter of 15th September 1766 sought to establish a committee to investigate the legitimacy of the *foros*. However, the scope of its work seems to have been very limited from the start: a delegation sent to the Desembargo do Paço (The Supreme Court of Justice for the Kingdom of

Portugal), in representation of the 'religions', Catholic charities and hospitals and other 'powerful', lead by the Superintendent for Tobacco in the Kingdom of the Algarve, Agostinho Álvares da Silva, questioned the type of contracts to which the royal charter referred and defended the legitimacy of the *foros* and *censos* practised in the region.

The first meeting of the committee, held on 16th June 1767, was presided over by the Judge of the District of the Algarve and was composed of the ministers nominated in the charter. The main topic of discussion was the clarification of the legal nature of the *censos* considered lawful or unlawful, and the type of judgments that needed to be issued. However, in the face of several questions originated with the first committee meeting, according to the President Judge himself, there were no further meetings had by the committee or any royal clarification of the questions raised.

This committee would be reactivated by charter issued on 16th January 1773, giving a clear sign that its function in the previous decade had not been fulfilled. This time it was specifically defined that the committee was to be held in the cities of Faro and Tavira, presided once more by Judge José António de Oliveira Damásio, who had by this time occupied the office of General Superintendent for Customs in the South Provinces. The problems with this new committee were soon to be felt: a few months after its reactivation, on 4th of August, a new charter would expand the first one, denouncing the subterfuge employed by original landowners, who alleged the existence of very old contracts for which they no longer possessed titles they could present to the committee. And, just like in the previous decade, the reinstitution of this committee would also get a new delegation sent to the Desembargo do Paço, which the Marquis of Pombal would classify as 'rash'.[9] This delegation was sent by the cathedral chapter of the Dioceses of the Algarve, a group which would be greatly affected by the new *foros* and *censos* legislation, and who therefore opposed it.

The committee would have gathered a few times but the shortage of documentary sources about its existence and operation don't allow us to expand on its action or effectiveness. However, despite the undertaken effort, the charter that would be issued during the reign of Queen Maria I, on 15th July 1779, would make clear that the previous charters of 16th January and 4th August 1773 were not complied with. It referenced that, given the fact that the deadlines for presentation of the titles for *censos* and *foros* were not complied with and that, according to the previous law, these should be therefore considered null and extinct, the Queen forgave the lack of compliance and established a new deadline of four months for the presentation of these titles.

It's interesting to point out that the lack of compliance with the royal dispositions for the regulation of the *foros* and *censos* was not exclusive to

9 Library and Historic Archive of the Ministry of Public Works, Transport and Communication, MR 14, fl. 43.

the 60s and 70s in the eighteenth century. In the seventeenth century, the publication of the charter of 13th of December 1614 – which fixed, for the first time, the rates for the *censos* and *foros* at 5% for *censos perpétuos a retro*, 10% for one lifetime *censos* and 8.3% for two lifetimes – gave rise to the need for the publication of another charter, a few years later, specifically directed toward the region of the Algarve: the charter of 14th October 1641, which stipulated that it was compulsory to respect the 5% tax in all "*foros*, contracts and *censos* celebrated before the issue of this charter, as well as after".

There is, however, an example of success for the Pombaline legislation issued between 1760 and 1780: the letter of law issued on 13th March 1772. This declared null all titles in the Serra de Tavira, absolving its inhabitants of all the rents that had been 'extorted' from them until then by Manuel Vaz Velho, and giving them full domain over the land they inhabited and exploited. There is no register of any *décima* tax paid in 1779 by Manuel Vaz Velho for income obtained from properties located in the Serra de Tavira, which signifies the success of the letter of law from seven years prior. Furthermore, this measure would anticipate something that would only become a reality in the following century, with regards to liberal agrarian reforms: a transfer to the farmers of the full domain of leased or rented properties.

It is in this letter of law that the greatest impact the Pombaline landowning reform had in the Algarve resides. The other measures seem to have faced a slew of difficulties, product of the existence of an unequal society, headed by a minority regional elite of great landowners, whose economic interests were deeply invested in the region for generations.

V. Conclusions

The Kingdom of the Algarve seems to constitute, as we tried to demonstrate, an interesting case study with regards to the close relationship between landownership and regional social context. Its peripheral position in the Kingdom of Portugal, and relative isolation and neglect from which it had suffered for centuries, allow to explain, in great measure, why these types of landownership contracts – which did not respect the law and only benefited the interests of a regional elite – were allowed to proliferate. The region-specific Pombaline legislation, in the 60s and 70s of the eighteenth century, would demonstrate that, in a society still characterized by a strong manorialism-type system, the announced changes, which posed a risk to old and deeply rooted interests, would not be successfully implemented.

These changes intended to alleviate the heavy charges levied by the original landowners on the farmers who exploited the land, and, consequently, allow for a greater investment in agriculture, generally contributing toward the economic 'restoration' and growth of the region. It's then logical to infer, given the failure in the application of the reform charters, that the desired economic growth did not come to pass, at least where agricultural activities are concerned. A report elaborated in 1790, by the academic Lacerda Lobo, from the Lisbon Royal Academy of Sciences, allows us to attest that, by the end of the eighteenth century, the agricultural situation in the Algarve was as precarious or more than in the previous decades and that the application of new reforms was urgent (Lobo, 1812).

The investigation is still ongoing and we've only analysed a small sample regarding the examples of Faro and Tavira. Despite this, considering the representative value of these two localities in the region, we can reach some preliminary conclusions.

We were able to establish a correlation between land distribution and social inequality. This allowed to test, at a regional level, the theory that societies in which there exists a greater inequality in wealth distribution, and where a strong social elite thrives, there is a tendency toward the creation of institutions that protect the interests of this wealthy minority, making them less effective in the promotion of economic development (Engerman & Sokoloff, 2002). In this particular case, one can further elaborate that the presence of a local elite became a factor of resistance against the landowning legislative reform, which threatened the existent entrenched manorialist-type regime.

Here are the main conclusions we reached in our analysis so far:

i. Evident predominance of small property, with landholding revenue unequally distributed (as revealed by the Gini coefficient);
ii. Landholding focused on a small number of landowners, composed in their majority by the dominant social classes, revealing a clear correlation between property distribution inequality and social inequality in the region;
iii. The interests of the dominant elite prevented the effective application of the property rights reform, perpetuating illegal usurious practises, stifling the region's economic growth.

The analysis presented still lacks great development and it's only a starting point for reflection about the issue of landownership and development of rural societies in the end of the Old Regime, of which the Algarve is only one case study. It's necessary to not only further explore the data collected in the regional and national historical archives but also to establish comparative parallels with other Portuguese regions and also other European rural areas, which would allow the creation of framework for the Algarve case. There is also the need to widen the theoretical and methodological sphere, in order to assess what other explicative models – beyond the correlation between inequality and economic growth – can help understand the particular case of the Algarve, at the end of the eighteenth century.

Bibliography

Congost, R., J. Gelman and R. Santos (eds) (2016) *Property Rights in Land*, London.

Congost, R. and R. Santos (2010) 'Working out the frame: from formal institutions to the social contexts of property', in R. Congost and R. Santos (eds) *Contexts of Property in Europe: The Social Embeddedness of Property Rights in Land in Historical Perspective*, Turnhout, pp. 15-38.

Correia, J. E. H. (1997) *Vila Real de Santo António. Urbanismo e Poder na Política Pombalina*, Porto.

Costa, L. F., P. Lains and S. M. Miranda (2011) *História Económica de Portugal, 1143-2010*, Lisboa.

Engerman, S. L., and K. Sokoloff (2002) 'Factor endowments, inequality, and paths of development among New World economies', *Economía: Journal of the Latin American and Caribbean Economic Association*, 3, 1, pp. 41-88.

Faísca, C. M. and B. Lopes (2015) 'Desigualdades de rendimento no Alentejo do Antigo Regime: Arraiolos, Avis e Portalegre (1690-1725)', *Análise Social*, 215, L (2º), pp. 330-354.

Lana-Berasain, J. M. (2003) 'Agricultural transformation, landownership, and markets in inland Spain: the case of Southern Navarre, 1600-1935' in E. Hillbom and P. Svensson (eds), *Agricultural Transformation in a Global History Perspective*, London, pp. 26-50.

Lobo, C. B. L. (1812) 'Memória sobre a agricultura do Algarve, e melhoramento, que pode ter', *in Jornal de Coimbra*, vol. I, Lisboa.

Magalhães, J. R. (1993) *O Algarve Económico 1600-1773*, Lisboa.

Magalhães, J. R. (2012) 'O Algarve nos séculos XVII e XVIII: uma sociedade cristalizada', in J. R. Magalhães, *O Algarve da Época Moderna*, Coimbra, pp. 281-291.

Reis, J. (2017) 'Deviant behaviour? Inequality in Portugal 1565-1770', *Cliometrica*, 11, 3, pp. 297-319.

Rodrigues, L. (2015a) 'Censo consignativo' in J. V. Serrão, M. Motta and S. M. Miranda (dir.), *e-Dicionário da Terra e do Território no Império Português*, Lisboa.

Rodrigues, L. (2015b) 'Censo reservativo' in J. V. Serrão, M. Motta and S. M. Miranda (dir.), *e-Dicionário da Terra e do Território no Império Português*, Lisboa.

Santiago-Caballero, C. (2013) 'Land inequality and agrarian per capita incomes in Guadalajara, Spain, 1690-1800', in E. Hillbom and P. Svensson (eds), *Agricultural Transformation in a Global History Perspective*, pp. 160-179.

Santos, R. (2012) 'Direitos de propriedade fundiária e estratificação social rural: um contributo sociológico', in A. Garrido, L. F. Costa and L. M. Duarte (eds), *Estudos em Homenagem a Joaquim Romero Magalhães: Economia, Instituições e Império*, Coimbra, pp. 277-293.

Santos, R. (2004) 'Economic sociology of modern *Latifundium*. Economic institutions and social change in Southern Portugal. Seventeenth-nineteenth centuries', *Sociologia: Problemas e Práticas*, 45, pp. 23-52.

Santos, R. and J. V. Serrão (2013) 'Property rights, social appropriations and economic outcomes: agrarian contracts in Southern Portugal in the late eighteenth century', in G. Béaur et al. (eds), *Property rights, Land Markets and Economic Growth in the European Countryside (Thirteenth-Twentieth Centuries)*, pp. 475-494.

Serrão, J. V. (2000) *Os Campos da Cidade: Configuração das Estruturas Fundiárias da Região de Lisboa nos Finais do Antigo Regime*, Lisboa.

Serrão, J. V. (2017) 'Extensive growth and market expansion, 1703-1820', in D. Freire and P. Lains (eds), *An Agrarian History of Portugal, 1000-2000: Economic Development on the European Frontier*, Leiden/Boston, pp. 132-171.

GUIDO ALFANI, MATTEO DI TULLIO

4 Inequality, growth and taxation in the countryside of the Republic of Venice, c. 1450 - c. 1750

I. Introduction

Recent years have seen a flourishing of studies on preindustrial inequality, which have added considerably to our knowledge of inequality dynamics in preindustrial times.[1] We now have good-quality, data-rich reconstructions of long-term trends in (mostly wealth, sometimes income) inequality for many parts of Italy (Alfani, 2015; 2017; Alfani and Sardone, 2015; Alfani and Ryckbosch, 2016; Alfani and Ammannati, 2017; Alfani and Di Tullio, 2019), Spain (Santiago Caballero, 2011; García Montero, 2015; Alfani, 2017), Portugal (Reis, 2017), the Low Countries (Van Zanden, 1995; Ryckbosch, 2016; Alfani and Ryckbosch, 2016; Alfani, 2017), Germany (Alfani, Gierok and Schaff, 2020) and Sweden (Bengtsson et al., 2017). Other research has focused on single years for which exceptionally good information is available, for example in Spain in 1759 (Nicolini-Ramos Palencia, 2016a; 2016b) or in Poland in 1578 (Malinowski and Van Zanden, 2017). This broad research campaign has reached beyond Europe, as preindustrial inequality has also been explored for Anatolia under the Ottoman Empire (Canbakal, Filiztekin and Pamuk, 2018), for the pre-revolutionary United States (Lindert and Williamson, 2016), and for Japan in the late Tokugawa period (Saito, 2015). Interestingly, compared to earlier research that tended to focus more on urban environments and on urban sources, today the rural environments are being explored much more systematically. Indeed, most of the recent reconstructions of long-term inequality trends for broad territorial aggregates, namely all those that have been produced by the ERC-funded project *EINITE – Economic Inequality across Italy and Europe 1300-1800*[2]

1 The research leading to these results has received funding from the European Research Council under the European Union's Seventh Framework Programme (FP7/2007-2013)/ ERC Grant agreement No. 283802, EINITE-Economic Inequality across Italy and Europe, 1300-1800 as well as under the European Union's Horizon 2020 Framework Program/ ERC Grant agreement No. 725687, SMITE-Social Mobility and Inequality across Italy and Europe, 1300-1800.

2 www.dondena.unibocconi.it/EINITE

Guido Alfani • Bocconi University, Dondena Centre and IGIER

Matteo Di Tullio • Bocconi University, Dondena Centre

Inequality in rural Europe (Late Middle Ages – 18th century), ed. by Guido ALFANI and Erik THOEN, CORN, 18 (Turnhout, 2020), pp. 65-79.

 DOI 10.1484/M.CORN-EB.5.121948

(as well as those being produced by a new project, *SMITE – Social Mobility and Inequality across Italy and Europe 1300-1800*), have included a specific analysis of the countryside, in order to keep track of potentially different dynamics between urban and rural environments.

This chapter makes use of data collected by the EINITE project for a group of rural communities in the Italian domains of the Republic of Venice – the area usually called the *Terraferma*. The data refer specifically to the provinces of (from West to East): Bergamo in current-day Lombardy, and Verona, Vicenza and Padua in current-day Veneto. There, rural property tax records are often available from the mid-fifteenth century, and can be used to measure wealth inequality. We find that during the early modern period, the general trend was for inequality to grow. This phenomenon may possibly be associated with economic growth during the fifteenth and maybe the sixteenth century, but continued even after the mid-seventeenth century, when a long period of economic stagnation began in the Republic. In this period, other forces proved able to cause an increase in inequality. The increase in (regressive) taxation may have been a crucial factor – especially in rural areas, which tended to be affected by a higher fiscal burden per unit of wealth compared to cities.

II. Inequality trends in the countryside of the Republic of Venice: an overview

Thanks to recent research, the Venetian *Terraferma* can now be counted among the areas of Europe for which we have the most systematic information about economic inequality (especially of wealth) from the end of the Middle Ages covering the entire early modern period. The information available for the rural areas is particularly striking, due to the fact that at least in some provinces rural areas were subject to a homogeneous system of direct taxation on real estate. This eases data analysis considerably. It facilitates building distributions representative of broad territorial aggregates – the entire countryside surrounding a prominent city and subject, at least to some degree, to the control of the city, or what we will refer to as a *contado* – without the need to turn to complex, potentially error-prone and often simply impossible, conversions of values reported in different denominations. A precise account of the sources available for the *Terraferma* and of their limitations is provided elsewhere (Alfani and Di Tullio, 2019). Here it will suffice to note that the information we use has been collected from fiscal records usually called *estimi* in Italy and present also in some other southern European areas (they are called *compoix* or *cadastres* in France and similarly in north-eastern Spain and elsewhere). These sources provide information about the taxable wealth owned by each household. They always includes real estate (lands and buildings), which was by far the main component of wealth in preindustrial rural societies, and sometimes other items as well, like capital invested in trade. The main limitation of these sources is that only rarely do they include the propertyless, that is, those households that had no taxable wealth. However, such households are usually very few in number (in the range of 3-8% of the total), as even tiny properties were recorded (like a small orchard or a fraction of a vineyard). Consequently although the exclusion of the propertyless from inequality measurement leads to systematic under-estimation of inequality levels, the distortion is very limited, as will also be discussed at the end of this section. More importantly, empirically we find that including the propertyless does not change the direction of the trend (see Alfani, 2015; 2017; Alfani and Di Tullio, 2019 for further discussion).

Our sources, then, allow reconstruction of household-level distributions of wealth. Unfortunately, for rural areas this is usually impossible for periods earlier than the mid-sixteenth century (the oldest *estimi* available, in the *Terraferma* as well as elsewhere, tend to refer to cities only[3]). The main exception is Arzignano, in the countryside of Vicenza. For Arzignano, which was an important rural town placed at the entrance to the Chiampo Valley and positioned between the two large cities of Verona and Vicenza, seven *estimi* survived, covering the entire period from 1449 to 1756. The community consisted of various localities with an overall population of between 550 and 1,000 households during the three centuries covered. Based on this information, it has been possible to reconstruct the series of Gini indexes of wealth inequality reported in Figure 1.[4] The figure also includes a similar series for Romano in the *contado* of Bergamo, beginning in the early sixteenth century, as well as two shorter series representative of the entire *contadi* of Padua and Verona, covering the periods 1550-1700 and 1600-1750 respectively. To facilitate comparisons between communities, measures have been clustered around reference years (50-year breakpoints from 1450 to 1750).

Overall, the information we have for the *Terraferma* suggests that rural wealth inequality tended to increase continuously from the late Middle Ages onwards. This is particularly clear in the case of Arzignano, where the Gini index was 0.486 in 1450, grew to 0.55 by 1550, 0.738 by 1650 and finally reached the quite high value of 0.768 by 1750. Inequality growth was monotonic in Romano, too (from 0.694 *c.* 1500 to 0.762 *c.* 1650) and nearly monotonic in the *contado* of Padua. Of the areas or communities included in the figure, only in the *contado* of Verona do we find a phase of overall inequality decline that covers the second half of the seventeenth century. During the eighteenth century, though, strong inequality resumed, reaching a Gini of 0.763 in 1750 (from 0.651 in 1600).

---

3 The main exception is Tuscany: see Alfani and Ammannati, 2017.

4 In the standardized form used here, the Gini index varies between values 0 and 1, with a value of 0 corresponding to perfect equality (i.e. all individuals have the same wealth) and 1 corresponding to perfect inequality (i.e. one individual owns all the wealth present within the boundaries of the community).

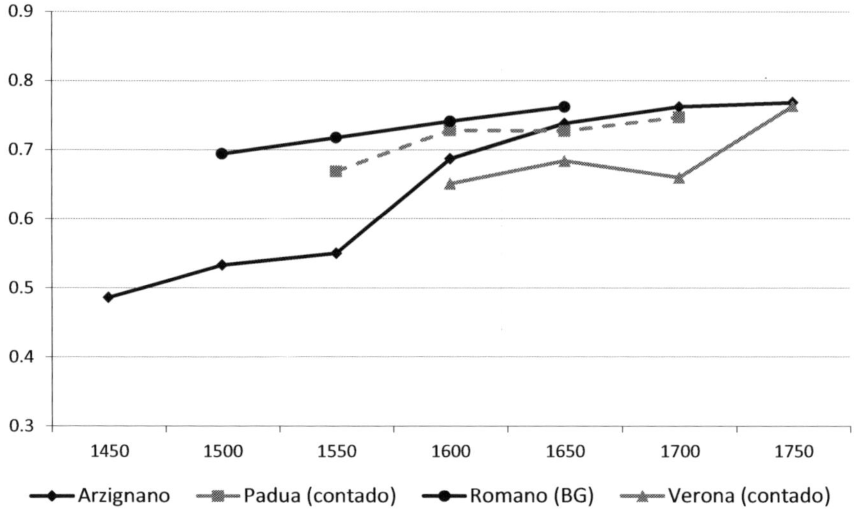

Figure 4.1. Long-term trends in rural inequality (Gini indexes of wealth concentration, propertyless excluded)

Notes: Measures organized around reference years when needed.

These inequality levels were generally lower than those reported for cities at the same point in time. For example, in Padua around 1600 the urban Gini was 0.788, much higher than the rural Gini of 0.728. One century later, the distance between the two had reduced only marginally (0.799 versus 0.747). This is an empirical regularity which had already been reported by Herlihy (1978) in his study of the 1427 Florentine *catasto*, and which has been confirmed by many recent studies of preindustrial inequality for Italy (Alfani, 2015; Alfani and Sardone, 2015; Alfani and Ammannati, 2017) as well as for other areas of Europe like Spain (Nicolini-Ramos Palencia, 2016a: 760). Moreover, the level of rural inequality we found for the rural areas of the *Terraferma* are in line with those found in other parts of Italy. In the countryside of the Sabaudian State in current-day Piedmont, the Gini was equal to 0.633 in 1450 in the village of Vigone, and grew to 0.733 by 1700. At the same date, it equaled 0.579 in Cumiana (Alfani, 2015, 1069). In the *contado* of Florence in Tuscany, the Gini was 0.546 in 1500, 0.613 in 1600, 0.737 in 1700 and finally reached 0.855 by 1800 (Alfani and Ammannati, 2017, 1084). The measures reported for the Sabaudian State and the Florentine State refer to inequality in ownership of real estate (propertyless excluded) and consequently they are entirely comparable to those we provide for the *Terraferma*.

In the two rural areas for which we have more detailed information, the *contadi* of Padua and Verona, the overall tendency for inequality growth in

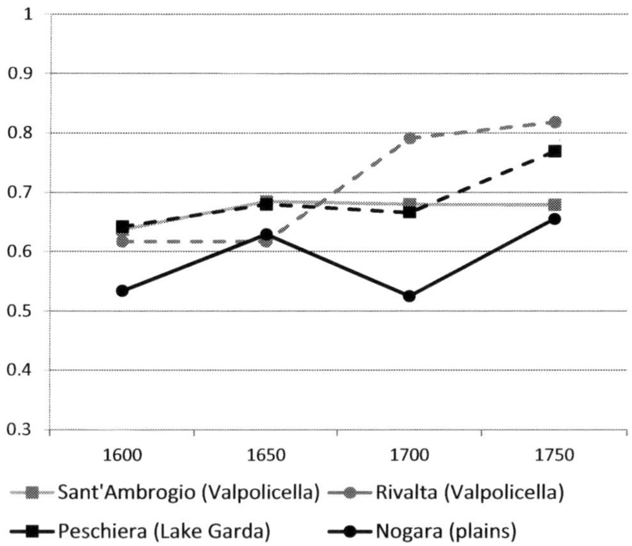

Figure 4.2. Inequality in the contado of Verona (Gini indexes of wealth concentration, propertyless excluded)

Notes: Measures organized around reference years when needed.

the long run is confirmed looking at each single community. For Verona, our series is the merger of nine communities, a selection of which is presented in Figure 2. Taking only the extreme years, 1600 and 1750, between them we find inequality growth in 7 communities out of 9. In the *contado* of Padua, for which we have complete coverage (i.e. our distribution includes all rural households of the entire province), the data are divided into 12 *podesterie* or *vicarie*, themselves administrative units that include a few distinct communities each. Considering again only the extreme years, 1550 and 1700, we find inequality growth in 11 out of 12 *podesterie/vicarie*. So overall, during the early modern period we find a tendency for inequality to grow in 86% of the sub-areas that we can distinguish in the *contadi* of Padua and Verona (18 out of 21).

The similar tendencies found across the rural areas surrounding Verona and Padua are even more interesting considering that within these broad territories there was considerable variation in the morphology of the land as well as in the agrarian model and in the crop regime. This is the case especially for Verona, whose territory went from pre-Alpine valleys in the North to the lowlands close to the Po River in the South. A specific study of how these differences might have affected (or not) the level and the trend in preindustrial wealth would surely be useful. For now, though, it will suffice to say that by simple visual inspection and by a preliminary analysis of the available measures, it is very difficult to detect significant differences dependent upon environmental factors. This can be seen in Figure 2, where of the seven communities constituting our sample for the *contado* of Verona, two – Sant'Ambrogio and Rivalta – are located in an hilly pre-Alpine area (the Valpolicella), one is fully in the plains (Nogara), and Peschiera is located on the shores of the Lake Garda, with its distinctive micro-climate and easy access to plentiful fish resources. In all three, inequality grew during 1600-1750, with a temporary interruption in Nogara in the second half of the eighteenth century, which may be the only peculiarity of the lowlands (as it is also found in the bordering community of Visegna). The reasons for this, however, are currently unclear.

As mentioned in the introduction, we have standardized our distributions by removing the propertyless, in the few instances when they were recorded alongside owners of real estate. Given that the propertyless were by definition those placed at the very bottom of the distribution (with a value of zero), this distorts systematically the Gini values towards lower levels. In this sense, the Gini indexes of wealth inequality that we have presented so far ought to be considered lower-bound estimates of the actual inequality. We would like to know, though, how great we can expect the inherent distortion to be. For some years only, our sources allow an estimation of this distortion as they also exceptionally include the propertyless. In particular in the *contado* of Padua the propertyless were included in 1627 and 1684. Propertyless households amounted to 3.1% and 8.1% of the total population in these two years. If we include them in the calculation of inequality measures, the Gini index increases by just 1.1% in 1627 (from 0.728 to 0.736) and by 2.5% in 1694 (from 0.747 to 0.766). We have more information about the prevalence of the propertyless in cities of the *Terraferma* (particularly in Padua and Bergamo), and the related distortion caused to inequality measures has been found to be equally limited (Alfani and Di Tullio, 2019: 102-105). Even more importantly, the rural and the urban data available for the *Terraferma* (as well as for other parts of Italy, for example the Sabaudian State/Piedmont: Alfani 2015) suggests that during the late medieval and early modern period, removing the propertyless never changes the trend (from growing to declining, or vice versa). Quite the contrary: adding the propertyless accentuates the trend towards growing inequality that we have reported from *c.* 1450 to the end of the eighteenth century.

These findings are consistent with the general literature on poverty, which suggests that across Italy, the numbers of the poor grew during the early modern period (Pullan, 1978; Woolf, 1988). This can also be seen in Figure 3, where a series representing the entire rural area of the Venetian *Terraferma* is shown with and without the propertyless (the series has been produced following the method introduced in Alfani, 2015. For details about its construction, see Alfani and Di Tullio, 2019: 181-199). Aggregating

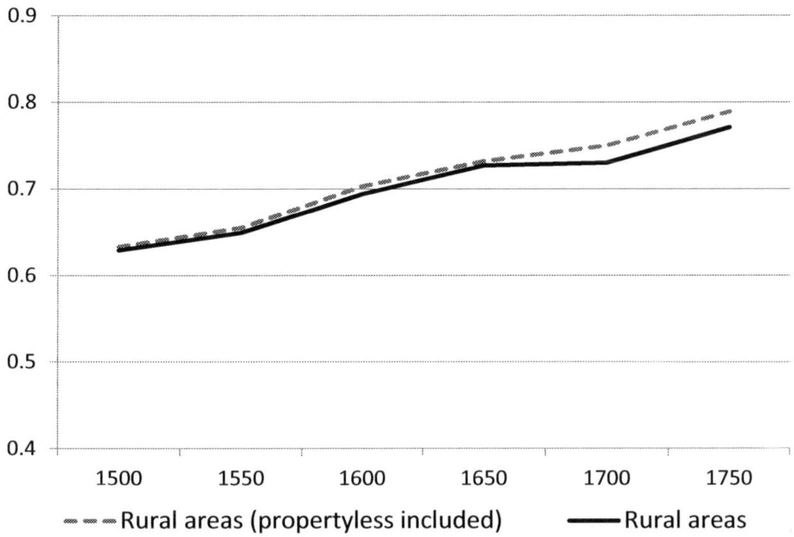

Figure 4.3. Inequality in rural areas of the Republic of Venice (Gini indexes of wealth concentration)

the data, the overall tendency for rural inequality to grow continuously throughout the early modern period is even more clear: the Gini was 0.629 in 1500, 0.694 in 1600, and finally peaked at 0.771 in 1750, which is the last year for which we have some information for wealth distribution in the rural *Terraferma*. Adding to this an estimate of the prevalence of the rural propertyless (itself a somewhat bold estimate based on exceptional information of the kind discussed above: see Alfani and Di Tullio, 2019: 193-196), we get a slightly steeper tendency towards growth: from 0.633 in 1500, to 0.703 in 1600 and 0.789 in 1750. Interestingly, the terrible 1630 plague, which killed 35% of the population of North Italy (except in Liguria, which was mostly unaffected) and possibly up to 40% of that of the *Terraferma*, does not seem to have arrested the tendency for inequality to grow. This is in stark contrast with what seems to have been the case at the time of the fourteenth-century Black Death (compare Alfani and Ammannati, 2017; Alfani and Murphy 2017).[5]

5 For an explanation of the inability of the 1630 plague to reduce inequality, see Alfani and Di Tullio, 2019: 112-121. For the general significance of this plague for northern Italian economic and demographic history, see Alfani, 2013b and Alfani and Percoco, 2019.

III. The long-run determinants of rural inequality growth: some reflections

The tendency for wealth inequality to grow in the rural areas during the early modern period as reported in the first section of this chapter is not limited to the Republic of Venice, it is also found in the other areas of Italy that so far have been the subject of systematic research into distributive dynamics. In particular, the tendency towards monotonic inequality growth found in the *Terraferma* are not only analogous to those reported for other areas, but might even be a relatively low-intensity example of more general dynamics. Indeed, if we compare the change in the Gini indexes during 1500-1750, we find that the 22.6% increase (from 0.629 to 0.771) found in the Republic of Venice compares favourably to the 29.2% increase which has been reported for the countryside of the Sabaudian State (from 0.586 to 0.757: Alfani, 2015) and especially to the 45.8% increase found in the Florentine State (from 0.546 to 0.796: Alfani and Ryckbosch, 2016). Figure 4 provides a representation of these tendencies, showing how the Venetian countryside turned from being the most unequal of the three areas considered in the sixteenth century to possibly being the least unequal at the end of the eighteenth century and surely considerably less unequal than the Tuscan countryside.

More than the differences among the trends, however, it is their substantial similarities that needs to be explained – even more so if we consider that these tendencies seem to have been common to other European areas, including the Low Countries, where some evidence of rural inequality growth exists for both the northern (Van Zanden, 1995) and the southern (Alfani and Ryckbosch, 2016: Appendix) regions.

It is not the objective of this chapter to provide an overall analysis of different possible explanations of inequality change in preindustrial times, a task which has been accomplished elsewhere (Alfani, 2019; Alfani and Di Tullio, 2019). Instead, we will now focus on certain specific aspects of rural inequality growth, and specifically on those that seem to be able to explain the clear underlying tendencies that have been detected for Italy and that may also be representative of the rural areas of Western Europe more generally.

A first important point, is that preindustrial inequality growth (either rural or urban) could not be presented simply as a by-product of economic growth. Indeed, economic growth may contribute to explaining some cases, like that of the Dutch Republic after it gained independence and went through its Golden Age. It seems, in fact, that this case has been pivotal in spreading among economic historians the idea that inequality grows together with per capita GDP, ever since the seminal article by Van Zanden on Holland (1995). This view has recently been reinforced by Van Bavel who argued, for some specific periods and areas including the Dutch Republic during the seventeenth century, that inequality increase was associated with the development of market economies, which may have led to growth in inequality of both income and wealth through increases in the efficient

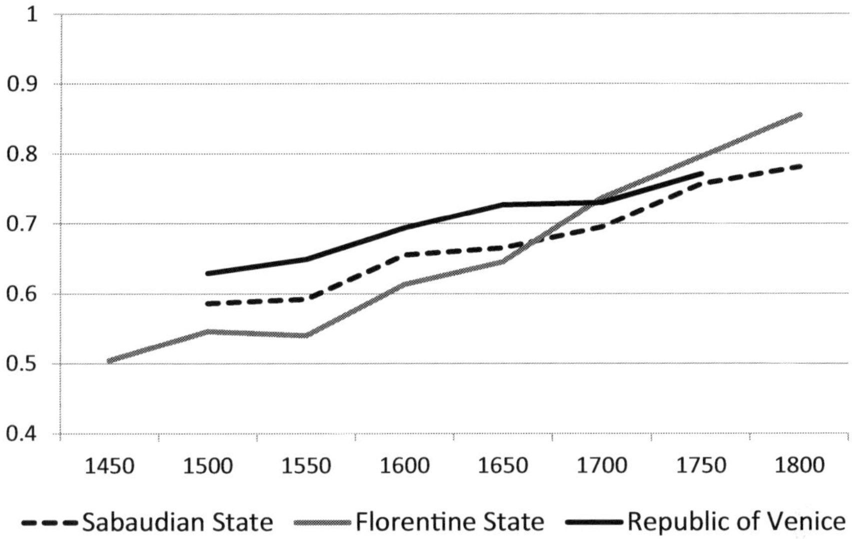

Figure 4.4. Inequality in rural Italy. Republic of Venice, Sabaudian State and Florentine State compared (Gini indexes of wealth concentration, propertyless excluded)

scale of trade and production, growing opportunities for financial dealing and speculation, growing investment opportunities (favouring the elites) in landed property and in shares of the public debt (Van Bavel, 2016: 192-193). This picture, however, does not seem to be able to explain correctly the case of central-northern Italy during the early modern period (or even that of the southern Low Countries: see Alfani and Ryckbosch, 2016), especially when rural areas are considered. Looking at this from a large-scale perspective, it is easy to understand why economic growth could not explain inequality growth in the Republic of Venice: after having managed to mostly keep its economic and political position for a surprisingly long time and in the face of increasingly harsh competition –in many different ways– from the new powers in Europe and the Mediterranean, from the mid-seventeenth century Venice finally lost its centrality in the European economy as a consequence of the damage wrought by the plague of 1629-1630 and by the War of Candia of 1645-1669 against the expanding Ottoman Empire (Alfani and Percoco, 2019). Indeed, the War of Candia stretched to the limit the economic possibilities of the state and favoured increases in the per capita fiscal burden, with the important distributive consequences discussed below. Decline, relative and absolute, was even more clear in the Florentine State from the first decades of the seventeenth century, and even the Sabaudian State –the only rising power among Italian pre-unification states– went through a long phase of economic stagnation during the seventeenth century, deeply marked by the 1630 plague and by civil war (Alfani, 2015). This assessment is based on the general literature concerning these areas, but it is also confirmed by the currently available estimates of per capita GDP in central-northern Italy (see discussion in Alfani and Ryckbosch, 2016) – estimates that, as a matter of fact, do not seem to incorporate much data specifically related to the Republic of Venice.

Of other possible explanations for long-run inequality growth in preindustrial times, one that seems particularly relevant for explaining changes in wealth inequality in rural areas has to do with the historical process known as 'proletarianization' – i.e. the process leading a share of the European population, growing throughout the early modern period, to lose the ownership of the means of production, thus becoming dependent on selling their labour for wages. This view, which is clearly rooted in the Marxist tradition of economic history, has also been strongly argued for by Tilly (1984), and more recently has been counted among the co-causes of inequality growth in some European areas, especially the Low Countries (Ryckbosch, 2016; Alfani and Ryckbosch, 2016).

Many specific historical processes have been presented as a component of an overall tendency towards proletarianization, from the spread of the putting-out system to the rural enclosures movement. For Italy, many studies have detailed the crisis of small peasant property with the subsequent concentration of wealth in many areas, especially from the second half of the sixteenth century when population pressure on the available resources became acute (Cattini, 1984; Alfani, 2013a: 76-77; Alfani, Mocarelli and Strangio, 2017). Famines, like the terrible one which affected the whole of the Italian peninsula from 1590 to 1593, accelerated the process (Alfani, 2011), which also involved the crisis of common or 'communal' property, again to the advantage of economic elites (Alfani and Rao, 2011; Di Tullio, 2014). In the Republic of Venice, we have some evidence of proletarianization in the growing share of propertyless households, including in rural areas (see Section 1). The 1630 plague reduced their prevalence only temporarily, thereafter the tendency became again oriented towards an increase.

Proletarianization was a general, pan-European phenomenon (Tilly, 1984: 26-36; Van Zanden, 1995: 656-658; Alfani and Ryckbosch, 2016), hence it seems to be particularly suitable for explaining distributive tendencies that appear to have been broadly common across the continent. However, proletarianization was somehow connected to demographic developments, as phases of acute crisis of small ownership tend to coincide with major famines on a continental scale (Le Roy Ladurie, 1966; Kamen, 1976; Alfani, 2013a: 76-77; Alfani and Ó Gráda, 2017), which usually occurred during phases of intense demographic pressure on resources (Alfani and Ó Gráda, 2018). The close connection with famines tends to create 'waves' of proletarianization. Herein lies a problem: a wave-like process does not seem to be able to explain the continuous, monotonic character of preindustrial inequality growth in the Italian and European countryside.

Many other factors have also been considered capable of promoting inequality growth in the long run, from demographic factors (demographic pressure per se, not only due to its ability to trigger proletarianization) and urbanization to institutional factors; see Alfani (2019) and Alfani and Di Tullio (2019) for a detailed analysis of each. Here we will focus on one specific institutional development, which presents two particularly desirable features: it was a pan-European phenomenon, and it progressed in a basically monotonic way during the early modern period in most areas of the continent – which is exactly what we need in order to explain general trends of the kind shown in figure 4. This process is the rise of the fiscal-military state, which was first suggested as a cause or fundamental co-cause of early modern inequality growth by Alfani (2015) for the case of the Sabaudian State, an argument generalized and explored in greater depth by a few subsequent studies (Alfani and Ryckbosch, 2016; Alfani and Ammannati, 2019).

From *c.* 1500, the growing cost of warfare increased states' financial needs. In turn, a larger and more efficient military allowed for concentration of coercive power, providing the means to impose a growing fiscal extraction. This led to the deepening of states' fiscal capacity and to increases in the per capita fiscal burden (Bonney, 1999; Yun Casalilla and O'Brien, 2012). For example, in the period *c.* 1550 to 1780, per capita fiscal pressure more than trebled in the Sabaudian State, increased six-fold in France and almost seven-fold in England and the Dutch Republic. Fiscal pressure increased also in the Republic of Venice, but more moderately – by about 70% (consider that in 1550, fiscal pressure in the Republic of Venice was relatively high to begin with). Such increases were able to produce, by themselves, greater inequality as the structure of the preindustrial fiscal systems was overall *regressive*: the effective tax rates paid by those at the top were lower than those suffered by the bottom of society. In the case of the Venetian *Terraferma*, it has been estimated that the effective fiscal rate weighing on the poorest 10% of the population might have been as little as 20-25%, and as much as 55-60% higher than that paid by the richest 5% (Alfani and Di Tullio 2019). The regressive structure of the fiscal levy did not change much during the early modern period, and as a consequence, post-tax inequality was systematically higher than pre-tax inequality: exactly the opposite of what we expect today, given that we have become used to progressive fiscal systems.

A regressive fiscal system was the consequence of a regime of systematic privilege, enrooted in law and institutions as well as in a culture that favoured nobles over commoners, citizens over rural dwellers, and so on. The process of the rise of the fiscal-military state and of the parallel increase in the per capita fiscal burden involved all European states independently from their economic conditions, as all had to play the same game if they were to protect themselves, or to be able to project military power outside their boundaries (Alfani, 2015; Alfani and Ryckbosch, 2016; Alfani and Di Tullio, 2019). While the structure of the fiscal system did not change much, the per-capita fiscal burden did grow very significantly, as seen above. It is this that increased the overall ability of the fiscal system to extract more and more inequality over time. This facilitates the conclusion that "the increase in the per capita fiscal burden is a feature of early modern Europe way more homogeneous and continuous in time than any other factor which has been proposed by earlier research as the possible cause of the widespread tendency for inequality to grow. Consequently, we have identified a common factor that surely favoured the increase in economic disparities across the continent" (Alfani and Di Tullio, 2019: 178-179). This view is further strengthened by the consideration that the main reasons for collecting more and more resources – war and the service of public debt, itself mostly accumulated to pay for war and defence – did not lead to inequality reduction as the consequence of state expenditure, differently from what we are used to today when welfare and social spending represent the largest component of the public budget. On the contrary: in preindustrial settings, state expenditures probably further favoured inequality growth (Alfani and Di Tullio, 2019: 165-174), although this specific aspect requires further research.

As mentioned above, one of the reasons why the fiscal system was overall regressive was that the rural dwellers were taxed more than those residing in the city. As on average they were poorer than urban dwellers, they tend to concentrate in the lower part of the overall distribution, contributing to explain why there was a steep difference in the effective fiscal rate. Indeed, in the case of the Republic of Venice, around 1550 rural dwellers accounted for 92% of the poorest 10% of the population, declining monotonically thereafter. They were 88% of the population in the second and third wealth deciles, 83% in the deciles from fourth to seventh, 58% in the eighth, 50% in percentiles 80-95, and finally, just 33% among the richest 5%. But discrimination of rural dwellers was not the only source of regressiveness of the fiscal system – hence additional factors weighed on rural dwellers, structurally contributing to keep them into the lower parts of the distribution. This has a number of consequences. First, it might explain why the tendency for preindustrial inequality growth is usually even more marked and clear in rural areas compared to cities. Second, it may have led to systematically lower opportunities for upward mobility in the country compared, again, to the city – a point which, however, is currently simple conjecture. Equally imperfect is our knowledge of the exact measure of the fiscal disadvantage suffered by rural dwellers. In an earlier study (Alfani and Di Tullio, 2019), we hypothesized that during the early modern period, rural dwellers paid between 10 and 20% more taxes per unit of wealth than the urban dwellers – but again, this is basically an educated guess. These are simply examples of the gaps that remain in our knowledge of the factors shaping distributive dynamics in the Italian and European countryside. Indeed, while there is no doubt that increasing taxation related to the rise of the fiscal-military state played a very important role in leading preindustrial inequality to grow, many of the subtleties of the actual mechanisms at work need further research to be clarified and compared properly across time and space. Consequently, there is to hope that research on preindustrial rural inequality will intensify in the upcoming years.

Bibliography

Alfani, G. (2011), 'The famine of the 1590s in Northern Italy. An analysis of the greatest "system shock" of the sixteenth century', *Histoire & Mesure*, 26, 1, pp. 17-49.

Alfani, G. (2013a), *Calamities and the Economy in Renaissance Italy*, Basingstoke.

Alfani, G. (2013b), 'Plague in seventeenth century Europe and the decline of Italy: an epidemiological hypothesis', *European Review of Economic History*, 17, pp. 408-430.

Alfani, G. (2015), 'Economic inequality in Northwestern Italy: a long-term view (fourteenth to eighteenth centuries)', *The Journal of Economic History*, 75, 4, pp. 1058-1096.

Alfani, G. (2017), 'The rich in historical perspective: evidence for preindustrial Europe (ca. 1300-1800)', *Cliometrica*, 11, 3, pp. 321-348.

Alfani, G. (2019), 'Wealth and income inequality in the long run of history', Diebolt, C. and Hupert, M. (eds), *Handbook of Cliometrics*, 2ns Edition, Berlin-Heidelberg, forthcoming.

Alfani, G. and Ammannati, F. (2017), 'Long-term trends in economic inequality: the case of the Florentine State, *c.* 1300-1800', in *Economic History Review*, 70, 4, pp. 1072-1102.

Alfani, G. and Di Tullio, M. (2019), *The lion's share. inequality and the rise of the fiscal state in preindustrial Europe*, Cambridge.

Alfani, G., Gierok, V. and Schaff, F. (2020), 'Economic inequality in preindustrial Germany: a long-run view (fourteenth to nineteenth centuries)', *Stone Center Working Paper Series* no. 03.

Alfani, G., Mocarelli, L. and Strangio, D. (2017), 'Italy', in Alfani G. and Ó Gráda, C. (eds), *Famine in European History*, Cambridge, pp. 25-47.

Alfani, G. and Murphy, T. (2017), 'Plague and lethal epidemics in the pre-industrial world', *Journal of Economic History*, 77, 1, pp. 314-343.

Alfani, G. and Ó Gráda, C. (2017) (eds), *Famine in European History*, Cambridge.

Alfani, G. and Ó Gráda, C. (2018), 'The timing and causes of famines in Europe', *Nature Sustainability*, 1, pp. 283-288.

Alfani, G. and Percoco, M. (2019), 'Plague and long-term development: the lasting effects of the 1629-1630 epidemic on the Italian cities', *Economic History Review*, 72, 4, pp. 1175-1201.

Alfani, G. and Rao, R. (2011) (eds), *La gestione delle risorse collettive. Italia settentrionale, secoli XII-XVIII*, Milano.

Alfani, G. and Ryckbosch, W. (2016), 'Growing apart in early modern Europe? A comparison of inequality trends in Italy and the Low Countries, 1500-1800', *Explorations in Economic History*, 62, pp. 143-153.

Alfani, G. and Sardone, S. (2015), 'Long-term trends in economic inequality in southern Italy. The Kingdom of Naples and Sicily, 16th-18th centuries: first results', paper given at the Economic History Association Annual Meeting, Nashville.

van Bavel, B. (2016), *The Invisible Hand? How market economies have emerged and declined since AD 500*, Oxford.
Bengtsson, E., Missiaia, A., Olsson, M. and Svensson, P. (2017), 'Wealth inequality in Sweden, 1750-1900', *Economic History Review*, 71, 3, pp. 772-779.
Bonney, R. (1999) (ed.), *The rise of fiscal state in Europe (1200-1815)*, Oxford.
Canbakal, J., Filiztekin, A. and Pamuk, Ş. (2018), *Inequality of Income and Wealth in the Ottoman Empire, 1500-1800*, Paper given at the World Economic History Congress, Boston.
Cattini, M. (1984), *I contadini di San Felice. Metamorfosi di un mondo rurale nell'Emilia dell'età moderna*, Torino.
Di Tullio, M. (2014), *The Wealth of Communities. War, resources and cooperation in Renaissance Lombardy*, Farnham.
García-Montero, H. (2015), 'Long-term trends in wealth inequality in Catalonia, 1400-1800: Initial Results', *Dondena Working Paper*, 79.
Herlihy, D. J. (1978), 'The distribution of wealth in a renaissance community: Florence 1427', in Abrams, P. and Wrigley, E. A. (eds), *Towns in Societies: Essays in Economic History and Historical Sociology*, Cambridge, pp. 131-157.
Kamen, H. (1976), *The iron century: social change in Europe, 1550-1660*, London.
Le Roy Ladurie, E. (1966), *Les Paysans de Languedoc*, Paris.
Lindert, P. H. and Williamson, J. G. (2016), *Unequal gains. American growth and inequality since 1700*, Princeton.
Malinowski, M. and Van Zanden, J. L. (2017), 'Income and its distribution in preindustrial Poland', *Cliometrica*, 11, 3, pp. 375-404.
Nicolini, E. A. and Ramos Palencia, F. (2016a), 'Decomposing income inequality in a backward pre-industrial economy: Old Castile (Spain) in the Middle of the 18th Century', *Economic History Review*, 69, 3, pp. 747-772.
Nicolini, E. A. and Ramos Palencia, F. (2016b), 'Comparing income and wealth inequality in pre-industrial economies: Lessons from 18th-century Spain', *EHES Working Papers*, 95.
Pullan, B. (1978), 'Poveri, mendicanti e vagabondi (secoli XIV-XVII)', Vivanti, C. and Romano, R. (eds), *Annali della Storia d'Italia*, I, *Dal feudalesimo al capitalismo*, Torino, pp. 981-1047.
Reis, J. (2017), 'Deviant behaviour? Inequality in Portugal 1565-1770', *Cliometrica*, 11, 3, pp. 297-319.
Ryckbosch, W. (2016), 'Economic inequality and growth before the industrial revolution: the case of the Low Countries (fourteenth to nineteenth centuries)', *European Review of Economic History*, 20, pp. 1-22.
Saito, O. (2015), 'Growth and inequality in the great and little divergence debate: a Japanese perspective', *Economic History Review*, 68, 2, pp. 399-419.
Santiago-Caballero, C. (2011), 'Income inequality in central Spain, 1690-1800', *Explorations in Economic History*, 48, 1, pp. 83-96.
Tilly, C. (1984), 'Demographic origins of the European proletariat', in Levine, D. (ed.), *Proletarianization and Family History*, Orlando, pp. 1-85.

Woolf, S. J. (1988), *Porca miseria. Poveri e assistenza nell'età moderna*, Roma-Bari.
Yun-Casalilla, B. and O'Brien, P. K. (2012) (eds), *The Rise of Fiscal States: A Global History. 1500-1914*, Cambridge.
van Zanden, J. L. (1995), 'Tracing the beginning of the Kuznets Curve: Western Europe during the Early Modern Period', *Economic History Review*, 48, 4, pp. 643-664.

DAVIDE CRISTOFERI

5 Socio-economic inequalities in fifteenth-century Tuscany: the role of the *mezzadria* system*

I. Why a new study on inequality in Tuscany? Goals of the article

The role of share-cropping in the interrelations between economic evolution and socio-economic inequalities, as well as its rationale, have been intensively debated (e.g. Cheung, 1969; Stiglitz, 1974; Hoffman, 1996; Galassi, 2000; Ackerberg and Botticini, 2000; Emigh, 2009). Nevertheless, Tuscany in the Renaissance period still offers an attractive case-study (see the recent contribution of: van Bavel, 2016: 97-144; Malanima, 2018) thanks to the important structural changes of the Tuscan Late Medieval economy and to the presence of very rich archival records.

Past and recent studies have focused on the Tuscan fiscal censuses, especially on the tax records of the city-state of Florence, to draw patterns of socio-economic inequality as well as of the spread of lease-systems, often at macro-level (Cherubini, 1974: 231-312; Conti, 1965a and 1965b; Herlihy and Klapisch-Zuber, 1985). Historians have stated the relevance of the so called *appoderamento*, i.e. the land consolidation process driven by Tuscan city-dwellers, who purchased, organised and managed the farmland in the so-called *poderi* (= landholdings) at the end of Middle Ages (Conti, 1965a and 1965b; Cherubini, 1974; Pinto, 1987; Piccinni, 2006a. For a comparison with the North-Sea area, see: van Bavel and Hoppenbrouwers, 2004). Scholars have studied, furthermore, the main leasing system used in this process, which was the *mezzadria*, a peculiar kind of share-cropping (Imberciadori, 1951; Giorgetti, 1974; Piccinni, 1992; Emigh, 2009) and have given attention

* This paper presents the first results of a study of the impact of sharecropping on socio-economic inequality trends in fifteenth-sixteenth century Tuscany. It is part of the GINI (*Growth, Inequality and Institutions*) project funded by Ghent University and supervised by Thijs Lambrecht, Erik Thoen, Koen Schoors and Eric Vanhaute (all Ghent University). My research also profited from input by Guido Alfani (Bocconi University): https://research.flw.ugent.be/en/projects/inequalities-and-growth-late-medieval-mezzadria-tuscany-15th-early-16th-c. I am grateful to all of them for their helpful comments and remarks as well as to Ilaria Becattini for her contribution to the data entry.

Davide Cristoferi • Ghent University

Inequality in rural Europe (Late Middle Ages – 18th century), ed. by Guido ALFANI and Erik THOEN, CORN, 18 (Turnhout, 2020), pp. 81-101.

 DOI 10.1484/M.CORN-EB.5.121949

to other elements such as fiscal systems and labour regulations (Ginatempo, 1989; Piccinni, 2006b; Cohn, 2007). Moreover, recent studies have shown an increasing economic inequality within the Tuscan rural communities and towns in the course of the Late Middle Ages towards Early modern times (Alfani and Ammannati, 2017. See also Herlihy, 1978 and for a comparison between Central-Northern Italy and the Low Countries: Alfani and Ryckbosch, 2016).

However, we do not as yet have any in-depth studies at our disposal to explore the causes and to understand the social structures and the mechanisms behind the increasing Gini indexes calculated. This is to a large extent due to the complexity and the large amount of available sources. Florentine fiscal records, for instance, are extremely difficult to interpret and it is also very time-consuming to analyse the influence of Florentine landlords on inequality patterns (Alfani and Ammannati, 2017: 1076-1079). What still remains to be studied is how social relations and institutions, especially property rights and share-contracts, influenced the mechanism of redistribution of wealth and of incomes from land in Late Medieval Tuscany. Moreover, there is a need to measure in a more profound way to what extent inequality developed and how important the regional differences in this respect were. Furthermore, which social categories within the peasantry and the landlords did or did not take advantage of this evolution and how this should be measured in the most appropriate way (see also: van Bavel and Hoyle, 2010; Béaur et al. 2013; Thoen and Soens, 2015) still needs to be investigated.

Let's first focus on the features of the *mezzadria* system and on the socio-economic environment in which it developed. *Mezzadria* was a short-term contract (1-5 years, 3 on average) between two legally-free actors. It divided half (= *mezzo* in Italian) of the input and of the output between the lessee and the lessor. It provided, however, also informal bonds to increase the dependency between both parties. The landowner, often a well-off city-dweller, was highly involved in the management of land tenure. The contract also provided very precise obligations for the tenant regarding crops choices, agricultural techniques, seasonal activities and it often stipulated that the former had to live with his family in the farmhouse of the landholding. This way *mezzadria* generally warranted a high labour input of the whole peasant family, often constrained to work exclusively on the *mezzadria* landholding (*podere*) (Ginatempo, 2002). This was usually a coherent land tenure composed of different plots of different sizes – cultivated through a polyculture system (cereals, vineyards, olive trees, fruit trees, industrial crops, wood). The system, however, allowed both actors (lessor and lessee) to cope with different market constraints: labour and food shortages, access to scarce land and credit.[1] The

1 In the literature, there are three main explanations for the spread of share-contracts in different times and places: 1) the risk-sharing hypothesis: landlords use *mezzadria* to attract risk-averse tenants in times of labor shortages; 2) the moral-hazard/multi tasking hypothesis: landlords use it to monitor tenants' efforts and protect valuable assets on the farm, resulting in lower transactions costs; 3) the imperfect capital market hypothesis: tenants and landlords use it to cope with imperfect capital markets. See: Cheung, 1969;

key point for peasantry and landlords was the negotiation of income shares, on the basis of the factors listed above as well as to the city-state's fiscal system, controlled by urban landowners.[2] This way, the Tuscan share-cropping contract became a 'battlefield' of both opposite and converging interests. It created a complex checks and balances system to secure power positions for the lessors and subsistence for the lessees, mainly via the redistribution of income from land (Mucciarelli and Piccinni, 1994; for a comparison with Late Medieval England, see: Goddard, Langdon and Müller, 2010).

In this paper, we focus on a spatial micro-scale to analyse the impact of *mezzadria* on socio-economic inequality at the beginning of fifteenth century, which is almost halfway of the process of *appoderamento*. The area under study belonged to the *contado* – the territory of the Florentine State close to its capital – whose taxation was organised in ecclesiastical districts, called *pievi*.[3] Known as the *pieve* of San Giovanni in Petroio in Mugello, 30 km north of Florence, with a surface of around 50 km^2 (4.900 h.) (Figure 5.1),[4] its social and pedological features were quite uniform. The *pieve* comprised and ruled five parishes and their hamlets, organised as well in small rural communities. In 1427, it counted 929 inhabitants divided over 174 households with a rather

Hoffman, 1984; Galassi, 1992; Ackerberg and Botticini, 2000. However, in Tuscany, investment in land was considered also as a form of capital insurance, of social prestige, of food insurance and also as a form of leisure, as the multitudes of villas and palaces they have built shows: Herlihy, 1981; Pinto, 1987; Lillie, 2011.

2 The short periods covered by the contracts make the situation of the lessee uncertain, increasing their dependence on the lessor. At the same time, the landowners are dependent on labour supplies. Urban elites coped with the emergence of stricter tax and labour policies to sustain their power position (based on control over capital and land). This increased after the Black Death, when labourers demanded more favourable labour conditions. However, many peasants preferred not to switch to other contracts or to become wage labourers: *mezzadria* was still the best private system of sustainment available. This way, at the beginning of the fifteenth century, *mezzadria* appeared already as the main leasing contract used in Central Tuscany. See: Herlihy, 1968, 1978 and 1981; Epstein, 1994; Piccinni, 2006b; Cohn, 2007; Emigh, 1996 and 2009.

3 *Pieve* = [// lat. *plēbs plēbis*] was used in Northern Italy. It indicated a minor ecclesiastical district of a diocese. The *pieve* consisted out of a church with a baptistery which ruled a territory with parishes and chapels (treccani.it/vocabolario/pieve). The territorial organisation of the *pievi* was used by the Late Medieval Florentine Republic to split up its territory in fiscal districts: see Conti, 1966, pp. 1-30.

4 The area of San Giovanni covers lengthwise the central-western part of Mugello, it borders the fortified village of Barberino west-northwards and those of Scarperia and San Piero a Sieve eastwards. It is located between 288 and 445 m. a.s.l. and it belongs to the valley of the river Sieve, surrounded from the North to the East by the Apennines (between 1.300-1.500 m a.s.l.) and from the East and the South by high hills and small mountains (between 600-900 m. a.s.l.). The landscape is characterised by oaks, chestnuts and beech woods as well as by pasturages on the slopes and to the top of the Apennines and on the southern high hills. Along the riverside, there was a long, narrow and fertile plain, which was intensively cultivated as were the northern hills. The climate is continental: arid in summer though mild in winter, rainy in autumn and spring, allowing the cultivation of vineyards as well as grain cropping in the whole valley. Olive trees were scarce at that time, and landholdings usually had parts of chestnuts woods. See: Righini, 1956, pp. 15-29 and 70-144.

low population density: around 19 people per km² (Table 5.1). The *pieve* was characterised by a considerable presence of Florentine landlords as well as of *mezzadria* contracts.

The micro-level of analysis has reduced the complexity of data-collection, but not its extent: a wide range of information has been collected for almost 1,000 inhabitants. This method allowed also to cross-reference and discuss coherent indexes of wealth concentration and to explore (part of) income from land. Furthermore, it has been possible to match the Florentine landlords with their estates and with their sharecroppers, an operation often missed in former studies.

The database on which this study is based was derived from the registers of the Catasto made in 1427-1429, the first fiscal census and cadastral survey of the Florentine Republic. It describes all the real estates, the livestock, the financial assets of all the households of the Florentine State (also the property less) and provides information such as position, land use, leasing system, value, output, lessors, lessees etc. The Catasto provided a tax system for each fiscal category: in our case, the Florentine city-dwellers, the inhabitants of the *contado* (the actual provinces of Florence and Prato), the religious and welfare institutions of cities and countryside.[5] However, the Catasto describes the Florentine rural society from a (at that time) fiscal perspective. For instance, data on land surface, usually roughly measured, are muddled up or not fully reliable, while landholdings and plots of land scattered in the territory could be recorded together within the same taxable asset, not taking into account the original agrarian structure. As a consequence, we have decided not to address land productivity here and to refer in general to landholdings or plots of land as *land units* (see Conti, 1966: 21-131). The term landholding will be used only when indicated in the description of the Catasto (= *podere* in Italian).

5 See: State Archive of Florence (from now on: ASF), Catasto. Each taxpayer had to declare for his property the following data: 1) the average income in money or in kind; 2) whether it was leased out or rented; 3) the character of the lease contract and the name of the lease-holder or of the owner; 4) the location as well as the kind of land use. The assessable value of each real estates of the *city* householders was calculated by Florentine officials capitalising at 7% of the declared income, whereas properties of rural inhabitants were just recorded with the value declared by their owners. Furthermore, the taxpayer had to indicate similar information for livestock: 5) the race; 6) the number; 7) the value; 8) the property rights or the leasing system as well as the name of the lessor or of the lessee. The same was true also for credits and debts, that is 9) the amount and 10) the name of the creditors as well as of 11) the debtors. Finally, the householder should also declare the structure of his family and the age of the members. However, from the total sum 200 golden florins was deducted for each family member (more or less the yearly living cost). The result (*sovrabbondante*) was taxed for the 0.5% plus a variable sum (between 2-6 golden pounds) for every adult male of the family. The assessable value of the *rural* householders, however, was taxed at a rate of 0.187% plus a tax of 1-4 golden pounds for each adult male. There is also a kind of system, less severe, used only for *religious* institutions, and another one for the people of the Florentine *distretto*. See: Conti, 1966, pp. 21-131; Alfani and Ammannati, 2017, pp. 1074-1076.

Table 5.1. Population of the pieve of San Giovanni in Petroio (1427-1429)

Parishes	Villanuova	Latera	Campiano	Spugnole	Lucigliano	Total
Households	51	48	17	46	12	174
People	289	290	76	197	77	929

Source: Author's database from ASF, Catasto 177, cc. 396r-543v.

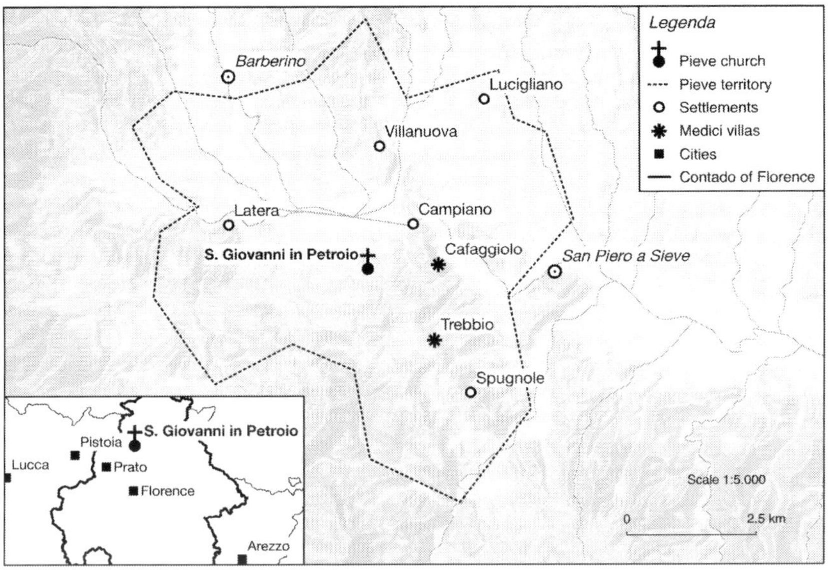

Figure 5.1. The territory of the pieve of San Giovanni in Petroio (15th c.)

Source: Elaboration of the author from: Klapisch-Zuber, 1983 and Pirillo, 2015: 103-107.

II. The socio-economic inequalities in San Giovanni in Petroio (Mugello, 1427-1429)

II.1 Socio-economic inequalities within the rural society

The data from the Catasto provide us with proxies to assess economic inequality within the peasantry of San Giovanni in Petroio. The tax recorded (called *catasto*) was the sum of the taxes on wealth (the *estimo*) and on *per capita* tax of male labour forces (the *testatico*, all the men between 15-69 years of age) of each household. As a consequence, the distribution of the *estimo* tax between the households of Petroio provides a good gauge of the wealth distribution in that area (Figure 5.2). If we exclude the propertyless (50 households), the result is very similar (0,61) to the pattern calculated in the same way in the Florentine *contado* at the beginning of fifteenth

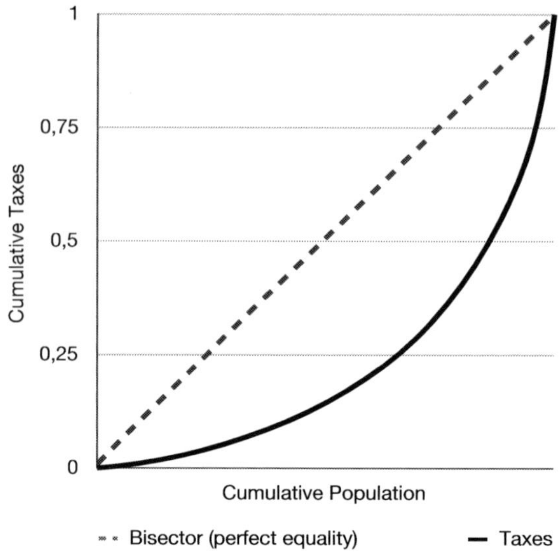

Figure 5.2. Wealth inequality in San Giovanni in Petroio (1427-1429): Gini index of distribution of taxes (estimo) (propertyless excluded)

Source: Author's database from ASF, Catasto 177, cc. 396r-543v. The Gini has been calculated on the 174 households of S. Giovanni in Petroio. The formula used to calculate the Gini coefficients of this paper is: $G = (2/(n-1)) * (\Sigma_i (F_i - Q_i))$, where (in our case), n is the number of individuals, i is the position of each individual in the ranking sorted by increasing wealth. The sum goes from 1 to $n-1$, F_i is equal to i/n, Q_i is the sum of wealth of all the individuals comprised between position 1 and i, divided by the total wealth of all individuals. See: Alfani, 2013.

century (0,57). It is likely that a slow increase of economic inequality had occurred after the decline triggered by the Black Death (Alfani and Ammannati, 2017: 1076-1081). However, when we examine the distribution of assets between all the 174 rural households, the Gini value calculated is higher: 0,73 (see Figure 5.3). The sustainability of this high unequal wealth distribution, as we will see in the next pages, is due to the fact that a large part of the rural population had income from lease-holding rather than from land property.

The disparity between the two outcomes was further explored by organising the 174 households of the *pieve* in four different fiscal classes. Table 5.2 uses the same criteria and definitions applied by the Florentine officials to group the rural taxpayers, based on the immovables and movables assessed in the Catasto (Conti, 1965b: 1-21). It shows that 29% of the householders did not have anything or just debts (*miserabili*), 44% were poor (*poveri*), that is assessed between 1-50 fl., 20% owned between 51-200 fl. (*mediani*) and only 7% were defined as well-off (*agiati*), with over 200 fl. In fact, 73%

Table 5.2. Distribution of assets per fiscal class in San Giovanni in Petroio (1427-1429)

Fiscal classes		**very poor**	**poor**	**middle**	**well-off**	
tax income		**0 fl.**	**1-50 fl.**	**51-200 fl.**	**over 200fl.**	**Total**
Households	total number	50	77	35	12	174
	%	29	44	20	7	100
Assets	total value (fl.)	0	1.837,7	3.812,8	4.789,3	10.440
	%	0	18	37	46	100

Source: Author's database from ASF, Catasto 177, cc. 396r-543v.

of the population lived in poverty, according to the criteria of the Catasto, with 14 fl. on average per householder, while only 12 families owned on average 28 times more.

Specifically, within the rural society of San Giovanni, the wealthiest class owned 46% of the assets, that is 42.5% of the land and 48.7% of the oxen. Furthermore, they lent 790 fl. or 61% of the credits. However, 35 households of the *mediani* shared with the well-off class the majority of taxable assets. Furthermore, this middle group mainly owned livestock (38% of total value) and had more debts in comparison with other classes (34.8% of total debt). Finally, the very poor were highly in debt (30% of the total debt), while the poor had borrowed less money (19% of the total debt) and owned more livestock (22% of the total value).[6] This pattern is clearly visible charting the index of concentration of different kinds of assets (Figure 5.3): the figure shows an unequal distribution of two factors of endowments like land (the main driver of assets value) and, especially, oxen (the main form of capital).

Behind the four fiscal classes of Table 5.2 we can identify different social categories, according to the taxpayers' declarations and to the classification developed by previous studies (see: Conti, 1965b: 1-21). This way, we can link wealth distribution to social position and professional activity, although these categories should be qualified: for example, leases did not impede wage or seasonal work.

Table 5.3 shows that in San Giovanni in Petroio there were, first of all, 69 sharecroppers, 15 farmers, 14 smallholders. In addition, 4 tenant holders were found, 3 craftsmen, 2 millers, a group of 16 inactive workers (widows, invalid, aged people) and 59 unspecified taxpayers. The farmers belonged to the

6 Source: Author's database from ASF, Catasto 177, cc. 396r-543v.

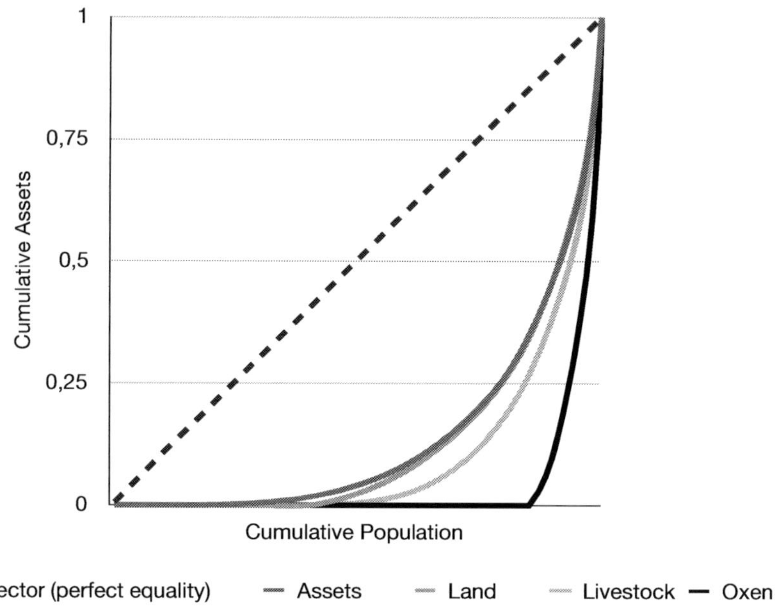

Figure 5.3. Wealth inequality in San Giovanni in Petroio (1427-1429): Gini index of distribution of assets (propertyless included)

Source: Author's database from ASF, Catasto 177, cc. 396r-543v. The Gini has been calculated on the 174 households of S. Giovanni in Petroio.

Table 5.3. Household structure and distribution of assets per social class in San Giovanni in Petroio (1427-1429)

Social classes	Households			Assets		
	total number	%	average members per h.	fl.	%	average per h. (fl.)
Share-croppers	69	38	6,1	2.178,8	22	31,6
Farmers	15	8	8,9	4.723,6	49	314,9
Smallholders	14	8	4,5	870,4	9	62,2
Tenant holders	4	2	6,3	150,5	2	37,6
Craftsmen	3	2	4,3	484,8	5	161,6
Millers	2	1	3	2,5	0	1,3
Not working householders	16	9	1,5	1.287,3	13	80,5
Unspecified householders	59	32	3,8	198,1	2	3,4

Source: Author's database from ASF, Catasto 177, cc. 396r-543v. Family structures however could be influenced by life-cycle: young and old households were probably smaller than family halfway of their life cycle, having children and maybe old family members. See: Herlihy and Klapisch-Zuber, 1985, pp. 259-295 and Smith, 1985.

middle and the well-off class (respectively 6 and 9 households): they owned farmland valued at over 151 fl. They cultivated directly all or most of their land resorting to the credit market (they were in debt with 29% of the total debt) and to their own household labour force, since their families were the largest of San Giovanni in Petroio (8.9 members on average).[7] A certain Stefano, son of Giovanni from Villanuova, belonged to this group. He was the head of a household of 14 members together with his two sons, Giovanni and Benedetto, and their spouses. He owned a farmhouse and land to the value of 318 fl., yielding around 14 fl. on a yearly basis in grain and wine. He owned a pair of oxen and leased out 4 bovines to other peasants; if we count also his cows, mules and sheep, Stefano had invested in total 88 fl. in livestock and draught animals.[8]

Craftsmen as well as some of the inactive people also belonged to the well-off and middle classes. As expected, the formers were the most active on the credit market and were lending out an average of 56 fl. per taxpayer; however, they also invested in land (67 fl. per household). The invalids, aged people and widows had on average the second highest value of assets: around 80 fl. They probably used it as life insurance, since they refrained from asking for loans and usually did not declare other family members.[9]

The next group are the smallholders, divided between the poor and the middle class (7 households per class), with 43-46 fl. invested in land per taxpayer. One of them, called Mone, son of Salvi, had a six-member household and lived in S. Martino a Beriano, close to his grain-fields, woods and pastures (62 fl. of value). He yielded every year a value of only 4.5 fl. in grain, but he also gained revenues from 28 sheep taken in lease. His revenues were probably insufficient, since he was in debt for 24 fl. However, he had been accounted for as *mediano*.[10] The low number of smallholders' family members could suggest also that these people were just farmers at the final or first step of their life-cycle or impoverished farmers (see Emigh, 2009: 64-91; Thoen and Soens, 2015).

The 59 unspecified taxpayers of Table 5.3 – the majority probably landless peasants, share-tenants and wage labourers –, as well as the tenant holders, some of the inactive people, the millers and the sharecroppers, were the poorest inhabitants of San Giovanni in Petroio. Among the sharecroppers, 23 households did not have anything, 33 were poor and only 13 owned between 51 and 200 fl. (*mediani*). Almost the same ratio was found among the tenants outside the share-cropping system. Their scarce number – just 4 – seems to suggest that the

---

7 Source: Author's database from ASF, Catasto 177, cc. 396r-543v. Family structures, however, could be influenced also by life-cycle: young and old households were probably smaller than family halfway of their life cycle, with children and maybe old members. See: Herlihy and Klapisch-Zuber, 1985: 259-295; Smith, 1985.

8 For Stefano son of Benedetto: ASF, Catasto 177, c. 434v.

9 Source: Author's database from ASF, Catasto 177, cc. 396r-543v.

10 Source: Author's database from ASF, Catasto 177, cc. 396r-543v. For Mone son of Salvi: ASF, Catasto 177, c. 524r.

spread of *mezzadria* (69 sharecroppers) was almost completed in 1427, although the socio-economic situation was more nuanced. Both these groups usually had large families (over 6 members per household) and they lived in the farmhouses of the leased landholding. However, tenants had on average more livestock and oxen than sharecroppers (14 fl. vs. 6 fl. in livestock per household). It was most likely thanks to their capital and because they were landowners that these peasants were driven towards tenancy instead of share-cropping. This way, in some cases, they could integrate their revenues, increase their pastures and get a house. However, as we have seen, there were also *middle* class sharecroppers who owned land and oxen. For instance, two men called Simone and Giovanni, sons of a certain Antonio, led their household of 7 people working as sharecroppers in the landholding of a Medici member in Lucigliano: next to it, they owned property with the value of 160 fl. and had livestock estimated at 16.5 fl. Every year, they earned from the lease and their property over 58 fl. in total.[11]

So, in this section we have seen that in early fifteenth-century San Giovanni in Petroio wealth inequality was high (0.73) and that almost 75% of the rural population lived under the poverty level, without land and capital. Most of the poorest households were sharecroppers, accessing the farmland via *mezzadria*, suggesting in San Giovanni in Petroio a strong connection between the high inequality level found and the spread of the *mezzadria* system.

II.2 Economic inequalities between the rural and urban Florentine society

The high number of sharecroppers allows us to integrate also their landlords, living in Florence, into our analyses. Doing so, the unequal pattern of land property distribution shown above was a lot higher. The 103 rural inhabitants recorded as landowners owned almost half of the land units recorded in the Catasto of San Giovanni for a total value of more than 6,900 fl. (see Table 5.4). However, in the *pieve*, dating back to 1427 and for which we have access to the mentioned records, 58 Florentine city-dwellers owned land for 30,900 fl. while the 10 churches and parishes of the pieve had almost 2,900 fl. invested in land. Actually, the rural population had only 17% of the whole land value, while the Florentines had around 76% and the religious institutions of that *pieve* 7%.

The relevant contribution of Florentine property and, to a minor extent, of ecclesiastical property as well in wealth concentration has been explored also by using the so-called Theil index (Figure 5.4). This is a statistical measure (usually not standardised) which allows to decompose inequality on the one hand into the part that is due to inequality within the different groups of a given population and, on the other hand, into the part that is due to differences between these groups (Theil, 1967; Conceição and Ferreira, 2000: 2-16). Figure 5.4 plots the decomposition of the contribution to inequality of both

11 Source: Author's database from ASF, Catasto 177, cc. 396r-543v. For Simone and Giovanni sons of Antonio: ASF, Catasto 177, c. 540v.

Table 5.4. The land property distribution in San Giovanni in Petroio (1427-1429)

	# land-owners	# land units	share of land units (%)	share of land value (fl.)	share of land value (%)	average value per land-owner (fl.)
Florentines	58	143	39	30.876,8	76	532,4
Rural inhabitants	103	171	47	6.977,5	17	67,7
Institutions	10	51	14	3.041,1	7	304,1
Total	171	365	100	40.895,4	100	239,2

Sources: Author's database from: ASF, Catasto 177, cc. 396r-543v (for the 103 rural inhabitants); Catasto 64, cc. 362r; 66, cc. 127r, 190v; 67, c. 386r; 68, c. 104r; 69, cc. 366r, 513r; 72, c. 388r; 73, c. 19r, 111r; 74, c. 154v; 75, c. 282r; 76, c. 30r; 77, c. 23r, 220r, 393r; 78, cc. 24r, 106v, 127r, 178r, 208v, 227r, 330r, 420v, 427r, 439r, 483r, 526v, 560v; 79, cc. 33r, 76r, 156v, 242v, 311v, 321v, 323v, 424r, 429v, 481v, 483r, 515r, 565r, 577r, 588v, 605r; 80, cc. 59v, 281r, 389r, 497r, 535r, 540v; 81, cc. 36v, 151v, 220v, 262r, 451r; Monte 75, cc. 668r, 699v (for the 58 Florentines); Catasto 194, cc. 241r-337v (for the religious institutions). The term *land units* refers to landholdings and plots of land, following the organisation of the fiscal records of the Catasto (see Conti, 1966: 21-131).

the groups of rural and Florentine landowners. This way, on a total Theil index of 1.6737, we can see that in San Giovanni, land property inequality was first of all the result of the inequality within the group of Florentine landowners (39% of the total, that is 0.822 points) and then of that between this group and the others (29% of the total, that is 0.609 points). The contribution of inequality within the group of rural landowners as well as within the religious institutions is also relevant (9 and 12% respectively).

As shown by the Theil index, many of the Florentine landlords belonged to the wealthiest classes of the city. Nine were members of the Medici family, such as the father of Cosimo the Elder, Giovanni son of Bicci, and his cousin Averardo son of Francesco. They were the wealthiest landowners of that *pieve*, from where their family moved to Florence in the thirteenth century. Giovanni, who was assessed in Florence at 81,072 florins, owned in Petroio the *villa* of Trebbio and a value of 6,394 fl. of land, 465 fl. of cattle and 543 fl. of credit. Averardo, who had an assessable base of 16,496 fl., owned in the same parish the *villa* of Cafaggiolo, worth 3,850 fl. in land, 255 fl. in cattle and 397 fl. in credit. Other landowners in that area included other rich Florentine households, who admittedly possessed less prestige or assets there, such as the families of Cavalcanti, Strozzi, Macinghi and Ubaldini, the latter being heirs of the ancient feudal lords of Mugello, as well as members of the lower middle class of the city.[12] This explains the high level of inequality found within this group.

12 Regarding the Medici family and their real estates, especially in Mugello, see: Franchetti Pardo and Casali, 1978: 5-46, 65-111; Nanni, 1992. For the bank activity of the Medici family and especially of Giovanni son of Bicci and Cosimo see: De Roover, 1963. For the income-tax return of Giovanni son of Bicci see: ASF, Monte 75, c. 668r and followings. For that

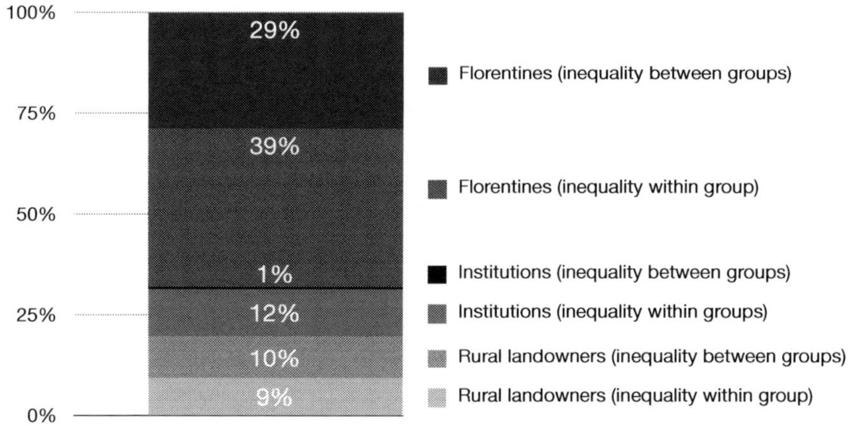

Figure 5.4. Decomposing the *Theil index* of San Giovanni in Petroio (1427-1429): contribution of Florentine, religious institutions and rural landowners to land property inequality

Sources: see Table 5.4. The formula used for the Theil index is: $T_{S.\ Giovanni\ in\ Petroio} = T' + T''$. T' is the inequality between the three groups, that is $T' = w_{Florentines} [\log (w_{Florentines} / n_{Florentines})] + w_{Ruralinhab} [\log (w_{Ruralinhab} / n_{Ruralinhab})] + w_{Relinst} [\log (w_{Relinst} / n_{Relinst})]$, while w is the wealth (land property value) shares for each group (the proportion of total land property value that every group has) and n is the population shares for each group. T'' is the inequality within each group and corresponds to the following formula: $1/n_{group} * {}^{n\ group}\Sigma_{i=1} [y_i / \mu_{group} (\log y_i / \mu_{group})]$, where n is the number of individual for each group, y is the income of each individual of that group and μ is the average land property value of that group (y/n). See: Conceição and Ferreira, 2000, pp. 17-30.

II.3 The role of mezzadria

As we have seen above, it is very probable that the city-dwellers controlled most of the land surface in San Giovanni. Of course, the land value data seem to indicate that they controlled the most fertile and most productive farmland of the *pieve* as a result of the process of *appoderamento* during the previous centuries. If we integrate in the calculation of asset distribution – which may be considered also as a proxy for income distribution – the values owned by Florentine landowners in the *pieve*, the Gini coefficient increases from 0,73 to 0,81,[13] moving apparently forward the 'inequality possibility frontier' of that

of Averardo son of Francesco see: ASF, Catasto 81, c. 451r and followings. For the other Florentine landlords see: ASF, Catasto 64, cc. 362r; 66, cc. 127r, 190v; 67, c. 386r; 68, c. 104r; 69, cc. 366r, 513r; 72, c. 388r; 73, c. 19r, 111r; 74, c. 154v; 75, c. 282r; 76, c. 30r; 77, c. 23r, 220r, 393r; 78, cc. 24r, 106v, 127r, 178r, 208v, 227r, 330r, 420v, 427r, 439r, 483r, 526v, 560v; 79, cc. 33r, 76r, 156v, 242v, 311v, 321v, 323v, 424r, 429v, 481v, 483r, 515r, 565r, 577r, 588v, 605r; 80, cc. 59v, 281r, 389r, 497r, 535r, 540v; 81, cc. 36v, 151v, 220v, 262r, 451r; Monte 75, cc. 668r, 699v.

13 The Gini has been calculated on the taxable assets of the 174 households of S. Giovanni in Petroio and of the 58 Florentine landowners. Source: Author's database from ASF, Catasto 177, cc. 396r-543v (for the 174 rural inhabitants); Catasto 64, cc. 362r; 66, cc. 127r, 190v; 67,

area (see: Milanovic, Lindert and Williamson, 2010). Such a high degree of wealth inequality among the rural inhabitants of San Giovanni and especially the inequality between its inhabitants and the Florentine landowners heavily influenced the access to factors of endowments such as land, capital and labour and required a mechanism to cope with it.

Florentines needed a leasehold system to save, improve and run their land investment. Furthermore, as has been showed before, most rural inhabitants could not afford oxen and credit to run a landholding as tenant holders. This was the result of land and credit market constraints: it made the leases in kind or in money not entirely suitable (van Bavel and Hoppenbrouwers, 2004; De La Roncière, 2005; Lambrecht and Schofield, 2009). Moreover, rural population needed somehow to have access to land to survive: the alternative was just to boost social conflicts or to move to Florence to look for better possibilities. This way, the risk was an exodus of labourers from the countryside towards the city, a decrease of the agricultural production and a downward movement of the value of urban investment in land property (Piccinni, 2006a and 2006b; Cohn, 2007).

The *mezzadria* contract provided exactly what both the actors were missing. Within the group of Florentine landowners, almost 80% of landholding (96% of the land value) was leased out in share-cropping. Indeed, other forms of leaseholds in money or in kind were applied to only 7% of land units, which amount to just 1% of the complete land value (Table 5.5). A similar pattern can be observed for the ecclesiastical property of Petroio: 1,405 fl. of land were leased out in share-cropping.[14] Through the share-cropping system, the Florentine lessors provided a wide range of investment as farmhouses, stables and service buildings as well as oxen and livestock. Furthermore, they also lent money and sowing seed to their sharecroppers to pay the running expenses and to supply the family needs (Piccinni, 1992; Ginatempo, 2002). This way the peasantry of San Giovanni had access to the land and the capital of the Florentines in exchange of their labour force, integrating their income with around 50% of the *mezzadria* yields.

Concerning the access to land, we can see that the value of the farmland leased out through sharecropping was over 29,000 fl., while the value of the oxen supplied also exceeded 1,000 fl. This way, the pattern of asset distribution within the whole rural population appears to be reversed (Table 5.6). The well-off (that is, mainly, the farmers) controlled just 11% of total land value, i.e. 247 fl. per household, while the poor and the very poor (mainly sharecroppers) had access to 67% of total land value. If we consider just the sharecroppers, they had access to almost 300 fl. of land per household. Moreover, the poor and

c. 386r; 68, c. 104r; 69, cc. 366r, 513r; 72, c. 388r; 73, c. 19r, 111r; 74, c. 154v; 75, c. 282r; 76, c. 30r; 77, c. 23r, 220r, 393r; 78, cc. 24r, 106v, 127r, 178r, 208v, 227r, 330r, 420v, 427r, 439r, 483r, 526v, 560v; 79, cc. 33r, 76r, 156v, 242v, 311v, 321v, 323v, 424r, 429v, 481v, 483r, 515r, 565r, 577r, 588v, 605r; 80, cc. 59v, 281r, 389r, 497r, 535r, 540v; 81, cc. 36v, 151v, 220v, 262r, 451r; Monte 75, cc. 668r, 699v (for the 58 Florentines).

14 Source: Author's database from ASF, Catasto 194, cc. 241r-337v.

Table 5.5. Tenant systems of Florentine land property in San Giovanni in Petroio (1427-1429)

Tenant systems	# land units	land units (%)	share of land value (fl.)	share of land value (%)	average value per land unit (fl.)
Leases in kind / money	10	7	344,0	1	34,4
Direct cultivation	12	8	578,7	2	48,2
Mezzadria	113	79	29.591,5	96	261,9
Unknown	8	6	396,4	1	49,6
Total	143	100	30.910,6	100	216,2

Sources: Author's database from: ASF, Catasto 64, cc. 362r; 66, cc. 127r, 190v; 67, c. 386r; 68, c. 104r; 69, cc. 366r, 513r; 72, c. 388r; 73, c. 19r, 111r; 74, c. 154v; 75, c. 282r; 76, c. 30r; 77, c. 23r, 220r, 393r; 78, cc. 24r, 106v, 127r, 178r, 208v, 227r, 330r, 420v, 427r, 439r, 483r, 526v, 560v; 79, cc. 33r, 76r, 156v, 242v, 311v, 321v, 323v, 424r, 429v, 481v, 483r, 515r, 565r, 577r, 588v, 605r; 80, cc. 59v, 281r, 389r, 497r, 535r, 540v; 81, cc. 36v, 151v, 220v, 262r, 451r; Monte 75, cc. 668r, 699v. The term *land units* refers to landholdings and plots of land, following the organisation of the fiscal records of the Catasto (see Conti, 1966: 21-131).

Table 5.6. Total amount of assets (owned and leased) per fiscal class in San Giovanni in Petroio (1427-1429)

Assets		share of land value			share of oxen value			share of livestock value			
fiscal classes		% households	fl.	%	per household (fl.)	fl.	%	per household (fl.)	fl.	%	per household (fl.)
very poor	0 fl.	29	8.068,5	29	161,4	477,5	30	9,5	223,6	11	4,5
poor	1-50 fl.	44	10.756,5	38	139,7	541,0	34	7,0	576,9	29	7,5
middle	51-200 fl.	20	6.418,1	23	183,4	325,8	20	9,3	655,7	33	18,7
well-off	over 200 fl.	7	2.967,0	11	247,3	256,0	16	21,3	543,0	27	45,3

Source: Author's database from: ASF, Catasto 177, cc. 396r-543v (for the 103 rural inhabitants); Catasto 64, cc. 362r; 66, cc. 127r, 190v; 67, c. 386r; 68, c. 104r; 69, cc. 366r, 513r; 72, c. 388r; 73, c. 19r, 111r; 74, c. 154v; 75, c. 282r; 76, c. 30r; 77, c. 23r, 220r, 393r; 78, cc. 24r, 106v, 127r, 178r, 208v, 227r, 330r, 420v, 427r, 439r, 483r, 526v, 560v; 79, cc. 33r, 76r, 156v, 242v, 311v, 321v, 323v, 424r, 429v, 481v, 483r, 515r, 565r, 577r, 588v, 605r; 80, cc. 59v, 281r, 389r, 497r, 535r, 540v; 81, cc. 36v, 151v, 220v, 262r, 451r; Monte 75, cc. 668r, 699v (for the properties of the Florentines); Catasto 194, cc. 241r-337v (for the property of the religious institutions).

very poor had access also to 65% of the most valuable oxen, and the well-off only to 16%. Finally, once we add up the land owned and the land leased, being the 'land used' within the rural population, the Gini coefficient plummets from 0,73 to 0,58 (Figure 5.5). Along with that, we should consider also that

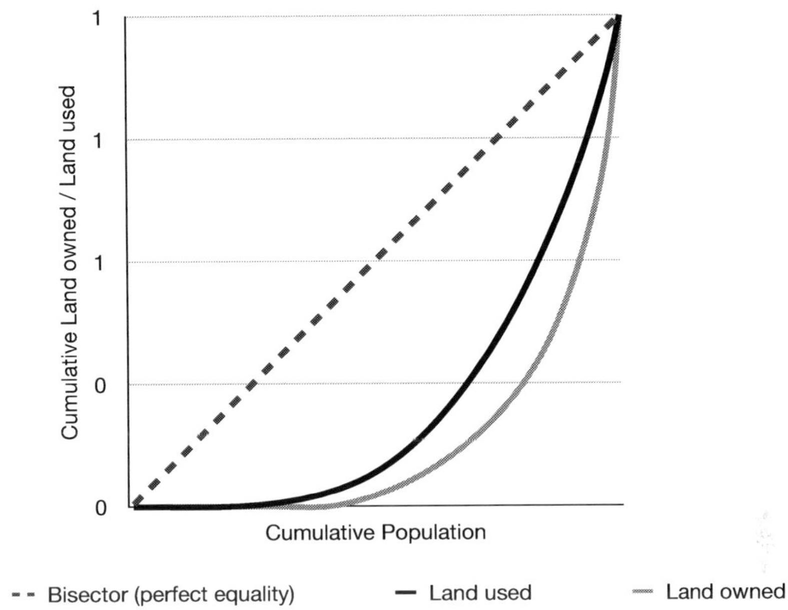

Figure 5.5. Wealth inequality in San Giovanni in Petroio (1427-1429): land used and owned

Source: Author's database from: ASF, Catasto 177, cc. 396r-543v (for the 103 rural inhabitants); Catasto 64, cc. 362r; 66, cc. 127r, 190v; 67, c. 386r; 68, c. 104r; 69, cc. 366r, 513r; 72, c. 388r; 73, c. 19r, 111r; 74, c. 154v; 75, c. 282r; 76, c. 30r; 77, c. 23r, 220r, 393r; 78, cc. 24r, 106v, 127r, 178r, 208v, 227r, 330r, 420v, 427r, 439r, 483r, 526v, 560v; 79, cc. 33r, 76r, 156v, 242v, 311v, 321v, 323v, 424r, 429v, 481v, 483r, 515r, 565r, 577r, 588v, 605r; 80, cc. 59v, 281r, 389r, 497r, 535r, 540v; 81, cc. 36v, 151v, 220v, 262r, 451r; Monte 75, cc. 668r, 699v (for the properties of the Florentines); Catasto 194, cc. 241r-337v (for the property of the religious institutions).

sharecroppers received on average around 25 fl. through the *mezzadria* system. Contracting a loan on the credit market or with the *mezzadria* lessor was quite different. The former, sooner or later, should be repaid by law, while the latter could be either contracted again among the actors, or paid with extra labour, or delayed or even let off. This is demonstrated also by the assessment criteria used in the Catasto: the officials never accounted as taxable assets the loans received by sharecroppers from their lessors, while they did so with the other kind of debts (Conti, 1966: 73-118).

Concerning the share of yields, the quality and quantity of the land as well as the investment of the lessors assured to the *mezzadria* landholdings the highest physical production of the *pieve.*[15] I calculated from the tax incomes

15 Unfortunately, it is not possible to calculate the land and the labour productivity, since the data available from the Catasto on land surface are scarce and not fully reliable. However, it

of the Catasto that these landholdings produced over 213 tons of wheat and 11,.000 litres of wine in 1427. This means over 4,000 fl. of the total agricultural output per year and around 36.6 fl. per landholding: this was seven times more than the mean output of the land cultivated by the farmers (5.1 fl.). Since in the *mezzadria,* contract revenues were usually divided in half, we can hypothesise that around 2,000 fl. of agricultural output produced by 69 sharecroppers was shared every year, i.e. almost 30 fl. per *mezzadria* household. Moreover, for 46 sharecroppers (of poor and middle fiscal classes), revenues from share-tenancy were added with yields from their directly managed estates. A further benefit of the *mezzadria* system for the peasants was the use of the garden and of the poultry: although not recorded in the Catasto as rent, it provided extra revenues from the market (Imberciadori, 1951).

This way, a landless peasant can have had some access to land, labour, credit and capital as oxen, livestock and sowing seeds. For instance, a certain Piero, son of Francesco, with Giovanni and Domenico as his sons, sharecroppers of Averardo de' Medici in Villanuova, had been assessed as *miserabili* in the Catasto. However, they leased two landholdings with a value of 596 fl., containing 4 oxen and 2 bovines of 50 fl. and a debt with the lessor Averardo of 92 fl. Their family, composed of 12 members, yielded on average almost 40 fl. per year.[16]

These data, however, do not allow us to measure the cost for the sharecroppers to have access to land. What we know from the existing literature is that this price may have been high: usually peasants were constrained to provide extra labour input or to renounce part of their share in favour of the landlord to repay their debts or their share of the input. Due to the increase of labour input (plantations, ploughing, levelling and removal of stones, creation of terraces and drainage) also the value of the *mezzadria* properties increased over time. As a consequence, we can hypothesise that the total amount of debts of sharecroppers with their lessors (over 1,700 fl.) as well as the value of the *mezzadria* landholding in San Giovanni in Petroio (over 30,900 fl.), could roughly indicate also the price paid in labour by the peasants to escape from inequality in input and output distribution. Moreover, the debts, the labour input paid as well as the uncertainty of the short-lease contract made the sharecroppers more dependent on their lessors, who could, for example, push them to accept less favourable labour conditions in times of high labour supply (Cherubini, 1991: 171-208; Epstein, 1994; Ginatempo, 2002).

---

is probable that the quantity and quality of the farmland purchased by the rich Florentine city-dwellers contributed more than capital and labour input on physical production. See for some estimation of *mezzadria* land productivity: Emigh, 2009, pp. 168-195; Nanni, 1992, pp. 13-20.

16 For Piero son of Francesco: ASF, Catasto 177, c. 396r.

III. Tentative conclusion

This exploration of socio-economic inequalities throughout a sample area of the *mezzadria* system can contribute to the general debate on inequality and growth in pre-industrial rural societies at three levels. First of all, this paper shows to what extent for research on inequality it could be useful to integrate indexes such as Gini and Theil with in-depth primary source-based social analyses. They make it possible to verify general explanations as well as to evaluate and measure the extent of exceptions. This exchange between the micro and macro level is important to better understand historical changes and to further enhance the legacy of previous studies (Piccinni, 2012: 1197-1206). Moreover, regarding the Florentine fiscal sources and especially the Catasto of 1427, we have studied the data collection for both rural and Florentine taxpayers together, which is uncommon in existing studies. This way, it has been possible to apply statistical analyses to the whole population, inhabitants and assets-owners together, shedding a new light on socio-economic inequality and on its composition. However, observing the role and relevance of 'external' investment is important to understand patterns of economic inequalities and development.

Secondly, in this paper I have tried to show the first results of a broader study of the Tuscan rural society. Of course, these first results will need further adjustments. Nevertheless, they have highlighted different patterns of wealth and income distribution in Tuscan rural society. On one hand, it has shown a high degree of economic inequality within the territory of San Giovanni in Petroio, in line with that of other rural communities of the *contado* of Florence. On the other, it has shown how this trend further increased once we integrate in our analyses the group of Florentine landowners, and how this integration is relevant since these landowners controlled most of the land. Finally, this paper has tried to show also why and how, in this stage of its existence, the share-cropping system called *mezzadria* partly coped with increasing wealth inequality. Indeed, the labour (income) organised in *mezzadria* was used to coping with the unequal distribution of factors of endowment (assets as land and capital-oxen). At the same time, it was determined by the unequal distribution of those factors. This suggests that these two trends, although connected, could be potentially divergent in the long term, according to the costs of access to land and capital established by the landowners. This cost was the main issue in the Florentine *contado*, and it was heavily influenced by institutions as the *mezzadria* contract, the credit, labour and land market and the policies of urban elites in the countryside. However, the Tuscan sharecropping comes out as most relevant: it made a poor rural society work (Pinto, 1990, 443-448).

Finally, this paper shows that it remains important to study in the future to what extent the condition of impoverished peasants was really improved by *mezzadria* compared to the period before the introduction of that system. One should also give more attention to the prices paid to have access to land. Furthermore, we can wonder how exactly and until when the wealth and income inequality through share-cropping really improved agricultural production and productivity in the Florentine *contado.*

Bibliography

Ackerberg, D. A. and Botticini, M. S. (2000), 'The choice of agrarian contracts in early renaissance, Tuscany: risk sharing, moral hazard, or capital market imperfections?', *Explorations in Economic History*, 37, pp. 241-257.
Alfani, G. (2013), 'Fiscality and territory. Ivrea and Piedmont between the fifteenth and seventeenth centuries', in Vester, M. (ed.), *Sabaudian Studies. Political Culture, Dynasty, & Territory 1400-1700*, Kirksville (MO), pp. 213-239.
Alfani, G. and Ammannati, F. (2017), 'Long-term trends in economic inequality: the case of the Florentine State, c. 1300-1800', *Economic History Review*, 70, 4, pp. 1072-1102.
Alfani, G. and Ryckbosch, W. (2016), 'Growing apart in early modern Europe? A comparison of inequality trends in Italy and the Low Countries, 1500-1800', *Explorations in Economic History*, 62, pp. 143-153.
Bavel, B. J. P. van (2016), *The Invisible Hand? How Market Economies have Emerged and Declined since ad 500*, Oxford.
Bavel, B. J. P. van and Hoppenbrouwers, P. (eds.) (2004), *Landholding and land transfer in the North Sea Area (late Middle Ages-19th Century)*, Turnhout.
Bavel, B. J. P. van and Hoyle, R. (eds.) (2010), *Rural economy and society in north-western Europe, 500-2000*, I, *Social Relations: Property and Power*, Turnhout.
Béaur, G. and Schofield, P. R., Chevet, J.-M., Perez-Picazo, M.-T. (eds.) (2013), *Property Rights, Land Markets and Economic Growth in the European Countryside (13th-20th Centuries)*, Turnhout.
Cherubini, G. (1974), *Signori contadini borghesi*, Firenze.
Cherubini, G. (1991), *Scritti toscani: l'urbanesimo medievale e la mezzadria*, Firenze.
Cheung, S., (1969), *The Theory of Share-Tenancy. With Special Application to Asian Agriculture and the First Phase of Taiwan Land Reform*, Chicago.
Cohn, S. K. (2007), 'After the Black Death: labour legislation and attitudes towards labour in late-medieval western Europe', *Economic History Review*, 60, 3, pp. 457-485.
Conceição, P. and Ferreira, P. (2000), 'The young person's guide to the Theil Index: Suggesting intuitive interpretations and exploring analytical applications', *UTIP Working Paper*, 14, pp. 1-54.
Conti, E. (1965a), *La formazione della struttura agraria moderno nel contado fiorentino*, III, 1. *Fonti e risultati sommari delle indagini per campione e delle rilevazioni statistiche (secoli XV-XIX)*, Roma.
Conti, E. (1965b), *La formazione della struttura agraria moderno nel contado fiorentino*, III, 2. *Monografie e tavole statistiche (secoli XV-XIX)*, Roma.
Conti, E. (1966), *I catasti agrari della repubblica fiorentina e il catasto particellare toscano (secoli XI-XIX)*, Roma.
De La Roncière, Ch. M. (2005), *Firenze e le sue campagne nel Trecento. Mercanti, produzione, traffici*, Firenze.
De Roover, R. (1963), *The Rise and Decline of the Medici Bank (1397-1494)*, Cambridge (MA).

Emigh, R. J. (1996), 'Loans and livestock. Comparing landlords' and tenants' declarations from the Catasto of 1427', *The Journal of European Economic History*, 25, 3, pp. 705-723.
Emigh, R. J. (1997), 'The spread of sharecropping in Tuscany: the political economy of transaction costs', *American Sociological Review*, 62, 3, pp. 423-442.
Emigh, R. J. (2009), *The Undevelopment of Capitalism: Sectors and Markets in Fifteenth-Century Tuscany*. Philadelphia (PA).
Epstein, S. (1994), 'Tuscans and their farms', *Rivista di Storia Economica*, 11, 1, pp. 11-23.
Franchetti Pardo, V. and Casali, G. (1978), *I Medici nel contado fiorentino: ville e possedimenti agricoli tra Quattrocento e Cinquecento*, Firenze.
Galassi, F. (1992), 'Tuscans and their farms: The economics of share tenancy in fifteenth century Florence', *Rivista di Storia Economica*, 9, 1-2, pp. 77-94.
Galassi, F. (2000), 'Moral hazard and asset specificity in the renaissance. The economics of sharecropping in 1427 Florence', in Kauffman, K. D. (ed.), *New Frontiers in Agricultural History*, London, pp. 177-206.
Ginatempo, M. (1989), *Crisi di un territorio*, Firenze.
Ginatempo, M. (2002), 'La mezzadria delle origini. L'Italia centro-settentrionale nei secoli XIII-XV', *Rivista di Storia dell'agricoltura*, XLII, pp. 49-110.
Giorgetti, G. (1974), *Contadini e proprietari nell'Italia moderna. Rapporti di produzione e contratti agrari del secolo XVI ad oggi*, Torino.
Goddard, R., Langdon, J. and Müller, M. (eds.) (2010), *Survival and Discord in Medieval Society. Essays in Honour of Christopher Dyer*, Turnhout.
Herlihy, D. (1968), *Santa Maria Impruneta: a rural commune in the Late Middle Ages*, in Rubinstein, N. (ed.), *Florentine studies: politics and society in Renaissance Florence*, London, pp. 242-276.
Herlihy, D. (1978), 'The distribution of wealth in a renaissance community: Florence 1427', in Abrams, P., Wrigley, E. A. (eds.), *Towns in societies: essays in economic history and historical sociology*, Cambridge, pp. 131-157.
Herlihy, D. (1981), 'The problem of the "return to the land" in Tuscan economic history of the fourteenth and fifteenth centuries', in *Civiltà ed economia agricola in Toscana nei secc. XIV-XV: problemi della vita delle campagne del tardo medioevo*, Pistoia, pp. 401-416.
Herlihy, D. and Klapisch-Zuber, Ch. (1985), *Tuscans and their families: a study on the Florentine Catasto of 1427*, New Haven (CT).
Hoffman, Ph. T. (1984), 'The economic theory of sharecropping in early modern France', *Journal of Economic History*, XLIV, 2, pp. 309-319.
Hoffman, Ph. T (1996), *Growth in a traditional society. The French countryside 1450-1815*, Princeton (NJ).
Imberciadori, I. (1951), *Mezzadria classica toscana con documentazione inedita dal IX al XIV secolo*, Firenze.
Klapisch-Zuber, Ch. (1983), *Una carta del popolamento Toscano negli anni 1427-1430*, Milano.
Lambrecht, Th. and Schofield, P. R. (eds.) (2009), *Credit and the rural economy in North-western Europe, c. 1200-c. 1850*, CORN Publication Series 12, Turnhout.

Malanima, P. (2018), 'Italy in the Renaissance: a leading economy in the European context, 1350-1550', *Economic History Review*, 71, 1, pp. 3-30.
Milanovic, B., Lindert, P. H. and Williamson, J. G. (2010), 'Pre-industrial inequality', *The Economic Journal*, 121, pp. 255-272.
Mucciarelli, R. and Piccinni, G. (1994), 'Un'Italia senza rivolte? Il conflitto sociale nelle aree mezzadrili', *Annali dell'Istituto Alcide Cervi*, 16, pp. 173-205.
Nanni, P. (1992), *Lorenzo agricoltore. Sulla proprietà fondiaria dei Medici nella seconda metà del Quattrocento*, Firenze.
Piccinni, G. (ed.) (1992), *Il contratto di mezzadria nella Toscana medievale*, III, *Contado di Siena 1348-1528. Appendice: la normativa 1256-1510*, Firenze.
Piccinni, G. (2006a), *L'evoluzione della rendita fondiaria alla fine del Medioevo*, in Cortonesi, A. and Piccinni, G., *Medioevo delle campagne. Rapporti di lavoro, politica agraria, protesta contadina*, Roma, pp. 57-95.
Piccinni, G. (2006b), *La politica agraria del comune di Siena*, in Cortonesi, A. and Piccinni, G., *Medioevo delle campagne. Rapporti di lavoro, politica agraria, protesta contadina*, Roma, pp. 207-292.
Piccinni, G. (2012), 'Signori contadini borghesi. Una recensione tardiva', Balestracci, D. et al. (eds.), *Uomini Paesaggi Storie. Studi di storia medievale per Giovanni Cherubini*, Siena, pp. 1193-1206.
Pinto, G. (1987), 'I mercanti e la terra', Cipolla, C. M. and Cardini, F. (eds.), *Banchieri e mercanti di Siena*, Roma, pp. 221-290.
Pinto, G. (1990), *L'agricoltura delle aree mezzadrili*, Gensini, S. (ed.), *Le Italie del tardo Medioevo*, Pisa, pp. 433-448.
Pirillo, P. (2015), *Forme e strutture del popolamento nel contado fiorentino, III, Gli insediamenti al tempo del primo catasto (1427-1429)*, Roma.
Righini, G. (1956), *Mugello e Valdisieve. Note e memorie storico-artistico-letterarie*, Firenze.
Smith, R. (ed.) (1985), *Land, Kinship and Life-Cycle*, Cambridge.
Stiglitz, J. E. (1974), 'Incentives and Risk Sharing in Sharecropping', *Review of Economic Studies*, 41, pp. 219-255.
Theil, H. (1967), *Economics and Information Theory*, Chicago (IL).
Thoen, E. (2004), '*Social agrosystems* as an economic concept to explain regional differences. An essay taking the former county of Flanders as an example (Middle Ages-19th century)', in Bavel, B. J. P. van, and Hoppenbrouwers, P. (eds.), *Landholding and land transfer in the North Sea Area (late Middle Ages-19th Century)*, Turnhout, pp. 47-66.
Thoen, E. and Soens, T. (2015), 'The family or the farm: a Sophie's choice? The late medieval crisis in Flanders', in Drendel, J. (ed.), *Crisis in the later Middle Ages: beyond the Postan-Duby paradigm*, Turnhout, pp. 195-224.

PINAR CEYLAN

6 Land regime and social stratification in sixteenth century Ottoman rural Manisa*

A longstanding presumption in traditional Ottoman historiography is the notion that inequality in the empire was low and stagnant before the nineteenth century – in sharp contrast to growing and more dynamic regions of the pre-industrial world. Some scholars have suggested that the Ottoman land regime, which was characterised by state ownership of land and peasant small holdings, and the Islamic principles that tasked the state with the role of protecting its subjects and providing for their subsistence, created and maintained an egalitarian social structure (Barkan, 1937, 1956; İnalcık, 1994; İslamoğlu, 1994; Kuran, 2010; Robinson 2009; Timur, 1989). For centuries, it is noted, the central Ottoman state proved itself capable of protecting its *dominium eminens* over arable lands to the detriment of the development of a landed class. State-owned lands, meanwhile, were equally distributed among independent small producers, holding hereditary usufruct rights and protected from over-exploitation by landlords. Furthermore, several historians have argued that such an institutional environment ensured that commercial expansion in the early-modern era did not typically result in the formation of large estates or force peasants into serfdom or wage labor on large holdings – a number of exceptions in the Balkans and Western Anatolia notwithstanding. Instead, production for the market occurred largely on small plots cultivated by independent peasants, even after Ottoman agriculture was exposed to increased European demand for its products (İslamoğlu, 1994; Keyder, 1991).

In line with this account, historians have provided us with a rigid and schematic picture of Ottoman rural society prior to the nineteenth century, dividing it into two large blocks – the ruler and the ruled. According to this discourse, there was a monolithic class of direct producers, consisting of a mass of undifferentiated, independent, taxpaying, and small-holding peasants, as well as a surplus-extracting class that was composed of dependent state agents who earned revocable and typically modest agrarian incomes and exercised

* This research is part of the GINI project, supported by Gent University and conducted jointly by the Economics and History Departments. I am particularly grateful to Prof. Erik Thoen and Assoc. Prof. Hülya Canbakal for their invaluable comments and remarks on this paper.

Pinar Ceylan • Ghent University

Inequality in rural Europe (Late Middle Ages – 18th century), ed. by Guido Alfani and Erik Thoen, CORN, 18 (Turnhout, 2020), pp. 103-122.

 DOI 10.1484/M.CORN-EB.5.121950

limited authority over the peasantry. Standing at the centre of this picture was the Ottoman state, the distributor of rights, privileges, stipends, offices, and immunities. It would not be misleading to argue that subscribing to this idealised version of the Ottoman rural economy and society would make the study of rural inequality in the pre-modern context a largely dead-end effort.

In an effort to demonstrate why studying rural inequality in the Ottoman context is legitimate and rewarding, however, this study critically and emprically examines some rooted assumptions concerning pre-modern Ottoman rural society. It does so by focusing on the Western Anatolian district of Manisa during the sixteenth century. Shortly after its conquest at the turn of the fifteenth century, Manisa was integrated into the larger Ottoman system of taxation, provisioning, and trade as an important agricultural zone, becoming one of the core provinces of the empire in which the classical land regime prevailed[1] (Barkey and van Rossem, 1997).

The main sources employed for this study are tax registers[2] for Manisa from the year 1531. These documents were written during the reign of Suleiman the Magnificent – the height of the Ottoman state's central power. Accordingly, Manisa in the early sixteenth century provides a cogent snapshot of the Ottoman institutional arrangements concerning rural production at a time when the classical land regime predominated.

Ultimately, this study illustrates that, in contrast to the simplified portrayal of Ottoman rural society in traditional historiography, the empire's land regime was extremely complicated during the classical period. Neither the surplus-extracting class nor the class of direct producers was monolithic and homogenous. Even in the central state's heyday – and in a region where the classical Ottoman land regime was firmly ensconced – there was significant diversity in the extraction and distribution of the agrarian surplus, as well as in the legal status and real conditions of the direct producers. The empirical evidence from Manisa confirms the existence of a complex, hierarchical system among the different groups on the basis of their fiscal obligations, privileges, and right to income derived from the land. The findings of the present study provide grounds to question the widely cited but empirically untested assumption of an 'egalitarian' rural society in the Ottoman Empire during the classical period.

I. Western Anatolia and the Ottoman district of Manisa

In the sixteenth century, Manisa was the centre of the Ottoman province of Saruhan in Western Anatolia. The administrative district covered an area

---

1 The Ottoman classical land regime was implemented in the Balkans, Anatolia and Syria. In many of the more distant areas, such as Eastern Anatolia, Iraq, Egypt, Yemen, Wallachia, Moldavia and the Maghreb, the Ottoman central administration did not alter the existing land regimes either to a limited extent or not at all (Pamuk, 2009).

2 See Appendix 6.1 for details.

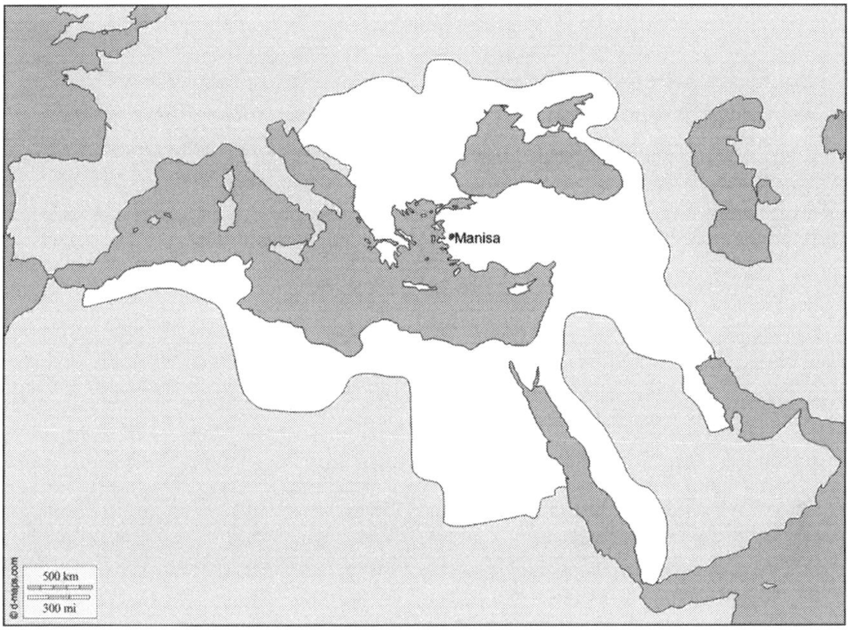

Figure 6.1. The Ottoman Empire in the seventeenth century

of around 250,000 hectares. Boasting fertile valleys and rich river basins, Aegean Anatolia has been a prosperous and densely populated region since ancient times. Rich agricultural production, as well as a geographical position that facilitated close trade relations with other parts of the Mediterranean, shaped the region's economy over many centuries (Emecen, 1989). After the Ottoman conquest, the region supplied the imperial capital with grain and other foodstuffs, while also exporting significant quantities of wheat, cotton, raisins, figs, alum, carpets, wool and hides to European markets.

Two developments in the medieval era had long-lasting impacts on the rural landscape. First, several villages inhabited by the autochthon population were invaded by nomadic Turcoman tribes fleeing the Mongols in the mid-thirteenth century, resulting in the establishment of a substantial number of temporary or periodic settlements – most of which evolved into villages over time. During this period, a peasant-nomad dichotomy began to crystallise. Although many nomads eventually became settled in this part of Anatolia in the following centuries, the presence of nomadic and semi-nomadic groups remained a feature of the rural economy well into the nineteenth century (Planhol, 1959).

The second important development was the Ottoman conquest. In the early fourteenth century, Turcoman groups established various small principalities along the Aegean coastline, extending their rule over Western Anatolia. At the turn of the fifteenth century, the region fell under Ottoman control. The subsequent introduction of the Ottoman land regime in the region resulted in the replacement of the pre-conquest landlords with a new landlord class, as well as the reorganisation of agricultural production within a new institutional environment, although traces of the previous institutional setting were not completely eradicated. As in the Balkans, Syria and Palestine, peace and the better protection of peasants under this new regime in Western Anatolia fostered a substantial increase in cultivated arable land, population, and urban development in the two centuries that followed (İnalcık, 1994).

II. The idealised version of the Ottoman land regime

The Ottoman land regime is often associated with 'state ownership of land', which in economic terms, refers to the inalienability of property rights over land and the central state's control over the distribution of agrarian rent. In the core lands of the empire (Anatolia and the Balkans), a significant share of arable land was registered as *miri* (state) land, meaning that, in principle, it could not be bought, sold or inherited by private individuals. Only the state could exercise the legitimate authority to establish or transfer proprietary rights on these lands. On this legal basis, surplus was extracted from the peasantry within a tax collection and revenue sharing system known as the *tımar* system, which emerged in the fourteenth century. Under this system, members of the ruling class, particularly military groups, were centrally assigned annual revenue grants that were accompanied by certain privileges, immunities and authorities. The source of these revenues was the taxes collected from direct producers, implying that the Ottoman surplus extraction mechanism was characterised by the extraction of rent in the form of tax revenues (Keyder, 1991).

In its simplified form, this surplus extraction and distribution mechanism led many scholars to consider the Ottoman surplus extracting class as a state-dependent group that lacked opportunities to concentrate wealth and power in its own hands. Accordingly, the Ottoman state's policy to curtail the power of independent centrifugal forces and its success in impeding the development of a propertied hereditary noble class have often been proposed as a fundamental determinant of the Ottoman socio-political order over many centuries. In this respect, scholars have frequently emphasised the grant of rights to collect rural tax incomes (instead of territorially determined property rights over land), the modest size of the revenues, and (at least in principal) the non-hereditary, service-dependent and revocable nature of these revenue grants allocated within the *tımar* system as factors radically distinguishing the Ottoman surplus extraction mechanism from its European counterparts.

Another characteristic feature associated with this idealised version is the limited power of the surplus extracting groups over direct producers. On land integrated into the *tımar* system, the organisation of agricultural production generally relied on small family holdings that were occupied by peasant households, who possessed hereditary usufruct rights and cultivated with a pair of oxen and family labour (Keyder, 1991). These holdings were given to the peasants under the *tapu* contract, a perpetual lease agreement granting the peasant certain rights[3] and stipulating various obligations,[4] and making him the "hereditary tenant in perpetuity" (Barkan, 1937: 399). The individual who leased the land under *tapu* (title-deed) was registered at a certain village as the subject of the *tımar* holder. These registered peasants were obliged to cultivate the land in their possession and pay personal and agricultural taxes to the *tımar* holder and provide him with certain services.

Among others, Genç (2014: 12) claims in this line of thought that these institutional arrangements granted great autonomy to the peasant: "Within the limits set by the law, the relation of the peasant with the state-owned land in his possession was not different than under private ownership. He perceived the land as his own. The peasant cultivated the land together with his family at his own will, reaped the yields himself, consumed what is left after taxation, and recognised that it will be bequeathed to his son upon his death". As such, many historians consider Ottoman direct producers to have been a 'free' or 'independent' peasantry, with little, if any servile obligations.

According to the traditional view, the hereditary character of the peasant's usufruct rights, along with the prohibition of the unjustified expropriation of the peasant, set important limits on the landlord class's power over direct producers. By expressly prohibiting landlords from possessing and cultivating land reserved for peasants, agricultural laws provided a safeguard that prevented this class from concentrating land in its hands. The *tımar* holder was responsible for collecting the assigned dues and supervising the territory and the way it was possessed and used by peasants (to ensure that the latter did not alter the status and use of the land), but did not have the authority to intervene in the organisation of agricultural production. At the same time, local landlord groups, who were responsible for administration and revenue collection, had no jurisdictional authority over people or the land. Jurisdictional authority

3 The usufruct rights of the peasant were guaranteed by a title deed (*tapu*). The land in his possession could not be taken from him at the landlord's will unless the peasant violated the obligations deriving from his status. The usufruct rights over family holdings were hereditary; upon the death of the possessor, the holding was bequeathed to the eldest son without being divided among the heirs. Moreover, these peasants could engage in handicrafts. They could cultivate more lands then the amount of land registered on them, as long as they paid their taxes. There was no limitation over their marriages or the internal organization of production on their lands (İnalcık, 1994).

4 Without appropriate authorisation, a peasant in possession of a *tapu* contract could not transfer (by selling, donating, endowing, mortgaging, or leaving by will) his usufruct rights over the holding to a third party or change its use by converting it into a vineyard or orchard. If left uncultivated for three consecutive years in the absence of force majeure, holdings under *tapu* could be taken from the peasant and given to someone else. If the peasant left the holding and moved to another place, he was liable to pay a tax and could be summoned back within 10 years of his departure (İnalcık, 1994).

belonged to the central state, which exercised it through the Ottoman courts. Thanks to the separation of juridical and administrative practices, the Ottoman court, it is argued, could act as an institution independent of landed interests and play a significant role in protecting the peasants against over-exploitation by the landlord class by preventing the latter's arbitrary demands for rents and services beyond what was defined in the law (İnalcık, 1994; İslamoğlu, 1994).

The third characteristic feature in the traditional view of the Ottoman land regime concerns the distribution of property to land among the peasantry. Many scholars state that the Ottoman agrarian economy was characterised by small-scale production in which the usufruct rights over arable land were distributed among direct producers in an egalitarian way (Keyder, 1991). Such scholars argue that this created an undifferentiated peasant class in terms of their access to land. The Ottoman land tenure system was shaped by the central government's desire to keep peasants on their land so as to maintain a permanent and stable source of tax revenue (Teoman and Kaymak, 2008). According to Ottoman economic wisdom and the agricultural codes of the classical period, promoting agriculture, particularly the cultivation of grains to feed urban populations, and maintaining the agricultural tax base was the overriding priority. Accordingly, the arable land was distributed among direct producers in a way that ensured that as many peasant families as possible possessed enough land for their subsistence. Therefore, Ottoman agricultural laws limited the size of the plots given as peasant holdings to the area that could be ploughed by a pair of oxen and cultivated by family labour. And, at least in principle, the integration of small family holdings into big landed properties, as well as their fragmentation into smaller holdings, was prohibited by law (İnalcık, 1994). In Western Anatolia, the average size of a family holding ranged from 5.5 hectares on top-quality soil to 12-14 hectares on low-quality soil (Emecen, 1989: 223).

Overall, this simplified image of the Ottoman land regime, which was characterised, on one hand, by a surplus-extracting class that earned service-dependent, non-hereditary incomes from land and was limited in its power vis-à-vis the central state and direct producers, and, on the other, a small, independent peasantry with identical rights and obligations that cultivated family holdings of more or less equal size, has continued to shape our understanding of Ottoman rural society in the classical period. In fact, the protection of this egalitarian structure over the centuries – thereby inhibiting the concentration of land in the hands of a small group and the expropriation of peasants – remains a central theme in the literature, in which many have described it as a major cause of the empire's "failed transition to capitalism" (Keyder, 1991).

III. Institutional diversity in surplus extraction

However, the actual land regime of the classical period was much more complex than the simplified view presented by the historiography centred on the Ottoman state. To begin with, this simplified depiction relies largely on the association of the Ottoman surplus-extracting class with locally rooted cavalrymen,[5] who were responsible for supervising the use of land and who possessed limited powers and earned modest revenue in directly collecting taxes from the peasantry (Moutafchieva, 1988). This, in fact, was only part of the bigger picture of surplus extraction in the empire's core lands. In reality, there was a significant diversity in the forms of the extraction and distribution of the agrarian surplus, as well as a wide discrepancy in terms of the powers and the revenues earned by a multiplicity of actors involved in this process. As a result, significant social and economic stratification existed within the Ottoman surplus-extracting class.

Above all, the Ottoman system of land tenure was based on a fundamental distinction between state-owned land, on one hand, and *waqf* and privately owned land, on the other (Aytekin, 2009). *Waqfs* were pious institutions that served charitable purposes or institutions established to guarantee a perpetual revenue source for one's family and offspring. While a dominant share of arable land, particularly grain-producing areas, was under state ownership[6] in the core lands of the empire, *waqf* and freehold land were not marginal in many areas.

Property rights on such land were established by an imperial diploma granted by the sultan in return for distinguished services and loyalty. In certain cases, these rights were recognised as a continuation of the pre-Ottoman property rights of the local aristocracy. These diplomas guaranteed the *waqf* or freehold status of the defined land and the right to collect taxes (tithes and customary dues, at the same rates under state control) from the peasants, and prevented any intervention by outsiders, including local state authorities. Freehold estates could be bequeathed, sold, or made into a *waqf* without limitation. In the case of *waqfs*, the purpose of the grant was explicitly stated in the grant diploma, and unlike freehold estates, *waqf* lands could not be used for other purposes or transferred to other parties (İnalcık, 1994). However, these lands were also formally protected from interventions and appropriation by the state, although confiscation of both private and *waqf* property was not a rare practice, particularly at certain historical junctures.

Importantly, the *waqf* and private ownership was territorially determined, meaning it represented a territorial unit; this was in contrast to *tımar*-holders' property rights – the subject of which was 'a given income of a certain sum' from land. Among others, Moutafchieva (1988), rightfully highlights the differences in incentive structures created by these two different forms of

5 Cavalrymen were the backbone of the Ottoman field army from the fourteenth to the sixteenth centuries.

6 State-owned arable lands are believed to have accounted for around three-quarters of the total amount of arable land in the fifteenth and sixteenth centuries in Ottoman Anatolia and the Balkans (Moutafchieva, 1988).

property rights. According to her, the conditional nature of the *tımar*-holders' relationship with the land, the allocation of *tımar* revenues in the form of fixed income, and the limits imposed by the central government on their control over land and labour sums led to their 'disinterestedness' in the organisation of agricultural production. Because of the way *tımar*-holders' property rights were defined, they were not permitted to benefit from a potential increase in the revenue from the land. In contrast to this form of ownership, *waqf* and private ownership associated with territorially determined, long-lasting and relatively secure property rights over land provided the *waqfs* and freeholders strong incentives, giving them a free hand to extract the maximum income by increasing the size of these estates, attracting a larger labour force, and exercising greater pressure on the peasantry.

Alongside the difference in the legal basis of ownership; in the *tımar* system implemented on state-owned lands, there was a significant degree of diversity in terms of the size of the revenue grants, the authorities and privileges associated with different echelons of the *tımar* hierarchy, the actors involved in surplus extraction, as well as the revenue collection practices. Besides the cavalrymen, the sultan and members of his household, state officials from different ranks (such as the central bureaucracy; local military, religious, and administrative elites; and other low-ranking state officials), and several other low-level revenue holders extracted surplus from the peasantry in various forms using different channels.

Depending on their size, revenue grants under the *tımar* system were divided into three categories. The largest revenue category featured the sultan and the members of his household, high imperial bureaucrats, and provincial governors. Under this category, revenues directed to the sultan's treasury (imperial domains) were handled separately. The second category included revenues of considerable size that were held by lower-ranking governors or similar officers in the standing army. The third category consisted mainly of modest revenues assigned to cavalrymen, as well as incomes of relatively insignificant size that were allocated to castellans and other individuals in exchange for their services to the state or the sultan (Adanır, 1998). The *tımar* hierarchy, of course, did not only reflect an economic stratification or a ranking in annual incomes, but also a distribution of power. Although Ottoman agricultural laws did not stipulate any special arrangements for the exploitation of land, whose revenues were directed towards state dignitaries, high military officials, or local administrators, the power of control of these elites over producers were surely not comparable with the cavalrymen or other low-ranking *tımar* holders.[7]

7 An interesting question on this point that requires further research is whether, and to what extent, the *tımar*--holding political elite could influence the Ottoman court in the event of disputes with peasants.

Table 6.1. Distribution of rural tax revenues according to different forms and actors of surplus extraction

Revenues allocated to	**As %**
The sultan	19
Members of the imperial household, state dignitaries, provincial governors	9
Local administrators, mid-ranking military officials	7
Cavalrymen	51
Castellans and others providing certain services to the state and the sultan	7
Waqfs and private owners	6
Unidentified revenue holder	1
Total	**100**

Sources: Manisa tax registers, 1531 (See Appendix 6.1)

Both the differences in the legal basis of ownership, as well as the divisions within the *tımar* system, had significant implications in terms of the modalities of revenue collection from the direct producers. Typically, private owners or *waqfs* directed agents or retainers to collect their revenues. On the other hand, the sultan's revenues were either farmed or collected by government employees (Darling, 1996). Hence, in contrast to the direct supervision and tax collection on the lands, the revenues of which were allocated to cavalrymen, surplus extraction on the larger revenue units of absentee lords involved state agents, tax farmers and other intermediaries. This provides us a complex picture of Ottoman surplus extraction that involved a wide range of actors: *waqf* beneficiaries and freeholders who enjoyed significant power and, in several cases, possessed rights to income over significantly large areas, as well as actors from different layers of the *tımar* hierarchy.

Table 6.1 presents how rural tax revenues – in other words, the surplus extracted from direct producers in the Manisa region – was distributed according to different mechanisms and actors engaged in extraction. In the early sixteenth century, just half of the region's revenues were allocated to cavalrymen, the segment viewed to be the quintessential component of the Ottoman surplus-extraction mechanism. A significant share of rural revenues in the region were directed towards the sultan, members of his household, and state dignitaries, meaning the revenues were divided into larger tax units and collected through tax farming. On the other hand, the small *tımar* revenues granted to castellans and other service providers accounted for 7% of total income, while the *waqf* and private revenues together constituted 6% of overall revenues in the early sixteenth century. At first glance, this latter figure might suggest that *waqf* and freehold estates occupied a trivial place in sixteenth-century Manisa, but these were concentrated in the southern sub-district of Merkez, where they accounted for 40% of overall rural revenues.

This is illustrative of the region-specific character of property structures, and the necessity of studying micro and mezzo processes.

IV. The landholding structures of direct producers

Similarly, the class of direct producers in Manisa exhibited great variety – instead of a monolithic mass – in their legal status and real conditions. Empirical evidence reveals that there was significant variance within this class in terms of the conditions of access to land, as well as rights, duties, and tax burdens, ultimately resulting in a stratified and differentiated community of direct producers. Alongside the registered peasants who cultivated state-owned family holdings with title deeds and paid personal and agricultural taxes to the *tımar* holder, there were several other groups engaged in rural production, including settled or semi-nomadic groups with clan status living in the villages who were involved in agricultural activity as tenants or sharecroppers; registered peasants on *waqf* land or private estates; sharecropping peasants on imperial domains; peasants cultivating land under simple tenancy agreements; tax-exempt groups, including infantrymen, who possessed small holdings; owner-occupiers and more.

Table 6.2 shows the composition of the agrarian work force in Manisa in 1531, according to their legal status. The most striking finding relates to the share of the registered peasants holding family farms on *tımar* lands. This group is widely considered to have been the single most dominant labour class in Ottoman agriculture; indeed, several historians have estimated that they comprised more than 90% of overall agrarian labour.[8] However, once the groups with clan status and infantrymen cultivating their own holdings are integrated into the analysis, it becomes apparent that landed peasants on *tımar* lands constituted just 32% of the total adult males in the region.

The high percentage (25%) of groups with nomad-clan status living in villages, who were involved in agricultural activities is noteworthy. Since the early days of the Ottoman Empire, one of the state's major agrarian policies in the face of the high land-labour ratio in Anatolia was to 'revive' uninhabited arable land by sedenterising nomads (İnalcık, 1994). Evidence from the fifteenth and sixteenth century tax registers suggests that several

8 This assumption largely results from a bias introduced by the choice of sources. While most studies on Ottoman rural history rely on detailed land surveys, most have failed to account for the fact that these sources excluded two groups that constituted part of the Ottoman agrarian labour force: groups with clan status and infantrymen in possession of their own holdings. In regions like Western Anatolia, where there was a large population of nomad-clan origin, this has especially led to misinterpretations. In this regard, Emecen's (1989) comprehensive study is exemplary for not limiting itself to *tahrirs* and making use of a wide range of primary sources.

Table 6.2. Distribution of direct producers in Manisa (male adults, single and married) according to landholding types in 1531

	adult males (n)	as %
Groups with clan status living in villages*	905	25
Landed peasants on *tımar* land	1141	32
Landless peasants on *tımar* land	411	11
Landed peasants on *waqf* and freehold land	199	6
Landless peasants on *waqf* and freehold land	73	2
Sharecroppers on imperial domains	79	2
Tax-exempted groups	147	4
Infantrymen in possession of military farms**	429	12
Zemin holders	205	6
Total	**3589**	**100**

Sources: Manisa tax registers, 1531 (See Appendix 6.1); Emecen 1989

* Figure is taken from Emecen (1989). Only groups with clan status who were indicated as living in the villages in question were included in the agrarian workforce. Others were excluded from the table.

** Figure is taken from Emecen (1989) based on a register from 1545.

nomadic tribes that came to Western Anatolia in the mid-thirteenth century became sedentary over time – whether gaining the status of settled peasant or formally retaining nomad-clan status – and that the temporary settlements established by the nomads were transformed into permanent agricultural settlements. Several other tribes began to engage in transhumance, wandering between their winter lands (in villages in lowlands) and summer lands (in highlands), periodically engaging in agriculture, especially during harvests, in addition to their main occupation of animal husbandry and dairy farming (Emecen, 1989).

In the existing literature, not much has been said regarding the role of tribal groups in agricultural production or the conditions under which these groups accessed land. While it has been noted that the state provided certain advantages to these groups with the aim of encouraging their involvement in agricultural activities, it remains largely unknown how the real conditions of these groups differed from those of settled peasants. This notwithstanding, an important distinction between registered peasants and groups with tribal status concerned the nature of their landholding contracts. Instead of a title deed, tribes with nomad-clan status cultivated land under a simple rental agreement (*mukataa*), which stipulated the payment of a land tax proportional to the area cultivated, alongside tithes (İnalcık, 1994). Evidence from tax registers shows that landholding according to a simple tenancy contract was common in sixteenth-century Manisa and, unlike the conventional wisdom, it was implemented in densely populated areas, as well as uninhabited villages.

On the difference between these two forms, İnalcık (1994: 108) states: "While the simple rental contract was freely concluded between the state and an individual, the title deed implied a certain status stemming from an original 'subjugation' which entailed, in addition to the tithes, certain personal obligations such as the payment of [personal taxes]". Additionally, unlike the title deed, the simple renting contract did not recognize the rights such as the rights of transfer of the holding to another farmer, bequeathing to sons, and preeminent rights of acquisition by wife, daughter and brother (İnalcık, 1994). More important was the legal guarantee that the title deed represented in terms of long-standing property rights, which protected the peasant against expropriation and ensured the longevity of the family holding. Although the real nature of the simple tenancy contract has not been studied, it is highly likely that due to its limited scope, it did not provide such a guarantee, which constituted the legal basis of the secured position of the Ottoman peasantry against the surplus-extracting class.

It should also be recalled that simple tenancy contracts were not reserved for groups with clan status. Registered landless peasants and peasants who held title deeds over small pieces of land also cultivated plots – not given as family holdings – under simple tenancy agreements.[9] Alongside this significant difference among the registered peasants with regards to the contractual arrangements determining the conditions of landholding, a further differentiation existed between those settled on *tımar* lands and those on *waqf* lands and freehold estates, which constituted 6% of male adults in Manisa. Although in general, the latter were also organised into small family holdings, the regulations concerning the general status of peasants and land use were applied to the peasants settled on freehold and *waqf* lands as in the state-owned lands, while the same rent, tax, and dues constituted the income of the landowners. Several historians have highlighted the fact that the conditions of the peasantry on such land differed from the peasantry on *tımar* lands. On one hand, the peasantry on the freehold or *waqf* land enjoyed certain immunities and better protection. Thanks to the relative administrative and fiscal autonomy of the *waqfs* and freeholders, these actors in the rural economy were able to protect their peasants by providing them exemptions from extraordinary war taxes, a principal form of granting privileges within the Ottoman fiscal regime (Adanır, 1998).

However, protection against certain forms of appropriation by the state did not mean lower levels of exploitation by landlords. While the small *tımar*-holders' authority and power over the peasantry were limited by regulations, *waqfs* and the private owners of large estates exercised a wide range of authorities as far as the peasantry on the estates were concerned, meaning they enjoyed a large degree of freedom in the methods of exploitation they applied. Although

9 The data from the registers does not allow us to identify those who held land with simple tenancy agreements.

there is not much empirical evidence on the subject, Moutafchieva's (1988: 110) claims concerning *waqfs* and freeholders' position in the organisation of agricultural production seems highly possible:

> Unlike *tımar* land ownership, in *waqf* land ownership, the feudal landowner played an important organisational role in production. For this reason, the exploitation carried out by him yielded results that provided him with huge surpluses of agricultural products and these surpluses could inevitably be an object of exchange. Furthermore, in spite of the undoubted interest of the *waqf* owner in extracting a bigger rent in kind, which is fairly typical, in *waqf* land as well, rent was, for the most part, in cash.

A third differentiation among registered peasants concerned those settled on the sultan's lands, which were cultivated by sharecroppers and registered peasants. Although forms of exploitation on these lands have not been studied in detail until today, we know that the forms of landholding by direct producers were unequivocal, and their exploitation was not subject to general juridical requirements applying to other lands under *tımar*. Imperial domains were managed by state officials appointed by the central government with the prime aim of maximising revenues. It implied that producers on these lands directly interacted with the state, rather than intermediaries, and were subject to higher levels of exploitation. This concerned both the regular peasants who had settled on imperial domains and other populations with servile or semi-servile obligations (Pamuk, 2017).

Other direct producers in Manisa were the sharecroppers who appear under the categorisation of *ortakçı* in sixteenth-century tax registers. From the fourteenth to the sixteenth centuries, the term 'sharecropping' in the empire referred to two different institutional arrangements. The first was associated with the imperial domains and some rural *waqfs* and denoted a servile or semi-servile status. The status of sharecroppers in this sense was a location-specific, hereditary, and communal one that was granted to the population of specific agricultural zones (Cook, 1972). Land, seed, oxen, and domiciles were provided to producers of slave origin (usually non-Muslim captives) who were tied to the land. And after the seed for next cultivation was separated, the yields were shared between the landlord and the sharecroppers on a 50-50 division. These producers were exempt from personal, land-related and extraordinary taxes. From the late fifteenth century onwards, this labour form largely disappeared, as those with sharecropper status became regular peasants (Şahin, 1996).

But in Western, Southwestern and Inner Anatolia, sharecropping as an institutional arrangement with some servile features continued to exist. In sixteenth-century Manisa, certain village communities of nomad origin held the status of sharecropper on land whose revenues were directed towards the sultan or crown prince. These were concentrated in the southern sub-district of Yengi, which was characterised by the production of cash crops (particularly cotton). It seems that these communities enjoyed some flexibility and appeared somewhere between the sharecropper-slave of the fourteenth century and regular peasants in terms of their obligations and conditions. A particularity of the system as implemented in Manisa concerned the sharing of the surplus. Here, the landlord did not provide the seeds, so he only received one-third of the output. The second form of sharecropping was one that resulted from an incidental contractual arrangement of the type that any producer might engage in. In this form, the sharecropper was a producer-partner cultivating the land on his own terms. Emecen (1989) suggests that producer-partner sharecroppers were scattered here and there across Manisa, especially cultivating small freehold land. In particular, many tribes with nomad-clan status cultivated land as free sharecroppers in Manisa.

A fourth category of direct producers in sixteenth-century Manisa was tax-exempted groups, which consisted of those fulfilling certain duties for the state or the sultan (low-level religious officials, horse breeders, bridge builders, miners, tar extractors, salters, charcoal burners, or producers of gunpowder, oil and grease, et cetera), and infantrymen. These were assigned small holdings for their subsistence. In exchange for services provided, both groups were exempted from personal and land-related taxes, as well as extraordinary war taxes, although they were expected to pay tithes on the yields of their plots (Adanır, 1998). In sixteenth-century Manisa tax registers, the first group of tax-exempted producers appear in the listings of the settled adult male population in numerous villages (4% of all male adults). In some cases, tax exemptions were granted to the whole village community if the community as a whole fulfilled a certain duty assigned. The second group of tax-exempted rural producers were infantrymen (12% of all male adults). During times of war, these were paid a given salary, but during times of peace, they lived on the farms assigned to them in several Ottoman provinces. Infantries directly exploited these farms, which were not under the supervision of the *tımar* holder, whose interference was strictly forbidden. In the end, the infantries occupied an autonomous position within the boundaries of the certain piece of land reserved for them.

Finally, a fifth category that appeared in the tax registers was *zemin holders*. Regarding this type of holdings, Özel (2016) states that these were peasant holdings whose previous holders left no heir. These plots were hired by poor or landless peasants on the basis of simple tenancy agreement and without title deed. Those cultivating *zemin* plots constituted 6% of the male adult workforce in the early sixteenth century.[10]

Overall, the evidence presented above demonstrates that the direct producer class in sixteenth-century Manisa was far from a monolithic class enjoying the same rights, obligations, and conditions of access to land. And although

---

10 Alongside these categories, privately owned farms existed in early sixteenth century Manisa. Emecen (1989) detects 14 small private farms in the 1531 register. Due to the marginal share of this form, it was not included in the analysis.

the category of settled and registered peasants was a major component of the class of producers, it appears that it was not as dominant as widely accepted once the involvement of groups with clan status in agricultural production is integrated into the analysis. A further point concerning differentiation at the village level concerns social relations. Unfortunately, primary sources provide us at best fragmentary evidence, if none at all, on the structure of the village community. On this issue, İslamoğlu (1994: 12-13) suggests that the existence of taxes, imposed on the entire village community (such as taxes levied on non-Muslim subjects or extraordinary wartime taxes) implied a certain hierarchy among the peasants, since it would require "the presence of individuals who assumed the role of allocation of taxes among different households and who were instrumental in the collection of taxes, making sure no household defected from its obligations". And she adds that "the authority of such individuals might have derived from their seniority, from the extent of their holdings, and more importantly, from their ties with *tımar* holders, or state officials".

V. Conclusion

Revealing the significant level of institutional diversity that marked Ottoman rural society during the classical period, this study attempted to go beyond the idealised version of the Ottoman land regime, which constituted the basis of the widely accepted assumption that Ottoman agricultural society was an egalitarian one that featured a small independent peasantry undifferentiated within itself and a state-dependent landlord class with limited powers over direct producers. Empirical evidence from early sixteenth-century Manisa demonstrated that, despite the significant place of cavalryman in the Ottoman surplus-extraction mechanism and that of registered peasants holding land with title deeds in agricultural production, these social strata were far from representing monolithic blocs of single Ottoman landlords and direct producers. In fact, Ottoman rural society was composed of many actors with varying degrees of power, rights, authorities, and obligations, ushering in a marked socioeconomic hierarchy at the local level. Overall, the findings of this study herald the prospect of future research into inequality in Ottoman rural society.

Appendix 6.1 Primary Sources

This study employs three Ottoman tax registers from early-sixteenth century Manisa that are available at the Prime Ministry Ottoman Archives.

The Ottoman government obtained information on the empire's sources of revenue through periodic registers called *tahrir defters*. These documents included detailed information on taxpaying subjects and taxable resources (Coşgel, 2004). "The *tahrir defters* were vital to the financial administration and were used for a variety of purposes"; they served as official registers to establish legal claims to land, assess the empire's expected tax revenues, and to allocate the revenues among military and administrative officials (Coşgel, 2004).

The first register used is the *Mufassal Tahrir Defteri No. BBOA TD165*, (pp. 1-91 concern the district of Manisa), dating from 1531. In preparing *Mufassal* registers, officials conducted detailed land surveys on a village basis and determined revenue sources. The information in these registers was composed of three main parts. The introductory section included the village name, the administrative affiliation of the district, and the name of the fief-holders who were entitled to the tax revenues of the village. The second part provided a survey of the adult male population in the village and the amount of land possessed by each. Tax-exempted males, as well as landed and landless peasants who had settled in the village, were recorded here. The third part, meanwhile, listed different tax items (personal taxes, land taxes, tithes, et cetera).

The second register was the *İcmal Defteri No. BBOA TD72* dating from 1531, (pp. 1-32 concern the district of Manisa). These summary registers showed the distribution of the revenues from tax units allocated as *tımars* among those entitled to such revenues. For each *tımar* holder, a separate entry was arranged. Each entry recorded the name, title, and, occasionally, the position of the *tımar* holder. This was followed by information about the income he was entitled to. The income of a *tımar* holder could be a sum of tax revenues from different tax units (usually a single village, but in some cases, an aggregated tax unit composed of several villages located nearby), or the revenue from a single tax unit could be shared among multiple *tımar* holders. In this case, both the overall revenue of the tax unit and the share of the fief-holder from this amount were indicated in the entry.

The third register was the *Evkaf Defteri No. BBOA TD398* (pp. 1-60 concern the district of Manisa), dating from 1527-1528. While the *Mufassal* and *İcmal* registers were prepared for state-owned land, whose revenues were allocated to *tımar* holders, *Evkaf* registers were special lists recording only villages and land owned privately and by *waqfs*.

Appendix 6.2

Arable land according to legal status

	Legal status	**Surplus extractor**
Miri land	'State-owned' land that could not be bought, sold, or inherited by private individuals. The rights of usufruct were given to peasants.	The tax revenues generated on *miri* land were generally distributed within the *tımar* system and allocated as grants to members of the ruling class in return for services.
Waqf land	Land in the ownership of *waqfs* (religious-charitable institutions or family *waqfs*) that were held independently and administered under a charter by a trustee or trustees. Such land could not be transferred to other parties.	Tax revenues (personal taxes of the settled peasants, land-related taxes, etc.) were appropriated by the *waqfs*.
Mülk land	Privately owned land, granted to individuals as a special privilege. These became full property of the owner and could be bequeathed, sold, or made into a *waqf* without restriction.	Tax revenues on privately owned villages and large freehold estates were appropriated by private owners. For small plots of land cultivated by owner-occupiers, only tithes were paid to the relevant landlord.

Landholding types and categories of direct producers

Landholding by *tapu* contract	The characteristic Ottoman landholding form, which featured a perpetual lease agreement granting the peasant certain rights and stipulating obligations, as well as making him the hereditary tenant in perpetuity.	Peasants registered in a certain village and paying personal taxes to the landlord.
Landholding by *mukataa* contract	Landholding by a simple lease contract that did not stipulate for the holder, obligations of a perpetual lease agreement other than to deliver appropriate taxes to the landlord. Those who held land with *mukataa* did not enjoy the protections provided by the title deed.	Landless peasants; registered peasants holding small amounts of land under *tapu* who also cultivated other land under *mukataa*; groups with clan status

Landholding by tax-exempted groups	Holding of small farm units by those who were exempted from personal and land-related taxes, as well as extraordinary war taxes, in exchange for services provided to the state. Such people were liable to pay tithes on the yields of their plots.	Infantrymen and groups fulfilling certain duties for the state
Sharecropping	A landholding form with some servile features and generally associated with the imperial domains. The yields were shared between the landlord and the sharecroppers. Sharecroppers were exempt from personal, land-related and extraordinary taxes.	Sharecropper (*ortakçı*) village communities on imperial domains
Zemin	Holding on the basis of simple tenancy agreement, of plots whose previous holders left no heir	Poor or landless peasants

Bibliography

Adanır, F. (1998) 'The Ottoman Peasantries, *c.* 1360–*c.* 1860' in: T. Scott (ed.), *The peasantries of Europe from the fourteenth to the eighteenth centuries*, London, New York, pp. 269-312.

Aytekin, E. A. (2009) 'Agrarian relations, property and law. An analysis of the Land Code of 1858 in the Ottoman Empire', *Middle Eastern Studies*, 45, 6, pp. 935-951.

Barkan, Ö. L. (1937) Osmanlı İmparatorluğu'nda Çiftçi Sınıfların Hukukî Statüsü. *Ülkü: Halkevleri Dergisi*, 56, 10, pp. 147-158.

Barkan, Ö. L. (1939-1940) 'XV. ve XVI. Asırlarda Osmanlı İmparatorluğu'nda Toprak İşçiliğinin Organizasyonu Şekilleri', *İstanbul Üniversitesi İktisat Fakültesi Mecmuası*, I, 1, 2, 4, pp. 29-74; 198-245; 397-447.

Barkey, K. and Van Rossem, R. (1997) 'Networks of contention: villages and regional structure in the seventeenth-century Ottoman Empire'. *American Journal of Sociology*, 102, 5, pp. 1345-1382.

Berktay, H. and Faroqhi, S. (1992) *New Approaches to State and Peasant in Ottoman History*, London.

Coşgel, M. (2004) 'Ottoman Tax Registers (Tahrir Defterleri)', *Historical Methods: A Journal of Quantitative and Interdisciplinary History*, 37, 2, pp. 87-102.

Cook, M. A. (1972) *Population Pressure in Rural Anatolia, 1450-1600*, London.

Darling, L. (1996) *Revenue-Raising and Legitimacy: Tax Collection and Finance Administration in the Ottoman Empire 1550-1650*, Leiden.

Emecen, F. M. (1989) *XVI. Asırda Manisa Kazası*, Istanbul.

Genç, M. (2014) 'Klasik Osmanlı Sosyal-İktisadi Sistemi ve Vakıflar', *Vakıflar Dergisi*, 42, pp. 9-18.

İnalcık, H. (1994) 'State, Land, and Peasant', in H. Inalcik and D. Quataert (eds), *An Economic and Social History of the Ottoman Empire*, Cambridge, pp. 103-178.

İslamoğlu-İnan, H. (1994) *State and Peasant in the Ottoman Empire, Agrarian Power Relations and Regional Economic Development in Ottoman Anatolia during the Sixteenth Century*, Leiden.

Keyder, Ç. (1991) 'Introduction. Large-scale commercial agriculture in the Ottoman Empire?', in Ç. Keyder and F. Tabak (eds), *Landholding and Commercial Agriculture in the Middle East*, pp. 1-16, Albany.

Kuran, T. (2010) *The Long Divergence. How Islamic Law Held Back the Middle East*, Princeton.

Moutafchieva, V. P. (1988) *Agrarian Relations in the Ottoman Empire in the 15th and 16th Centuries*, East European Monographs, No. CCLI, New York.

Nagata, Y. (1979) '16. Yüzyılda Manisa Köyleri, 1531 Tarihli Saruhan Sancağına Ait Bir Tahrir Defterini İnceleme Denemesi', *İstanbul Üniversitesi Edebiyat Fakültesi Tarih Dergisi*, 32, pp. 731-758.

Özel, O. (2016). *The Collapse of Rural Order in Ottoman Anatolia: Amasya 1576-1643*, Leiden.

Pamuk, Ş (2009) 'Changes in Factor Markets in the Ottoman Empire, 1500-1800', *Continuity and Change*, 24, 1, pp. 107-136.

Pamuk, Ş. (2017) *Osmanlı-Türkiye İktisadi Tarihi 1500-1914*, Istanbul.

Planhol, X. (1959) 'Geography, Politics and Nomadism in Anatolia', *International Social Science Journal*, XI, 4, pp. 525-531.

Robinson, J. (2009) 'The political economy of inequality', *Economic Research Forum Working Paper (No. 493)*.

Şahin, C. (1996) *A Comparative Study of Sharecropping System throughout the Ages in the Ottoman Empire*, (Unpublished thesis, Bilkent University).

Teoman, Ö. and Kaymak, M. (2008) 'Commercial agriculture and economic change in the Ottoman Empire during the nineteenth century: A comparison of raw cotton production in western Anatolia and Egypt', *The Journal of Peasant Studies*, 2, 35, pp. 314-334.

Thoen, E. (2004) 'Social agrosystems' as an economic concept to explain regional differences, An essay taking the former County of Flanders as an example (Middle Ages-19th century)', in B. J. P. van Bavel and P. Hoppenbrouwers (eds), *Landholding and Land Transfer in the North Sea Area (late Middle Ages – 19th Century)* (CORN 5), Turnhout, pp. 47-66.

Timur, T. (1989) *Osmanlı Çalışmaları İlkel Feodalizmden Yarı Sömürge Ekonomisine*, Ankara.

DANIEL R. CURTIS

7 All equal in the presence of death? Epidemics and redistribution in the pre-industrial period*

Catastrophic events throughout history have led to redistribution in economic resources, and in the twentieth century, nowhere is that seen more dramatically than in the aftermath of the two World Wars as overall wealth shrank dramatically (Piketty, 2014). Following Piketty's book, the same 'equalizing' thesis has also been applied to history going further back in time. For example, Branko Milanovic has gone as far as to suggest that "epidemics and wars alone can explain most of the swings in inequality [referring to premodern Spain]" (2016: 480), while ancient historian Walter Scheidel has argued that the only time socio-economic inequalities levelled themselves out before the Industrial Revolution was during episodes of mass violence or sudden catastrophic mortality (2017). These views are important, but they also create concerns, because they inadvertently downplay the effects of active human intervention via political processes – history suggests that reducing inequality by peaceful or less destructive means is rather difficult (Scheffer et al., 2017), which is discouraging for today with societies experiencing gross inequalities in access and ownership of resources. Accordingly, even if it is certainly not any of the above-mentioned authors' intentions,[1] these narratives might be taken up by those ideological or pressure groups that dismiss progressive taxation or welfare systems as simply doomed to fail. Indeed, as a rather perverse incentive structure, *The Economist* noted that "some may see civilisational collapse as a price worth paying for the Utopia they might build in the rubble",[2] and *The New Statesman* going even further by quoting Scheidel himself with the thought

* This chapter benefitted from funding by the Nederlandse Organisatie voor Wetenschappelijk Onderzoek (NWO) in the form of a VIDI grant (grant no. 016.Vidi.185.046) in the project 'Positively Shocking! The Redistributive Impact of Mass Mortality through Epidemic Diseases and Violent Conflict in Early Modern Northwest Europe'.

1 A central tenet behind Piketty's argument connecting the World Wars and equitable redistribution is that egalitarian policies developed in the aftermath of this conflict – the welfare state which included new public services and social security systems: 2014, 368-375.

2 https://www.economist.com/books-and-arts/2017/03/02/the-lessons-of-violence-and-inequality-through-the-ages [accessed 26/9/2018].

Daniel R. Curtis • Erasmus University Rotterdam

Inequality in rural Europe (Late Middle Ages – 18th century), ed. by Guido Alfani and Erik Thoen, CORN, 18 (Turnhout, 2020), pp. 123-142.

 DOI 10.1484/M.CORN-EB.5.121951

that in the future "only all-out thermonuclear war might fundamentally reset the existing distribution of resources".[3]

Given the wide-ranging appeal of narratives such as this, it is important that we critique the individual empirical components from which they are composed. This chapter, which mainly focuses upon the line of argumentation put forward by Scheidel and Milanovic, forms such a critique by limiting itself, in the main, to the role of epidemics and mortality spikes in pre-industrial Western Europe in the Middle Ages and early modern period – the period before the onset of the Industrial Revolution in the mid-eighteenth century.[4] The critique is divided into three issues. First, we look at the empirics behind the arguments – that is to say the basic quantity of examples and case studies providing the underlying empirical evidence for the 'equitable' redistributive impact of epidemic disease mortality. Second, we look at the logic supporting the redistribution trends – the causal mechanisms said to be behind the process. Third, we look at the indicators used in the redistributive process: on the one hand addressing some issues with the independent or causal variables invoked (i.e. raised mortality via epidemics), and on the other considering some issues with the dependent or outcome variables – that is the measurement of redistribution itself via wealth, property or income.

As one may expect, the amount of empirical evidence to support the 'equitable' redistribution effects of pre-industrial mortality shocks is somewhat smaller than that which can be assembled for the nineteenth- and twentieth centuries. Just a few years ago, a significant obstacle would have been the basic lack of empirical research being performed on pre-industrial inequality – so for example, the 'inequality possibility frontier' established in an important article of Milanovic, Peter Lindert and Jeffrey Williamson from 2011 was based on just eight data observations from before 1750 (261). That fundamental problem is much less acute nowadays: a plethora of works have been produced in recent years to reconstruct long-term premodern trends in inequality – many of which are outlined in other chapters of this book – even if more is still needed. Nevertheless, when one looks at the book of Scheidel, for example, in search of empirical support for the equitable distribution thesis *specifically*

---

3 https://www.newstatesman.com/politics/uk/2017/08/catastrophe-only-cure-inequality [accessed 26/9/2018]. Direct statement originally from Scheidel, 2017: 438.

4 Other inconsistencies are found in the distributive outcomes seen during European settlement of Latin America, but will be not be discussed in this chapter. For example, recent research has shown that an epidemic in 1570s Mexico that reduced the indigenous population by 70-90 per cent facilitated a process of elite concentration and farmed through large estates. Where collapse was less severe, indigenous villages were better able to maintain control of communal lands, hindering colonist encroachments: Sellars and Alix-Garcia, 2018. The notion that inequality decreased after the Antonine Plague of 165-180 CE in the Western Roman Empire also is not met with complete consensus: see, for example, a narrative (based on the archaeological record) of decreased living standards across broad sections of society, and a move towards a more extractive and less inclusive form of economic organization: Jongman, 2014: 95-97.

after mortality shocks in the period before 1750, it is clear that there is still a paucity of examples to choose from. Most of the qualitative evidence for the effects of the Black Death is taken from different examples from England, and then of the quantitative evidence, almost everything pertains to certain areas of late-medieval and early modern Italy based predominantly on the archival research of Guido Alfani and associates, one case for Augsburg (already discussed in van Zanden, 1995; and again expanded upon by Alfani, Gierok and Schaff, 2020), and some fragmentary cases for individual localities during the Roman period and Antiquity based on Scheidel's own expertise – though as recently pointed out, beyond Egypt, based on a handful of data points (Jongman, 2014: 78). Encouragingly, a new long-term study has recently been produced for Barcelona and its hinterlands, published after Scheidel's book, providing an index for inequality on annual basis by innovatively using 'marriage license books' from 1481 to 1880. This research loosely supports the 'leveling' effect of epidemics thesis, by pointing to general temporal associations between known plagues such as in 1647-1652 and reduced inequalities in economic distribution (Brea-Martínez and Pujados-Mora, 2018), although this association is not statistically demonstrated.

Why the reliance on Alfani, one may ask, if we have more and more quantifiable evidence for pre-industrial distribution? The answer lies in the temporal coverage. While we have time series evidence for early modern, and to a lesser extent late-medieval, real wages (often employed by Scheidel as indirect evidence for distributional changes), long runs of direct figures for pre-industrial wealth and property distribution, in particular, are hard to come by. Accordingly, it is incredibly rare for historians of the pre-industrial period to find a quantitative indicator for distribution immediately prior to a mortality or violent shock, and then the same quantitative indicator using the exact same source material immediately in the aftermath of the said shock – which hinders systematic research on the topic. Alfani's study into wealth inequality around the time of the 1629-1630 plague in Ivrea, a town in Northern Italy (2010a; 2010b), is perhaps the only evidence we have of this very systematic and temporally-focused type for anywhere in the world, and then his wealth distribution evidence for before and after the Black Death of the mid-fourteenth century is about as good as we can realistically expect to get for the medieval period – even if there are some chronological gaps between distributional markers and shock (2015; Alfani and Ammannati, 2017; also Ammannati, 2015).[5] Are select areas of the

5 This kind of research contradicted older studies that tended to either suggest that post-Black Death redistribution of landed wealth was not substantial (Campbell, 1984: 132), or starting out equitable, but over time moving in the opposite direction through consolidation (Herlihy, 1967, 185-190; 1978). Other literature argues that significant redistributive changes such as lasting consolidation were difficult because high epidemic mortality led to cases where elderly adults had nobody to pass their property on to, and thus families unable to maintain estates for more than one generation: Razi, 1993: 30.

pre-industrial northern and central Italian peninsula suitably generalizable to support an 'equalizing' thesis almost presented by Scheidel as a 'universal law' of human history?

Notwithstanding the paucity of basic empirical evidence linking and epidemics and redistribution, what is the generally posited logic behind this process? Exactly how did epidemics help redistribute resources in an equitable manner? One of the dominant explanations is said to be the destruction of people while keeping capital intact – realigning the balance in favor of labor (Acemoglu and Robinson, 2012: 96-101). This view has been well applied for mass mortality arising out of the Black Death, since regardless of whether scholars think that this severe first plague of the Second Pandemic was 'good', 'bad' or 'negligible' for aggregate economic development, most literature has supported the basic principle that it led to shifting ratios in labor and capital and helped raise real wages (Pamuk, 2007; Voigtländer and Voth, 2013a; Clark, 2016; Malanima, 2018; Campbell, 2016: 373-380; Humphries and Weisdorf, 2015; also for the First Pandemic Plagues: Pamuk and Shatzmiller, 2014), even if 'wage stickiness' and rising nominal prices meant this was not always with immediate effect (Munro, 2003) and some authorities tried to deliberately contain such wage rises (Cohn, 2007: 469-470). According to this line of reasoning, the gap between 'elites' such as lords and aristocrats and 'lower orders' such as peasants and laborers was narrowed, as higher wages, easier mobility, reduced extra-economic impositions, and greater opportunity to purchase property, meant most post-Black Death societies became less 'unequal' with improved living standards for survivors (Hatcher, 1994; Dyer, 2005; Cohn, 2016; Soens and Thoen, 2010). Another element of this logic, with specific regard to property redistribution after epidemics, is that sudden mass mortality could have some equitable effects, at least in the short- or medium term, because in certain conditions of partible inheritance, property was more likely to be divided up and fragmented between different heirs.

Although this kind of logic may be applicable for the Black Death – indeed recent work has tended to emphasize the equitable effects of mid-fourteenth-century mortality (Alfani and Ammannati, 2017; Ammannati, 2015) – it is not necessarily a given that the same logic can be applied for all pre-industrial epidemics. Actually, we should not assume all socio-economic responses to epidemic mortality spikes mirrored those of the Black Death in a universally applicable model where labor was destroyed and capital went untouched (Alfani and Murphy, 2017). In fact, many late-medieval and early modern epidemic diseases went hand-in-hand, often causally, with upsurges in conflict – with soldiers destroying buildings and infrastructure, consuming food stores, and ruining land – and therefore hitting capital too (Outram, 2002). Yet even regarding the direct effects of epidemics, capital damages took place, such as the formal public health regulations that called for the slaughter of roaming animals or the burning of goods coming from 'infected' environments (Alfani, 2013b: 101-103; Curtis, 2020). Frequently in the documentary records we find reference to the costs of cleaning and care-giving personnel within infected houses – and associated enforced cessation of business – making it more difficult for the poor to pay rents, tithes and taxes. Quarantine and isolation policies were not enforced in a uniform and egalitarian manner.

Accordingly, it is also not entirely clear that all examples move in the direction posited by Scheidel, Milanovic and others. In the immediate aftermath of the 1629-1630 plague in Ivrea, inequality in wealth was reduced temporarily (though only by 0.02 on the Gini coefficient between 1628 and 1630),[6] but by 1632 quickly returned to its pre-plague levels (Alfani, 2010: 63) – that is to say it had no impact on general inequality trends, despite the fact that Alfani has shown the 1629-1630 plague to have been exceptionally severe and disruptive in Northern Italy, and possibly even on a par with the Black Death of 1347-1352 (2013a). Going on to explain this finding, Alfani notes how early modern institutions by that time had been configured to limit the redistributive effects of strong mortality shocks – in particular through the mechanisms of property transfer and inheritance – and instead worked to preserve the 'status quo' of resource distribution (Alfani, 2010a; also, Di Tullio, 2018; on a broader conceptual level: van Bavel, 2016). Indeed, in some parts of Europe, such as the Kingdom of Naples, women were prevented from marrying as one tactic – forced to remain single and sent to live their lives at ecclesiastical institutions instead for fear of fragmentation of familial estates in conditions of equally partible inheritance among kin of both sexes (Curtis, 2015: 705).[7] The protection of familial and institutional estates meant that Southern Italian inequalities in the distribution of landed property were some of the sharpest in Europe by the eighteenth century (Curtis, 2013). Interestingly, Scheidel acknowledges this argument and important counter example (2017: 308) (which is the only example with a really convincing quantitative link between mortality shock and distributive outcome), and yet it plays no role in the overall construction of the bigger narrative.

It is also important to note that while the worst stages of the Black Death were not simultaneous to outright famine in Europe, it did occur on the back of an extended period of cold and wet now referred to as the tipping point in the transition from the Medieval Climate Anomaly to the Little Ice Age (Campbell, 2016: 277-284). Although the relationship between famine and plague is still unclear (many recent works disputing the direct connection: essays in Alfani and Ó Gráda, 2017; Curtis and Dijkman, 2019; Kelly and Ó Gráda, 2014), it is very much clear that many periods of famine did indeed lead to all kinds of other diseases connected to declines in nutrition, social unrest, migration and movement, and consumption of dubious replacement

6 Such a small temporary decrease does raise the question of to what extent that a reduction in wealth inequality of 0.02 had any discernible effects on the welfare and well-being of the inhabitants of the city.

7 Though, of course, male heirs receiving their share through death of a parent while female heirs received theirs as marital dowries.

foods (again the essays in Alfani and Ó Gráda, 2017). Plague and famine's connection may still be open for debate, but general epidemics and famine's connection has a strong consensus. This is important to note because while recent work has suggested an equitable impact of pre-industrial epidemic diseases, other literature has tended to emphasize the more inequitable potential impact of harvest failures, dearth and famines (again conceded in Scheidel, 2017: 332-333). The fact that epidemics and famines occur together, therefore, significantly complicates matters. Financial buffers ensured that the wealthy could often ride out periods when food prices went high, and thus were not forced to sell goods or even land like the poor (Galloway, 1988: 277). During the Great Famine of 1315-1317, it has been remarked that further social polarization occurred in the distribution of landholding, as the functioning of volatile and skewed land markets in a context of extreme population pressure led to plot fragmentation in many places (Campbell, 1984: 110-118; Jordan, 1996: 91; Schofield, 1997: 10-14; Bekar and Reed, 2013). Indeed, Bruce Campbell once remarked that this situation was not compounded by not by extra- economic extraction from lords, but through tenant on tenant extortion, based on economic disparities between the peasantry themselves (2005: 43).

The close link between epidemics and famines creates problems in the 'equalizing' logic employed by the likes of Scheidel because, quite clearly, an equitable mechanism of realignments in land-resources or capital-labor associated with epidemics can occur simultaneously with an inequitable redistribution mechanism linked to resource buffers and alienation. Curiously, most empirical research into the effects of famines and epidemics on distributive outcomes has tended to offer cases occurring during extremely high Malthusian pressures on resources – redistribution in densely-populated Tuscany after the Black Death, or in Northern Italy in 1629-1630, or other works on 1315-1317 Great Famine in England or the Southern Netherlands – but very few works looking at redistribution after mortality crises occurring in conditions of low Malthusian pressures, or systematically comparing the same localities between high and low pressures.[8] This is important to note because it has been suggested that the aggregate economic effects of the Black Death, for example, were very different in societies with pre-existing high land to labor ratios (van Bavel and van Zanden, 2004; Álvarez-Nogal and Prados de la Escosura, 2013). The same could easily be the case for economic redistribution too. Indeed, a demographic shock in years 536-537 CE in an area of eastern Sweden has been suggested to have produced the opposite redistributive outcome – an increasingly stratified Iron Age social structure with elite acquisition of large landholdings – all taking place within a context of already very low Malthusian pressures on resources (Löwenborg, 2012).

8 The absence of this broader conceptual comparison, at least for famines, was noted recently in Geens, 2018: 1048-1049.

It must be also iterated that the critique offered here is not merely one that argues against the 'equalizing' hypothesis established by Scheidel – indeed, some of the logic of the inequitable impact of famines described in the paragraphs above may also not necessarily be universally applicable. Socio-institutional mechanisms could conspire to limit moves towards social polarization too. For example, rather than complete societal collapse, rural peasants relied on a combination of reciprocal networks and relationships between individuals and groups at a local level – being offered credit, insurance, charitable sustenance and capital to ease the burden, and avoid having to alienate property as an act of last resort (Vanhaute and Lambrecht, 2011). During some medieval famines, scholars have even suggested a heightened communal sociability – trade switching to restricted local groups based on personal networks of trust and reputation (Slavin, 2014). Even in periods of significant harvest failure, where wealthy creditors could have taken advantage of less prosperous peers, not all creditor-debtor relations within rural communities were aggressively uni-directional (Schofield, 2008: 46-68; Briggs, 2009: 151-155, 190-193). In conditions of sharp economic polarity, tenants leasing land were allowed to fall into rent arrears after severe shocks, but this did not necessarily equate to 'structural debt' nor 'debt dependence' (Ogilvie, 2014: 272-274; Ogilvie, Küpker and Maegraith, 2012). The abbey of Mariënweerd in the Central Netherlands allowed more than 20 of its tenants during the famine of 1556-1557 to run into arrears for sums equivalent to one or two years of rent payment, which were continuously carried over to the next year and formed a type of interest-free credit, enabling these tenants to overcome the most difficult periods (van Bavel, 1993). Sometimes the wealthiest and most powerful segments of pre-industrial society had no desire to exploit those down the social hierarchy because their actual wealth and power was entirely composed from the maintenance and continued perpetuation of the community as a form of 'status quo' – satisfying other principles of conservation, defense and social reproduction (Di Tullio, 2014: 152).

Accordingly then, what this chapter is asserting is rather than an 'inevitable' model of redistribution after sudden mortality spikes, what we tend to see from the medieval and early modern periods in Europe are redistributive outcomes that do not move in a uni-linear direction, vary in intensity, and do not always last the same amount of time – that is to say are not always structural changes. While epidemic diseases did of course produce some equitable outcomes, this was not always the case – sometimes certain groups were able to instrumentalize these events to their benefit, while sometimes mechanisms were already set in place to stop resources moving hands in either direction. This diversity of outcome sometimes was connected to institutional 'layers' refracting the redistributive process in new directions, sometimes the pre-existing levels of inequality and population pressure on resources, and sometimes it was simply due to the coincidence of different things happening at the same time: disease and famine, disease and warfare, and sometimes all three together. The multiplicity of these existing or absent conditions and their combinations works against any kind of easily applicable overarching model or even framework. The rest of this chapter is now devoted to two areas where we can potentially move forward – with specific attention on the types of indicators of redistribution used. That is to say it is likely we can focus more explicitly and systematically on the independent variable of epidemic disease itself – disease characteristics, after all, were not all the same – and also on the outcome variables regarding the measurement of equality and inequality after these epidemics.

While a number of scholars have noted that post-epidemic socio-economic developments could be quite diverse, mostly this diversity is attributed to disease's interaction with various 'societal' variables such as the qualities of institutions (Pamuk, 2007; Epstein, 2000; van Bavel and van Zanden, 2004; Fochesato, 2018; Acemoglu, Johnson and Robinson, 2003), which implicitly follows an observation from a classic Robert Brenner paper that "different outcomes proceeded from similar demographic trends at different times and in different parts of Europe" (1976: 39). However, we also know that not all epidemic diseases displayed similar epidemiologic characteristics, and even the same outbreak of disease did not display uniform features across time or space. Indeed, pre-industrial epidemic diseases varied in severity, spread, and selectivity, and accordingly had differing effects on production factors (Alfani and Murphy, 2017).

This diversity in epidemiologic characteristics could easily have had consequences for the direction, intensity and scale of economic redistribution seen. For example, some diseases killed more 'universally' – disrespecting age, sex, and socio-economic status – the initial outbreak of the Black Death of 1347-1352 has been presented like that.[9] Other diseases, however – even other plagues – killed more selectively. Accordingly, to what extent were the redistributive effects of an epidemic focusing exclusively on the poor or poorer neighborhoods (i.e. a disease of poverty), different to an epidemic that killed rich and poor alike – in the process decimating not only the holders of physical capital, but also likely those with higher amounts of human capital (Alfani and Murphy, 2017: 335). Similarly, epidemics killing adults of reproductive and working age rather than the elderly or minors may have led to very different redistributive outcomes than those epidemics that just killed off the 'frail'. Not only were these adults of reproductive age the main 'earners' and had the most property or income that could be exposed to post-mortem redistribution, but these adults were the dominant 'care-givers' to the vulnerable – thus producing 'secondary vulnerabilities'. Conversely, epidemics killing off the frail may even have produced a rise in GDP per head

9 Although other literature in more recent years also argues for selective outcomes in the Black Death and the 'universal killer' categorization is over-stated: DeWitte, 2018; Curtis and Roosen, 2017. On the language of 'universality' used by contemporaries to describe plague signs: Carmichael, 2008: 18.

if working-adults were still standing – by logic of fewer 'non-earners'.[10] Some of the economic redistribution seen after epidemics was also dependent on the extent of their spatial spread. A significant part of the logic behind increased social mobility after epidemic outbreaks was the apparent 'inevitability' that rural inhabitants migrated to the cities to take up new urban vacancies from the depleted cities. But, as we now know, not all pre-industrial epidemics were simply 'urban afflictions' (Curtis, 2016a), and those epidemics with wider territorial spread could often hamper the process of rural-urban migration by simply destroying the reservoir of people in the countryside (Alfani, 2013a). Clearly again, these kinds of selective epidemiologic characteristics had the potential for very different economic consequences.

Finally, some attention has to be given to the outcome variables regarding the redistributive impact of epidemics. An initial hindrance to work on pre-industrial inequality some years ago was the continual vague confusion between economic indicators. Even in the recent work of Scheidel (2017), there is often an unsystematic distinction between the ways in which different measurements of inequality are given – frequently switching without warning between property, wealth, wages and income. In general, however, most recent work has started to become much more explicit and systematic with which type of economic inequality they are measuring. This is important in the specific case of the redistributive impact of epidemics, since it is clear that a disease that kills people but has limited effects on physical resources has potentially very different consequences for wages and income, than it does for wealth and property. We have also become more careful in the types of comparison of economic inequality that can take place. Indeed, in the work of Alfani, for example, we learn that the best forms of comparisons are not spatial – since these require different types of source material with differing rates of socio-economic exclusion – but temporal comparisons within the same locality over the longer term, which allow similar types of source material to be employed (if not entirely the same) (Alfani, 2015; Alfani and Ammannati, 2017; also Ryckbosch, 2016).

Nevertheless, we perhaps should also recognize that on some occasions there were inequalities occurring 'within' inequalities – elements less straightforward to quantify. For example, disease outbreaks could lead to heightened amounts of property transfer – leading to greater or lesser levels of inequality in property distribution. But simultaneous to basic areas of land changing hands between parties, diseases could also instigate changes and new developments in the terms of tenure given to those very same pieces of property. Alfani and Ammannati suggest, for example, that the Black Death in the Florentine State led in various localities to heightened equality in the

10 Recently, a negative economic burden of malaria was not found for areas of nineteenth-century Africa precisely because it was said to afflict the young "in whom society had invested few resources": Depetris-Chauvin and Weil, 2016: 1232).

distribution of property (2017). But at the same time, one of the effects of the Black Death was also an increasing move towards more amounts of property (in the Florentine *contado*) being held as part of sharecropping (*mezzadria*) arrangements, with urban parties providing the capital investments (Emigh, 2009).[11] Although no definitive answer shall be provided here, a question may be posited as to what the most 'important' development was in this case – at least in terms of living standards of ordinary rural inhabitants – changes in the actual distribution of the areas held by individual parties, or the terms by which this land was held? This point has wider significance when we think about the redistributive impact of epidemic diseases for landed property – a mortality spike may lead on the surface to two similar reductions in inequality in two localities (as, for example, measured by Gini coefficients of landholding), but with quite different tenurial statuses bringing quite different burdens to the owners and users. A further point to note is that post-epidemic redistribution could simultaneously move in very different directions – more property in the hands of certain types of owner (absentee urban elites, for example) could be compatible with heightened equality in the overall distribution of 'access' to the land at the 'user level' (as recently argued in the aftermath of floods: Curtis, 2016b; van Bavel, Curtis and Soens, 2018; van Cruyningen, 2014; and more as a general process in Dombrecht and Ryckbosch, 2017: 81). And as a final note of caution, we should also be aware that regardless of the redistributive impact of epidemics on wealth and property, social and economic stratification was entirely 'blocked off' for certain people in certain societies and thus impossible to cater for in the form of straightforward Gini coefficients: for example, regardless of the effects of the Black Death and recurring epidemics in the Kingdom of Valencia, it is clear that Muslims could not scale the feudal hierarchy of the Christian Kingdom (Baydal Sala and Esquilache Martí, 2014: 61, 64), despite comprising a third of the population (Torró, 2008: 186) and exhibiting their own internal social stratification.

It may be useful as a future direction to start focusing on other areas of redistribution, which move away from standard indexes of inequality measured in wealth, property, income and wages. Indeed, epidemics had redistributive qualities which extended far beyond those limited dimensions – a recent critique of Scheidel's book has correctly noted that aside from compression or dispersion of wealth and income, we still do not know that much about how violent and mortality shocks made different genders, races, and classes more secure or less vulnerable, within particular structures of inequality (Watts, 2018: 1593). For example, one such element of redistribution was the ways in which epidemic diseases opened up new opportunities for the young – or alternatively, created new challenges, restrictions and pressures to be faced. By this, we essentially mean new forms of inter-generational redistribution.

11 Although the move towards sharecropping had already begun before the Black Death, and was merely accelerated: see the classic Pinto and Pirillo, 1987.

In underdeveloped and developing countries today, unexpected deaths in adulthood, often during epidemic outbreaks, create significant social problems – creating orphaned children and uncared for elderly parents (Atrash, 2011), and the young survivors are left with reduced family of community support, few social networks, and poor access to food and healthcare, and all the while minors assume new roles as 'heads of household', principle care-givers, and earners (Ronsmans et al., 2010; Nilsson and De Vreyer, 2019). Despite the disciplines of economics and development studies using indicators such as care, protection, knowledge, skills and social networks in broader assessments for the economic impact of contemporary diseases, however, the historical focus on the economic impact of epidemics has remained mostly at the level of traditional economic indicators including GDP (Broadberry et al., 2015; Clark, 2016), urbanization (Voigtländer and Voth, 2013a), real wages (Pamuk, 2007; Malanima, 2018), property distribution (Alfani, 2010a; Scheidel, 2017), fertility (Voigtländer and Voth, 2013b; Foreman-Peck and Peng, 2018), and population recovery (van Bavel and van Zanden, 2004). Accordingly, the redistributive impact of epidemic diseases in terms of their effects on the life chances and opportunities for the young – sub-adults and children – has been entirely limited, with almost no systematic research. Underexploited orphanage records and records of guardianship offer an insight into the financial statuses of the young – not just how they were provided for – but also an insight into the financial pressures that multiple epidemic deaths in a short space of time could bring to a family (for a local study: Sas, 2008; also used as indirect measures of inequality in Dombrecht and Ryckbosch, 2017: 76, 79). In particular, still there is scope for research to be conducted at the micro level that meticulously employs a systematic comparison between the life chances and life-courses of children from a community that lose both their parents, children that lose one parent, and those that remain with both parents intact. Furthermore, initial research into the scarring effects of smallpox on young adults and children in eighteenth-century Sweden showed that these kinds of outbreaks could provide downward social mobility for those afflicted – especially on the marriage market (Sköld, 1996).

Pre-industrial epidemics also had redistributive consequences beyond those of wealth and property of individual owners. Indeed, the wealth of pre-industrial communities was not always tied up in what the individual owned, but what could be accessed via collective or common-pooled institutions (Di Tullio, 2018). Vital sources of economic resources – especially in the rural context – were provided by poor relief institutions, commons, and water boards, to name but a few. This is relevant since access to these resources was often either dependent on socio-economic status or the prior ownership of privately distributed economic resources – often land (in the case of the commons and water boards: Curtis, 2016c). Furthermore, all three of these institutions functioned well at 'optimal' levels of participation – a large amount of local people paying into a 'collective insurance system' such as the poor table (Van Onacker and Masure, 2015), or offering labor and service to maintain and regulate the commons (De Moor, 2010), or maintaining the upkeep of the water management infrastructure (Soens, 2009). A lot of previous attention has been put on the effects of population pressure on these institutions – and how these institutions were malleable and could withstand and negotiate such pressures (De Moor, 2008; more conceptually: Ostrom, 1990) – but almost nothing has been produced on the opposite tendency, and the effects of a destruction of people on their overall functioning. What did the sudden loss of a substantial proportion of the community via epidemic outbreaks mean for participation within these institutions? How were rights, obligations and modes of access redistributed accordingly? All this has been left out of the epidemics-redistribution literature so far, and yet resources provided via these collective institutions were often the most important for pre-industrial societies – especially in the countryside. So, to use just one example, in certain patrilineal systems, women who married 'outsiders' to their village, such as in Nonantola (Emilia Romagna, Northern Italy) after 1584, lost their rights to the common completely (Alfani and Munno, 2012). This kind of finding is highly relevant given that in the aftermath of epidemics, rates of nuptiality spiked and there was a smaller pool of local potential partners to choose from.

Another feature absent from the epidemics and redistribution literature – also even the general literature on pre-industrial inequality – is the gender dimension. This is important because explicitly considering epidemics' impact on women can lead to qualitative changes in our assessment of redistributive change. For example, as already mentioned, there is a view that the Black Death of the mid-fourteenth century, working in tandem with recurring epidemics, led to reduced inequalities in various medieval societies – and shown quantitatively through increases in real wages for laborers and peasants, or more equitable distribution of property and wealth. Recent work on wages from England, however, has shown that whatever long-term benefits occurred in the form of rising real wages for men after the Black Death, women did not share in these benefits (Humphries and Weisdorf, 2015) – or at least not all of them.[12] Bioarchaeological evidence supports this contention: women did not share in post-Black Death health benefits in the same way as men (DeWitte, 2018; Lewis, 2016). This is without considering all the new social inequalities that were produced during epidemics – authorities' crackdowns on prostitutes (as convenient scapegoats) and the banning of women from funerals during plagues (Curtis, 2020), the public shaming of women trying to hide infections in households (Carmichael, 1998: 145), the locking away of women under male

12 A similar situation has been seen in the first half of the seventeenth century in Leiden where people flocked to the city after epidemics to fill in vacancies within the booming textile industry, and although women found employment, and were an important component of the sector, men dominated many roles and benefited from high real wages: van Nederveen Meerkerk, 2010.

authority (Rose, 2018: 1006), and the increased inequalities – and therefore dangers – associated with the duties of household care and other medical provisioning (Cabré, 2008; Munkhoff, 1999; Winer, 2017). We need to also consider structural changes: recently it was suggested that significant crises exacerbated inequitable male-female distribution of property in medieval Brussels and surroundings, despite prevailing egalitarian partible inheritance practices (Bardyn, 2018). Accordingly, new kinds of inequality – between men and women – may have been forged, which run antithetical to the whole 'leveling' hypothesis.

A final element of post-epidemic redistribution that needs to be addressed is the differences between 'actual' distribution of economic resources in wealth, property and income, and what this actually meant for societies within their historical context: that is to say their perception of inequality and fairness. Indeed, trends in 'perceived distribution' need not have entirely mirrored the 'realities' of redistribution during and after epidemic outbreaks (Alfani and Frigeni, 2016; Cohn, 2016). For example, while an epidemic may have led to more equitable distribution of economic resources via realignments in labor-capital ratios or fragmentation of estates, there is also the possibility that these diseases also led to new kinds of social inequalities – especially with regard to discrimination against the poor. Did diseases that selectively victimized the poor (in terms of mortality) translate into prejudices and persecution; or conversely, did this set in motion new mechanisms to improve general welfare (Cohn, 2018)? This is an important point to make given literature has suggested that diseases such as plague developed into afflictions primarily associated with poverty (Slack, 1985), certainly by the sixteenth- and seventeenth centuries, and yet social recognition of the connection between the two did not always neatly follow chronologically (Cohn, 2010). Put simply: regardless of economic 'realities', how did epidemics change (if at all) the perception of the poor over time? And should we even care about the 'realities' of economic redistribution, if society at the time does not explicitly recognize this as an issue of significance or relevance?

To conclude, although the views of Scheidel, Milanovic, and others, about the largely egalitarian effects of epidemics appear logical – and are supported in some cases – we lack the empirical examples to fully prove this for the pre-industrial period up to now, or at least to offer this as a definitive universal principle characterizing much of human history. This is not down to a basic lack of interest or material on pre-industrial inequality – a field which has taken off in recent years, as the rest of this book shows. It is down to the difficulties of finding source material that can systematically show redistribution outcomes directly connected to an epidemic outbreak: redistribution closely before and closely after the mortality itself. When we do have such evidence, this is often in isolation (Alfani, 2010a), and so cannot be placed within a broad long-term scheme either: that is to say we do not have many redistribution markers both before and after epidemics using the same sources, and even when we do, it cannot be repeated for the same place looking at many different epidemics to build up a long-term picture. These limitations being the case, it may induce us to start looking more towards other facets of inequality – beyond the traditional 'economic' measurements of wealth, property, wages and income. The capacity for epidemics to shape gender-differentiated outcomes, and the broader vulnerabilities and welfare of children, the elderly, and migrants, for example, remain altogether unexploited avenue for productive research, but have obvious relevance for our interest in how diseases affect redistribution across societies and vulnerabilities of social groups within them.

Bibliography

Acemoglu, D. and J. Robinson (2012) *Why nations fail: the origins of power, prosperity and poverty*. New York: Random House.

Alfani, G. (2010a) 'The effects of plague on distribution of property: Ivrea, Northern Italy 1630', *Population Studies*, 64, pp. 61-75.

Alfani, G. (2010b) 'Wealth inequalities and population dynamics in early modern Northern Italy', *Journal of Interdisciplinary History*, 40, pp. 513-549.

Alfani, G. (2013a) 'Plague in seventeenth-century Europe and the decline of Italy: an epidemiological hypothesis', *European Review of Economic History*, 17, pp. 408-430.

Alfani, G. (2013b) *Calamities and the economy in Renaissance Italy: the Grand Tour of the Horsemen of the Apocalypse*. Basingstoke: Palgrave.

Alfani, G. (2015) 'Economic inequality in Northwestern Italy: a long-term view (fourteenth to eighteenth centuries)', *Journal of Economic History*, 75, pp. 1058-1096.

Alfani, G. and C. Munno (2012) 'Godparenthood and social networks in an Italian rural community: Nonantola in the sixteenth and seventeenth centuries', in G. Alfani and V. Gourdon, eds, *Spiritual kinship in Europe, 1500-1900*, Palgrave: London, pp. 96-123.

Alfani, G. and R. Frigeni (2016) 'Inequality (un)perceived: the emergence of a discourse on economic inequality from the Middle Ages to the age of revolutions', *Journal of European Economic History*, 45, pp. 21-66.

Alfani, G. and C. Ó Gráda, eds (2017) *Famine in European history*, Cambridge: Cambridge University Press.

Alfani, G. and F. Ammannati (2017) 'Long-term trends in economic inequality: the case of the Florentine State, *c*. 1300-1800', *Economic History Review*, 70, pp. 1072-1102.

Alfani, G., V. Gierok and F. Schaff (2020) 'Economic inequality in preindustrial Germany, ca. 1300-1850', *SocArXiv*, 3, pp. 1-98.

Alfani, G. and T. Murphy (2017) 'Plague and lethal epidemics in the pre-industrial world', *Journal of Economic History*, 77, pp. 314-343.

Álvarez-Nogal, C. and L. Prados de la Escosura (2013) 'The rise and fall of Spain (1270-1850)', *Economic History Review*, 66, pp. 1-37.

Ammannati, F. (2015) 'La Peste Nera e la distribuzione della proprietà del tardo medioevo', *Popolazione e Storia*, 16, pp. 21-45.

Atrash, H. K. (2011) 'Parents' death and its implications for children's survival', *Journal of Human Growth and Development*, 21, pp. 759-770.

Bardyn, A. (2018) 'The gender distribution of immovable property in late medieval Brussels (1356-1460)', *Continuity and Change*, 33, pp. 1-28.

Bavel, B. van (1993) *Goederenverwerving en goederenbeheer van de abdij Mariënweerd (1129-1592)*, Hilversum: Verloren.

Bavel, B. van (2016) *The invisible hand? How market economies have emerged and declined since AD 500*, Oxford: Oxford University Press.

Bavel, B. van, D. R. Curtis and T. Soens (2018) 'Economic inequality and institutional adaptation in response to flood hazards: a historical analysis', *Ecology and Society*, 23, art. 30.

Bavel, B. van and J. L. van Zanden (2004) 'The jump-start of the Holland economy during the late-medieval crisis', *Economic History Review*, 57, pp. 503-532.

Baydal Sala, V. and F. Esquilache Martí (2014) 'Exploitation and differentiation: economic and social stratification in the rural Muslim communities of the Kingdom of Valencia, 13th-16th centuries', in F. Aparisi Romero and V. Royo Pérez, eds, *Beyond lords and peasants: rural elites and economic differentiation in pre-modern Europe*, Valencia: University of Valencia Press, pp. 37-68.

Bekar, C. and C. G. Reed (2013) 'Land markets and inequality: evidence from medieval England', *European Review of Economic History*, 17, pp. 294-317.

Brenner, R. (1976) 'Agrarian class structure and economic development in pre-industrial Europe', *Past and Present*, 70, pp. 30-75.

Briggs, C. (2009) *Credit and village society in fourteenth-century England*, Oxford: Oxford University Press.

Broadberry, S. et al. (2015) *British economic growth, 1270-1870*, Cambridge: Cambridge University Press.

Cabré, M. (2008) 'Women or healers? Household practices and the categories of health care in late medieval Iberia', *Bulletin of the History of Medicine*, 82, pp. 18-51.

Campbell, B. (1984) 'Population pressure, inheritance, and the land market in a fourteenth-century peasant community', in R. M. Smith, ed., *Land, kinship and lifecycle*, Cambridge: Cambridge University Press, pp. 87-134.

Campbell, B. (2005) 'The agrarian problem in the early 14th century', *Past and Present*, 188, pp. 3-70.

Campbell, B. (2016) *The great transition: climate, disease and society in the late-medieval world.* Cambridge: Cambridge University Press.

Carmichael, A. (1998) 'The last past plague: the uses of memory in Renaissance epidemics', *Journal of the History of Medicine and Allied Sciences*, 53, pp. 132-160.

Carmichael, A. (2008) 'Universal and particular: the language of plague, 1348-1500', *Medical History Supplement*, 27, pp. 17-50.

Clark, G. (2016) 'Microbes and markets: was the Black Death an economic revolution?', *Journal of Demographic Economics*, 82, pp. 139-165.

Cohn, S. K. (2007) 'After the Black Death: labour legislation and attitudes towards labour in late-medieval Western Europe', *Economic History Review*, 60, pp. 486-512.

Cohn, S. K. (2010) *Cultures of plague: medical thinking at the end of the Renaissance*, Oxford: Oxford University Press.

Cohn, S. K. (2016) 'Rich and poor in Western Europe, *c.* 1375-1475: the political paradox of material well-being', in S. Farmer, ed., *Approaches to poverty in medieval Europe: complexities, contradictions, transformations, c. 1100-1500*, Turnhout: Brepols, pp. 145-173.

Cohn, S. K. (2018) *Epidemics: hate and compassion from the Plague of Athens to AIDS*, Oxford: Oxford University Press.

Cruyningen, P. van (2014) 'From disaster to sustainability: floods, changing property relations and water management in the south-western Netherlands, c. 1500-1800', *Continuity and Change*, 29, pp. 241-265.

Curtis, D. R. (2013) 'Is there an "agro-town" model for Southern Italy? Exploring the diverse roots and development of the agro-town structure through a comparative case study in Apulia', *Continuity and Change*, 28, pp. 377-419.

Curtis, D. R. (2015) 'An agro-town bias? Re-examining the micro-demographic model for Southern Italy in the eighteenth century', *Journal of Social History*, 16, pp. 646-664.

Curtis, D. R. (2016a) 'Was plague an exclusively urban phenomenon? Plague mortality in the seventeenth-century Low Countries', *Journal of Interdisciplinary History*, 47, pp. 139-170.

Curtis, D. R. (2016b) 'Danger and displacement in the Dollard: the 1509 flooding of the Dollard Sea (Groningen) and its impact on long-term inequality in the distribution of property', *Environment and History*, 22, pp. 103-135.

Curtis, D. R. (2016c) 'Did the commons make medieval and early modern rural societies more equitable? A survey of evidence from across Western Europe, 1300-1800', *Journal of Agrarian Change*, 16, pp. 646-664.

Curtis, D. R. (2020) 'Preserving the ordinary: social resistance during Second Pandemic Plagues in the Low Countries', in C. Gerrard, P. Brown and P. Forlin, eds, *Waiting for the ends of the world: new perspectives on natural disasters in medieval Europe*, London: Routledge, pp. 280-297.

Curtis, D. R. and J. Dijkman (2019) 'The escape from famine in the Northern Netherlands: a reconsideration using the 1690s harvest failures and a broader Northwest European perspective', *The Seventeenth Century*, 34, pp. 229-258.

Curtis, D. R. and J. Roosen (2017) 'The sex-selective impact of the Black Death and recurring plagues in the Southern Netherlands, 1349-1450', *American Journal of Physical Anthropology*, 164, pp. 246-259.

De Moor, T. (2008) 'The Silent Revolution: a new perspective on the emergence of commons, guilds, and other forms of corporate collective action in Western Europe', *International Review of Social History*, 53, pp. 179-212.

De Moor, T. (2010) 'Participation is more important than winning. The impact of social-economic change on commoners' participation in 18th-19th-century Flanders', *Continuity and Change*, 25, pp. 405-433.

Depetris-Chauvin, E. and D. N. Weil (2016) 'Malaria and early African development: evidence from the sickle cell trait', *The Economic Journal*, 128, pp. 1207-1234.

DeWitte, S. (2018) 'Stress, sex, and plague: patterns of developmental stress and survival in pre- and post-Black Death London', *American Journal of Human Biology*, 30, e23073.

Di Tullio, M. (2014) *The wealth of communities: war, resources and cooperation in Renaissance Lombardy*, Farnham: Ashgate.

Di Tullio, M. (2018) 'Cooperating in time of crisis: war, commons, and inequality in Renaissance Lombardy', *Economic History Review*, 71, pp. 82-105.

Dombrecht, K. and W. Ryckbosch (2017) 'Wealth inequality in a time of transition: Coastal Flanders in the sixteenth century', *Tijdschrift voor Sociale en Economische Geschiedenis*, 14, pp. 63-84.
Dyer, C. (2005) *An age of transition? Economy and society in England in the later Middle Ages*. Oxford: Oxford University Press.
Emigh, R. (2009) *The undevelopment of capitalism: sectors and markets in fifteenth-century Tuscany*, Temple University Press: Philadelphia.
Epstein, S. R. (2000) *Freedom and growth: the rise of states and markets in Europe, 1300-1750*. London: Routledge.
Fochesato, M. (2018) 'Origins of Europe's North-South divide: population changes, real wages and the 'Little Divergence' in early modern Europe', *Explorations in Economic History*, 70, pp. 91-131.
Foreman-Peck, J. and P. Zhou (2018) 'Late marriage as a contributor to the Industrial Revolution in England', *Economic History Review*, 71, pp. 1073-1099.
Galloway, P. R. (1988) 'Basic patterns in annual variations in fertility, nuptiality, mortality, and prices in pre-industrial Europe', *Population Studies*, 42, pp. 275-303.
Geens, S. (2018) 'The Great Famine in the County of Flanders (1315-1317): the complex interaction between weather, warfare, and property rights', *Economic History Review*, 71, pp. 1048-1072.
Hatcher, J. (1994) 'England in the aftermath of the Black Death', *Past and Present*, 144, pp. 3-35.
Herlihy, D. (1967) *Medieval and Renaissance Pistoia: the social history of an Italian town, 1200-1430*. New Haven: Yale University Press.
Herlihy, D. (1978) 'The distribution of wealth in a Renaissance community: Florence 1427', in P. Abrams and E. A. Wrigley, eds, *Towns in societies: essays in economic history and historical sociology*, Cambridge: Cambridge University Press, pp. 131-157.
Humphries, J. and J. Weisdorf (2015) 'The wages of women in England, 1260-1850', *Journal of Economic History*, 75, pp. 405-447.
Jongman, W. M. (2014) 'Re-constructing the Roman economy', in L. Neal and J. G. Williamson, eds, *The Cambridge History of Capitalism*, Cambridge: Cambridge University Press, pp. 75-100.
Jordan, W. C. (1996) *The Great Famine: Northern Europe in the early fourteenth century*, Princeton NJ: Princeton University Press.
Kelly, M. and C. Ó Gráda (2014) 'Living standards and mortality since the Middle Ages', *Economic History Review*, 67, pp. 358-381.
Lewis, M. (2016) 'Work and the adolescent in medieval England. AD 900-1550: the osteological evidence', *Medieval Archaeology*, 60, pp. 138-171.
Löwenborg, D. (2012) 'An Iron Age shock doctrine: did the AD 536-537 event trigger large-scale social changes in the Mälaren Valley area?', *Journal of Archaeology and Ancient History*, 4, pp. 1-29.
Malanima, P. (2018) 'Italy in the Renaissance: a leading economy in the European context, 1350-1550'. *Economic History Review*, 71, pp. 3-30.
Mann, M. (2012) *The sources of social power, vol. 3: global empires and revolution, 1890-1945*, Cambridge: Cambridge University Press.

Milanovic, B. (2016) 'Income inequality is cyclical', *Nature*, 537, pp. 479-482.

Milanovic, B., P. Lindert and J. G. Williamson (2011) 'Pre-industrial inequality', *The Economic Journal*, 121, pp. 255-272.

Munkhoff, R. (1999) 'Searchers of the dead: authority, marginality, and the interpretation of plague in England, 1574-1665', *Gender and History*, 11, pp. 1-29.

Munro, J. (2003) 'Wage stickiness, monetary changes, and real incomes in late-medieval England and the Low Countries, 1300-1500: did money matter?', *Research in Economic History*, 21, pp. 185-297.

Nederveen Meerkerk, E. van (2010) 'Market wage or discrimination? The remuneration of male and female wool spinners in the seventeenth-century Dutch Republic', *Economic History Review*, 63, pp. 165-186.

Nilsson, B. and P. De Vreyer (2019) 'When solidarity fails: heterogeneous effects on children from adult deaths in Senegalese households', *World Development*, 114.

Ogilvie, S. (2014) 'Choices and constraints in the pre-industrial countryside', in C. Briggs, P. M. Kitson and S. J. Thompson, eds, *Population, welfare and economic change in Britain, 1290-1834*, The Boydell Press, Woodbridge, pp. 269-306.

Ogilvie, S., M. Küpker and J. Maegraith (2011) 'Household debt in early modern Germany: evidence from personal inventories', *Journal of Economic History*, 72, pp. 134-167.

Onacker, E. Van and H. Masure (2015) 'Unity in diversity: rural poor relief in the sixteenth-century Southern Low Countries', *Tijdschrift voor Sociale en Economische Geschiedenis*, 12, pp. 59-88.

Ostrom, E. (1990) *Governing the commons: the evolution of institutions for collective action*, Cambridge: Cambridge University Press.

Outram, Q. (2002) 'The demographic impact of early modern warfare', *Social Science History*, 26, pp. 245-272.

Pamuk, S. (2007) 'The Black Death and the origins of the "Great Divergence" across Europe, 1300-1600', *European Review of Economic History*, 11, pp. 289-317.

Pamuk, S. and M. Shatzmiller (2014) 'Plagues, wages, and economic change in the Islamic Middle East, 700-1500', *Journal of Economic History*, 74, pp. 196-229.

Piketty, T. (2014) *Capital in the twenty-first century*, Cambridge MA: Harvard University Press.

Pinto, G. and P. Pirillo (1987) *Il contratto di mezzadria nella Toscana medievale. Il contado di Siena, sec. XIII-1348*, Florence: Olschki.

Razi, Z. (1993) 'The myth of the immutable English family', *Past and Present*, 140, pp. 3-44.

Ronsmans, C. et al. (2010) 'Effect of parents' death on child survival in rural Bangladesh: a cohort study', *Lancet*, 375, pp. 2024-2031.

Rose, C. (2018) 'Plague and violence in early modern Italy', *Renaissance Quarterly*, 71, pp. 1000-1035.

Ryckbosch, W. (2016) 'Economic inequality and growth before the Industrial Revolution: the case of the Low Countries (fourteenth to nineteenth centuries)', *European Review of Economic History*, 20, pp. 1-22.

Sas, B., (2008) 'Die Swaerigheyt des levens te Gierle tijdens de miserabele tweede helft van de 17de eeuw', *Heemkundige Kring Lille*, pp. 105-134.

Scheffer, M. et al. (2017) 'Inequality in nature and society', *Proceedings of the National Academy of Sciences*, 114, pp. 13154-13157.

Scheidel, W. (2017) *The great leveler: violence and the history of inequality from the Stone Age to the Twenty-First Century*, Princeton NJ: Princeton University Press.

Schofield, P. (1997) 'Dearth, debt and the local land market in a late thirteenth-century village community', *Agricultural History Review*, 45, pp. 1-17.

Schofield, P. (2008) 'The social economy of the medieval village in the early fourteenth century', *Economic History Review*, 61, pp. 39-61.

Sellars, E. A. and J. Alix-Garcia (2018) 'Labor scarcity, land tenure, and historical legacy: evidence from Mexico', *Journal of Development Economics*, 135, pp. 504-516.

Sköld, P. (1996) *The two faces of smallpox. A disease and its prevention in eighteenth- and nineteenth-century Sweden*, Umeå: Demographic Data Base Umeå.

Slack, P. (1985) *The impact of plague in Tudor and Stuart England*, London: Routledge.

Slavin, P. (2014) 'Market failure during the Great Famine in England and Wales (1315-1317)', *Past and Present*, 222, pp. 9-49.

Soens, T. (2009) *De spade in de dijk? Waterbeheer en rurale samenleving in de Vlaamse kustvlakte (1280-1580)*, Ghent: Academia Press.

Soens, T. and E. Thoen (2010) 'Vegetarians or carnivores? Standards of living and diet in late-medieval Flanders', in S. Cavaciocchi, ed., *Le interazioni fra economica e ambiente biologico nell'Europa preindustriale: secc XIII-XVIII*, Florence: Florence University Press, pp. 495-527.

Torró, J. (2008) 'Del almagram a las particiones de frutos. Las cargas agrarias en las aljamas musulmanas del reino de Valencia', in R. Vallejo and A. Furió, eds, *Los tributos de la tierra. Fiscalidad y agricultura en España (siglos XII-XX)*, Valencia: University of Valencia Press, pp. 185-222.

Vanhaute, E. and T. Lambrecht (2011) 'Famine, exchange networks and the village community. A comparative analysis of the subsistence crises of 1740s and the 1840s in Flanders', *Continuity and Change*, 26, pp. 155-186.

Voigtländer, N. and Voth, H-J. (2013a) 'The three horsemen of riches: plague, war, and urbanization in early modern Europe', *Review of Economic Studies*, 80, pp. 774-811.

Voigtländer, N. and Voth, H-J. (2013b) 'How the West "invented" fertility restriction', *American Economic Review*, 103, pp. 2227-2264.

Watts, M. J. (2018) 'It's all over now baby blue', *American Historical Review*, 123, pp. 1583-1595.

Winer, R. L. (2017) 'The enslaved wet nurse as nanny: the transition from free to slave labor in childcare in Barcelona after the Black Death (1348)', *Slavery and Abolition*, 38, pp. 303-319.

Zanden, J. L. van (1995) 'Tracing the beginning of the Kuznets curve: western Europe durin the early modern period', *Economic History Review*, 48, pp. 643-664.

WOUTER RYCKBOSCH

8 A regional comparison of social inequality & economic development in 16th-century Flanders*

I. Introduction

Does a more egalitarian social structure in the countryside lead to economic development, or does it hinder it? Development economists and historians of early modern Europe have answered this question – arguably of non-trivial importance in today's world of rising inequalities – in rather conflicting ways. Economists have found land inequality to be negatively correlated to growth on a general level (Deininger and Olinto, 1999; Neves, Afonso, and Silva, 2016), and have pointed to specific cases where divergent levels of economic development can at least partly be explained by differences in land inequality. It has been argued, for instance, that more egalitarian patterns of land use and ownership in East Asia (Taiwan and South Korea in particular) can help to explain its remarkable economic success in recent decades compared to Latin America, where land inequality remains high (Kay, 2002). Economic historians of Africa have pointed out that the vast levels of inequality in land ownership inherited from the colonial past drive the persistence of high income inequalities on the continent, and potentially impede economic development (Frankema, 2010). The oft-cited historical case of how more egalitarian levels of rural inequality could lead to more economically beneficial economic institutions and development is the contrast between the North and Latin American colonial institutions (Sokoloff and Engerman, 2000; Engerman and Sokoloff, 2005).

In contrast to this position, historians of pre-industrial Europe have generally been less certain about the relationship between land inequality and economic development. Traditional scholarship on the transition to

* This research came about in the context of the research project 'Economic growth and inequality. Explaining divergent regional growth paths in pre-industrial Europe (late middle ages – 19th Centuries', co-ordinated by Erik Thoen, Thijs Lambrecht, Eric Vanhaute and Koen Schoors at Ghent University. The author would like to acknowledge the helpful suggestions from Erik Thoen, Thijs Lambrecht, Tim Soens, Wouter Ronsijn, and Maïka de Keyzer.

Wouter Ryckbosch • Vrije Universiteit Brussel

Inequality in rural Europe (Late Middle Ages – 18th century), ed. by Guido Alfani and Erik Thoen, CORN, 18 (Turnhout, 2020), pp. 143-167.

 DOI 10.1484/M.CORN-EB.5.121952

agricultural capitalism during the early modern period tended to stress its connection to growing inequality in the ownership of the means of production in the English countryside as a result of the enclosure movement (Brenner, 1976). This was then contrasted instructively with the case of France, where a much more egalitarian peasant agriculture resulted in a seemingly endless 'histoire immobile' of economic stagnation (Le Roy Ladurie, 1966). This seemed to suggest that growing levels of land inequality were ultimately conducive to growth in early modern Western Europe. However, in recent decades, a revisionist view has gained currency, arguing that economic growth also could and did occur in more egalitarian, or at least less polarised, agrarian contexts, such as early modern France (Hoffman, 2000), or the open-field agriculture of sixteenth- and seventeenth-century England (Allen, 1992). A new consensus view on the relationship between land inequality and early modern economic development has not emerged from this, possibly also because rural historians have tended to pay attention mostly to seigniorial relationships, class conflict, and institutional structures of land ownership and tenure – all of which are clear aspects of rural inequality, but not as easily interpreted and integrated into economic debates as parameters of income or wealth inequality. In response to this, Daniel Curtis has called upon rural historians to confront the question of economic inequality more explicitly, for instance by calculating Gini coefficients of wealth, land ownership or land holdings (Curtis, 2013). The present paper seeks to take up this challenge.

In order to examine the relationship between land inequality and economic development in the European countryside, this paper will attempt to conduct a regional comparison within the County of Flanders. It has been well established that agrarian socio-economic structures diverged markedly between the different regions of the Flemish countryside from the fourteenth century onwards (Soens and Thoen, 2008; Thoen and Soens, 2015). However, to this date no attempt has been made to estimate the precise differences in land inequality throughout sixteenth-century Flanders, and to relate these to the question of economic development. This paper will explore whether this lacuna can be expected to be filled by using a collection of fiscal sources from the second half of the sixteenth century: the so-called *20th penny levies*. These fiscal sources allow for the study of the distribution in land use and ownership, as well as of the spread of peasant ownership and leasehold.

The paper starts out with a closer examination of the sources used, and of the methodological choices made in producing the measurements of rural inequality. After that, I introduce the different regions studied from the perspective of the social agro-system approach, and present the results in terms of land inequality, ownership and the spread of leasehold. As a final analysis, I will compare the findings with regards to (sub-)regional levels of inequality to aggregate levels of wealth per village, as measured from a different fiscal source. The paper concludes with general remarks on the historical connection between social relations in the countryside and economic development.

II. Sources: the sixteenth-century penny levies in Flanders

For the purpose of this paper, I have relied on the detailed fiscal records preserved in the aftermath of the wealth tax imposed by the Duke of Alva in 1569-1571. In the aftermath of a series of rebellious events undertaken by Calvinists and members of the lower nobility in 1566, king Philips II sent Alva to the Low Countries as governor. His mission was to restore the peace and the uncontested position of Catholicism. From his first entry into the Low Countries in August 1567, Alva also had clear ideas on how to improve the Habsburg's financial situation in the Low Countries (Craeybeckx, 1947; Maddens, 1972; Arnould, 1946). Central to those plans was the imposition of a series of new taxes that could be levied uniformly over all the provinces of the Low Countries, and without recurring negotiation with the Provincial Estates. One of those taxes was a 100th penny tax on all movable and immovable capital, based on the example of the Spanish *'alcabala'* taxes. The Estates of Flanders were the first in the Netherlandish provinces to consent to this exceptional levy in 1569, although with slight modifications. With regard to the 100th penny levy on capital, they agreed to i) a tax of 1% on the value of movable property, excluding household goods, jewellery and clothes, and above the value of 100 fl., to be levied primarily in the cities, and ii) a tax on real estate. Since the latter tax provides the basis of the analysis in this paper, it is worthwhile to consider its nature in somewhat more detail.

An ordinance from September 9th. 1569 stipulated how the tax was to be set and collected (Craeybeckx, 1948: 84). It was based mostly on Alva's initial proposition, modified slightly in view of some of the concerns raised by the Estates of Flanders. The 100th penny on real estate was in fact levied not as a capital tax of 1% as initially proposed, but as a tax on capital revenues. Land of all kinds was to be taxed at the 22nd penny (4.55%), while the rent of houses was taxed at the 16th penny (6.25%). Five-sixths of these sums were to be by the owner or landlord, and only one-sixth by the leaseholder or renter. In practice, the real estate levy would ultimately be converted to a more straightforward 20th penny on all types of real estate (van den Abbeele 1985). Exemptions were remarkably few. Castles and 'hoven van plaisance' ('country manors' or 'maisons de plaisance') were exempt, but not the other properties of noblemen and -women. Sacred places such as churches, chapels or cloisters were exempt, but not a cloister's property outside of its own enclosure. There was no explicit provision for the exemption of the poor, but since the brunt of burden fell on the owners rather than the users of the land, this presumably was deemed unnecessary.

How was the yearly revenue of these lands and houses assessed? The basis for the fiscal assessment was the mandatory submission of rental and lease contracts for all individuals. If no such contract was available, for instance, when the owner occupied or used the land or house him/herself, the local tax commissioners could determine the rental value of the property based on comparable properties in the neighbourhood. Those commissioners were appointed by royal officials among the local notables, and such an appointment could not be refused by law. Fraud in the self-declaration of property was punished with a severe financial penalty, a percentage of which went to those who had tipped off the authorities. This process, which took place across Flanders in 1570 and 1571, resulted in the redaction of local *cohieren*: registers which recorded the names of the owner and leaseholder, the (estimated) yearly rent or lease, and the levy based on that amount. Although this was not explicitly required by the 1569 ordinance, most of these registers also detailed the nature of the landed properties: the type of land, whether or not a homestead was present, etc. The type of capital levies imposed by Alva was not entirely new in the Low Countries. In the 1540s, several similar 10th and 20th penny taxes on the yearly revenue from real estate had been levied. One of the reasons why these registers have been much less systematically preserved than those from 1569-1572 is that the Estates were very concerned about keeping the regional distribution of wealth hidden from the central administration. They felt that having this information out in the open invited direct taxation without the required intervention of the Estates – which would drastically undercut their political leverage. In 1569, it was explicitly ordained that all registers had to be sent to the lord's Chambers of Account for inspection. As a result, a substantial collection of *cohieren* – local registers of the 100th penny tax on real estate – is available for study throughout Flanders (Van Twembeke, 1986; Cassiman, 1950).

The general revenues from this 100th penny tax – which was actually a 20th penny on revenue – has been used in a seminal study by M. A. Arnould in order to address the regional distribution of wealth in the 16th-century Southern Low Countries (Arnould, 1946). The local registers have also been used frequently for a variety of different studies – many of them focused on the reconstruction of agricultural activities in different regions of 16th-century Flanders and Brabant. In the 1970s and 1980s in particular, a large number of studies used these sources to reconstruct the local agrarian economic system and property structures (Deprez, 1956; Verbeke, 1988; van den Abbeele, 1985; De Ridder, 1985; Pée, 1971; Vandenbroeke and Van den Abbeele, 1991). However, to this date no systematic study has been undertaken of differences in land inequality between different agrarian regions based on these sources.

III. A regional analysis of land inequality

This paper aims to compare local and regional differences in land inequality based on the 1569-1571 penny levies in Flanders. The first step of the analysis provides a superficial comparison in farm size inequality between different regions, whereas the second step of the study brings the analysis to a more in-depth perspective on local levels of land inequality in a small number of case studies. Figure 8.1 brings together data on the land size distributions from 68 villages throughout Flanders, and aggregates those at the regional level. A total of 12,494 households were included in this analysis. It is clear that across most regions in Flanders smallholdings were dominant: in every region farms with less than 5 ha in cultivation were the dominant type of exploitation. Farms larger than 20 ha were exceptional everywhere, and nowhere did they account for more than 10% of all farms, except for the *polder* region in the Brugse Vrije. Unlike the other regions studied here, the northern part of the Brugse Vrije belonged to an area that has been described as 'coastal Flanders': a region that transitioned towards agrarian capitalism from the 16th century onwards (Thoen, 2004; van Bavel, van Cruyningen, and Thoen, 2010). Unfortunately, few 1569-1572 penny levies from this region have survived. To allow for a more instructive comparison, we use data on different but very similar taxes (*pointingen*) for the village of Oostkerke in 1570, as well as older penny levies from 1544 for the polder parishes of Waterland-Oudeman and Watervliet. Although the detail offered in these sources is less extensive than in the 1569-1571 penny levies, the basis of taxation was very similar, and therefore the results can be considered comparable. Comparing the farm size distribution in the Brugse Vrije polders with the other regions – all situated in 'inland Flanders' indicates that the social agrarian system was indeed very different between coastal and inland Flanders.

This does not mean that the social agro-system of inland Flanders was entirely homogeneous. According to Erik Thoen and Bas van Bavel, this region was characterised by the continued dominance throughout the late medieval and early modern period of peasant agriculture with a large degree of peasant ownership and a limited spread of leasehold. This does not mean that this region was based on subsistence farming or a lack of commercialisation, as the spread of proto-industrial activities, urban investments and commercialised agriculture indicate – hence Thoen's characterisation of the region as 'a commercial survival economy' (Thoen, 2001). Although the regional differences within inland Flanders appear to be fairly limited, some variation is nevertheless evident. In the Vier Ambachten, on the northern border of the County, smallholding appears to have been less prevalent, and larger farms were more numerous. The Oudburg, Land van Waas, and Land van Dendermonde regions occupied a middling position, with a notably larger group of middle-sized farms (1-5 ha and 5-20 ha) than elsewhere, a feature that persisted until the 19th century (Ronsijn, 2013). Further to the south of the County of Flanders, the Chattelny's of Kortrijk and Oudenaarde and the Land van Aalst were clearly dominated even more by (extreme) smallholding, combined with the limited – but crucial – presence of a few large landholders (Vermoesen, 2010). These latter regions were thus the clearest example of an agrarian landscape characterised by a 'commercial survival economy'.

This particular distribution of farm sizes was consistent with other regional characteristics (Table 1). Regions with a dominance of smallholding were also characterised by higher population density, and with a lower prevalence of leasehold. The comparison suggests that there was no clear-cut contrast

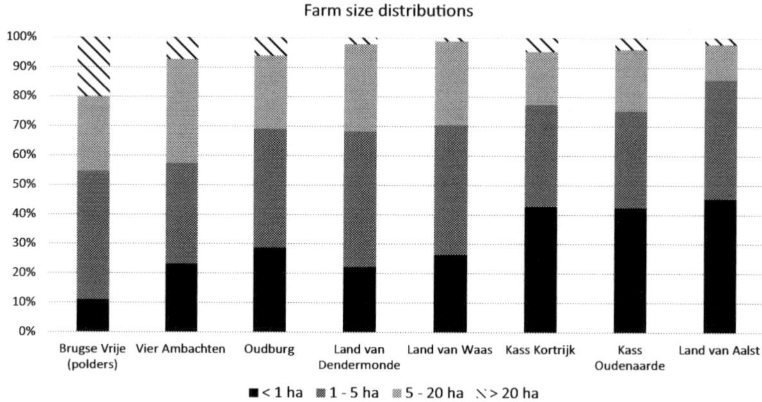

Figure 8.1. Types of farms per size category in different regions of Flanders, *c.* 1571-1572

Sources: Van den Abbeele 1985; De Ridder 1985; Deprez 1956; De Rammelaere 1962; Vandenbroeke and Van den Abbeele 1991; Pée 1971; Municipal Archives Ghent, *Oud Archief Stad Gent*, series 28: 44/183, 58/237, 4/17, 78/325; series 28bis: 2/32 (courtesy of Tim Soens); State Archives Bruges, *Bundels Brugse Vrije*, 271 (courtesy of Kristof Dombrecht).

Table 8.1. Summary statistics of agrarian property structures in Flemish regions, *c.* 1571-1572.

	% < 5 ha	Households per ha (density)	Share of acreage in leasehold	N (households in sample)
Brugse Vrije (polders)	54.33	0.10	73.60	416
Vier Ambachten	57.28	0.16	71.10	430
Oudburg	69.02	0.16	70.94	3,570
Land van Dendermonde	68.05	0.22	47.96	2,288
Land van Waas	70.48	0.23	51.00	2,713
Kass Oudenaarde	76.00	0.22	61.00	80
Kass Kortrijk	77.32	0.25	54.27	1,563
Land van Aalst	85.67	0.29	37.84	1,434

Sources: Van den Abbeele 1985; De Ridder 1985; Deprez 1956; De Rammelaere 1962; Vandenbroeke and Van den Abbeele 1991; Pée 1971; Municipal Archives Ghent, *Oud Archief Stad Gent*, series 28: 44/183, 58/237, 4/17, 78/325; series 28bis: 2/32 (courtesy of Tim Soens); State Archives Bruges, *Bundels Brugse Vrije*, 271 (courtesy of Kristof Dombrecht).

between large-scale, capitalist agriculture dominated by large leasehold farms in some regions, and survival-oriented peasant agriculture on the other hand. Instead, there seems to have been a continuum within Flanders where, more or less from north to south, regions became increasingly more dominated by peasant small-holding.

IV. In-depth analysis of local inequality levels

At the regional level, the analysis of the penny levies confirms the regional correlation between social structures (land inequality) and the nature of the agrarian economy. But how consistent are these findings at the local level? For the second part of the analysis, this paper uses the returns of the 100th penny levies (20th penny in practice) for nine case studies, each consisting of between one and three villages in the County of Flanders (Figure 8.2). The nine selected case studies (13 villages in total) are spread over four different soil types (polders, sand, sand-loam, and loam), six administrative regions (Brugse Vrije, Oudburg, Land Van Waas, Kasselrij Kortrijk, Kasselrij Oudenaarde, and Land van Aalst), and in the vicinity of six different cities (Brugge, Gent, Antwerpen, Aalst, Oudenaarde, Kortrijk). In terms of agricultural specialisation, prominence of proto-industrial activity, and landscape, these case studies capture much of the diversity in the Flemish rural panorama of the sixteenth century.

IV.1 Methodological obstacles

In the context of a rural society in which most income was derived from the land, it is useful to think of the distribution of land *use* as an approximation of the distribution of income in that society. On the other hand, the distribution of land ownership can serve as a rough approximation of wealth inequality. Although the 1569-1571 penny levies offer exceptionally detailed information on both land use and ownership, they are not perfect as sources of information on inequality. The most important obstacle is that the levies took the parish, village or fief as the basic unit within which taxation was distributed. Reconstructing land use and ownership that was spread across parochial boundaries thus presents some difficulties. There is only one exception, i.e. when farms containing parts within the jurisdiction of a different entity are leased or sold *en masse* – that is, together. These lands are then supposed to be taxed in the place of the main seat of the farm, i.e. the farmhouse (*pachthoeve*) or homestead (*hofstede*), or where the majority of the land is situated. Yet the situation is considerably more complex in the case of plot leases, as those were to be taxed and recorded in the parish where they were situated, even though their owners or leaseholders were not necessarily located there. These are called '*afgezetenen*', and are sometimes listed separately, but not always so.

In order to reconstruct the inequality and land use of households, including the land used and owned by such 'afzetenen' would significantly distort the picture. Generally speaking, these were mostly smaller plots constituting – almost as a rule – only a limited portion of the entire farm of these households. Therefore, any analysis that takes into account all farmers listed in these tax lists is bound to overestimate levels of land inequality since

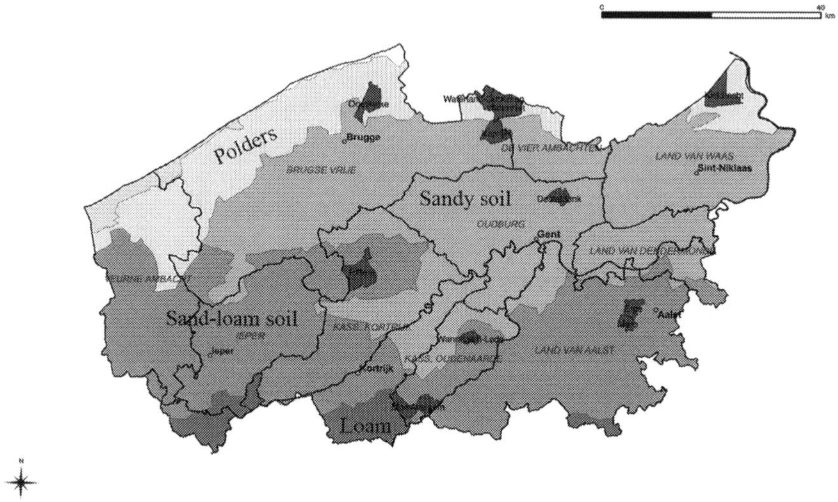

Figure 8.2. The case studies used in this paper in a map of the part of the County of Flanders that is currently situated in Belgium.

it would erroneously count many small parcels as independent households, while they were in fact part of larger farm units. A solution to this would be to only take those farmers into account who we know actually lived in the parish. This place of residence can be indicated by their ownership or lease of a farmstead or homestead. A comparison of the number of households without a homestead and the number of *afgezetenen* for those parishes for which we have this information (Erpe, Mere en Deerlijk), indicates that this indeed brings us significantly closer to the reconstruction of actual households and their farms per parish. In Deerlijk, for instance, 7% of the total acreage was in use by farmers without a homestead in the parish. More than half of this (4%) was used by people recorded explicitly as *afgezetenen*. In Mere, 30% of the total acreage was in use by people without a homestead in the parish. Of this 30% the largest part (23%) belonged to *afgezetenen*. In Erpe, a total of 36% of the total acreage in the parish was leased or owned by people without a homestead in the parish, and almost all of this was used by people who were explicitly recorded as *afgezetenen* (33%).

These examples show that although selecting only farms which did have a homestead in the parish for analysis is a reliable way of filtering out the *afgezetenen*, there are also some remaining plots of land which are not used by *afgezetenen* but neither have a homestead in the parish. The reasons for this may vary. Most of these people seem to have been relatives of households who did own or lease a farmhouse or homestead in the parish. It is therefore likely that they shared the house – and probably also the farm itself. This seems evident, for instance, in the case of Florentine De Baetchelier, who owned only 0.15 hectares of land without a homestead, and was recorded right next to Pieter

De Baetchelier – possibly her brother – who did own a farmstead (Municipal Archives Ghent, *Oud Archief Stad Gent*, series 28, 44/183). For the sake of the analysis of land use per household, the land held by such relatives who were recorded consecutively in the tax registers was added up so as to form a single household. For the few remaining landholdings without a homestead, a number of explanations are possible. Either they boarded with others, whether they were (obvious) relatives or not, or the plot with their actual homestead may have been exempt from taxation and thus left unrecorded. Such was probably the case for *Joncheer* Francois van Assche, or the *Heer* van Orsijn who both owned land in Deerlijk, but were not recorded as *afgezetenen* (Municipal Archives Ghent, *Oud Archief Stad Gent*, series 28, 11/51).

Focusing only on the households with a homestead in the parish thus offers clear advantages over reconstructing inequality from all land users in the parish. There is a risk of excluding some farms of those who were exempt from taxation, or who boarded in the houses of others, but that most likely constitutes only a minor distortion. One remaining issue, of course, is that this approach will never allow us to reconstruct the total size of all farms in so far as they included parcels in other parishes (unless they were bound 'en masse' with the land within the parish, cf. supra). However, it seems unlikely that this affected levels of inequality in a significant way. This can be tested by looking, again, at the case studies of Erpe and Mere – two small parishes situated next to each other. Of the 249 *afgezetenen* in Erpe, 39 were recorded as living in Mere. After tracing those in the tax list of the inhabitants of Mere, it is possible to establish the socio-economic profile of most of these households.[1]

Table 7.2 indicates that the lease or ownership of land in a neighbouring village was spread more or less proportionally over the different quintiles of the land use distribution. In all quintiles such land use in an adjacent village was common, even though in the richest quintile, the size was much larger. The final column indicates that for the lower quintiles, this land in neighbouring parishes constituted a larger part of their total farm size than for the higher quintiles. Since the size of these holdings outside of the parish were thus relatively larger for the smaller farmers, taking into account these land holdings leased or owned outside the parish boundaries has an overall smoothing effect upon land inequality in general. This is clear when comparing the Gini coefficient for land inequality in Mere with and without taking the land of the parish's *afzetenen* in Erpe into account: in the former case the Gini is slightly lower (0.59) than in the latter case (0.61).[2]

---

1 Only 33 of those 39 could be positively identified in Mere. The remaining 6 were probably relatives subsumed under other households that were recorded.

2 This trend is robust also when using alternative inequality measures. The Atkinson coefficient is 0.48 with the land in Erpe, compared to 0.50 without. The Theil coefficient is 0.66 with, and 0.70 without taking these land holdings into account.

Table 8.2. The social profile of inhabitants from Mere with land in neighbouring Erpe, 1571-1572

Quintile of land use in Mere	% of HHs with land in Erpe	Median Ha in Erpe (of HH with > 0)	% of a HH's land used in Erpe (median)
Qu 1 (poorest)	24%	0.37	55%
Qu 2	23%	0.33	27%
Qu 3	15%	0.46	26%
Qu 4	35%	0.29	10%
Qu 5 (richest)	31%	10.69	10%
Total (N = 96)	26%	28.34	17%

Source: Municipal Archives Ghent, *Oud Archief Stad Gent*, series 28, 44/183.

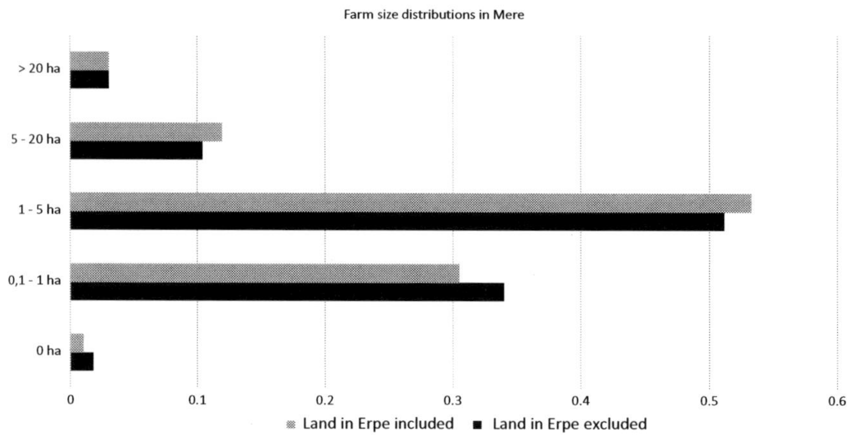

Figure 8.3. Comparing the land size distribution of the village Mere; lands leased or owned in the village Erpe are excluded or included

Source: Municipal Archives Ghent, *Oud Archief Stad Gent*, series 28, 44/183.

This implies that our inequality results based solely on the land used by each household within their respective parish (which is the only information available in the majority of cases) will tend to overestimate the level of inequality attested. However, it should be noted that the villages of Erpe and Mere analysed thus far are exceptional in the sense that they were both situated towards the border of their parochial boundaries, and both village settlements exhibited a tendency to converge (see Figure 8.4). It is quite likely that Erpe and Mere had a much more strongly inter-linked village population than most other neighbouring villages. This implies that for the majority of places the inequality bias will have been smaller than shown in this example. Nevertheless, since there is no practical way of resolving this problem, it is a type of *systematic error* which we will necessarily have to accept and take into

Figure 8.4. Detail from the Ferraris map (1777), showing Erpe (north) and Mere (south)

Source: De Grote Atlas van Ferraris. De eerste atlas van België. 1777. Kabinetskaart van de Oostenrijkse Nederlanden en het Prinsbisdom Luik (Tielt 2009). Also available online at https://belgica.kbr.be/.

account when interpreting the results. The problem is most pressing in as far as it affects regions and localities differentially. It is likely that the distortive effect caused by land held in other parishes will be the largest in (a) smaller parishes, and (b) in regions with more frequent small-scale plotleasing practices. The former is easy enough to gather from the tax registers themselves. As a proxy for the latter, we will use the share of total acreage held by *afgezetenen* within the parish as an approximation of the extent of land outside of the parish held by its inhabitants. Since the vast majority of *afgezetenen* lived in the immediately surrounding parishes, this can safely serve as a proxy for practices in land use in the other direction as well. This is evidenced both by the cases of Erpe and Pollare: only rarely did those who held (i.e. used) land in a parish live more than a couple of kilometres away from its borders (Figures 8.5 & 8.6).

IV.2 Local land inequality: the distribution of farm sizes

The first analysis presented here looks at the inequality in the size of land holdings: i.e. not in the ownership of land, but in its use. The Gini coefficient offers a summary statistic of a given distribution by summarizing the Lorenz curve which plots the cumulative shares of population and income. It ranges

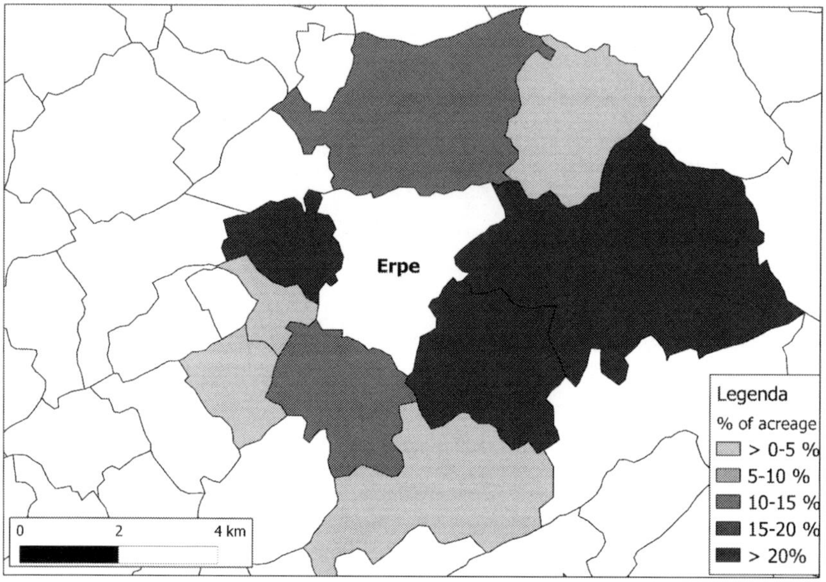

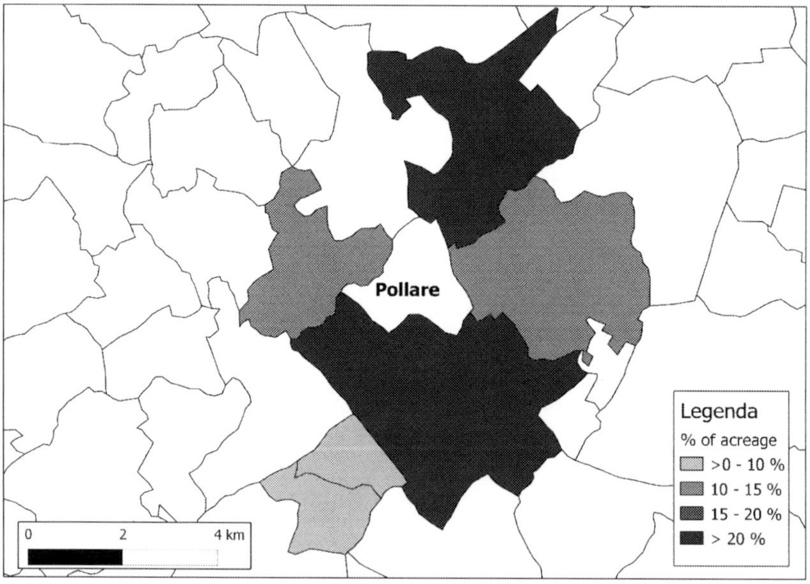

Figures 8.5 & 8.6 The location of *afgezetenen* in the villages of Erpe and Pollare, 1571-1572

Source: Municipal Archives Ghent, *Oud Archief Stad Gent*, series 28, 44/183; http://www.rikvanhauwe.be/pol/pol.20/tpp.overzicht.htm (august 2017).

Table 8.3. Inequality of land size holdings for a selection of case studies, 1571-1572

	Gini	Top 10% share	Top 5% share	Surface (ha)	N hh's
Brugse vrije (polder)					
Oostkerke	0.49	31%	17%	1,517	77
Waterland-Oudeman & Watervliet	0.62	43%	26%	2,845	341
Land van Waas (polder)					
Kieldrecht	0.61	41%	22%	1,489	130
Brugse vrije (sand)					
Kaprijke	0.58	41%	28%	1,429	291
Oudburg (sand)					
Desteldonk	0.52	37%	23%	575	101
Kasselrij Kortrijk (sand-loam)					
Pittem	0.63	38%	25%	2,455	278
Kasselrij Oudenaarde (sand-loam)					
Wannegem	0.65	44%	30%	365	53
Avelgem	0.67	54%	42%	976	281
Moen (loam)	0.62	48%	37%	776	174
Land van Aalst (sand-loam)					
Erpe & Mere	0.68	56%	38%	437	272

N.B. The data for Waterland-Oudeman & Watervliet is from 1544.

Sources: Municipal Archives Ghent, *Oud Archief Stad Gent*, series 28: 44/183, 58/237, 4/17, 78/325, 33/141, 32/137, 14/62, 47/197; series 28bis: 2/32 (courtesy of Tim Soens); State Archives Bruges, *Bundels Brugse Vrije*, 271 (courtesy of Kristof Dombrecht).

from 0 to 1, where the former denotes complete equality, and the latter complete inequality. Table 3 complements the Gini results with the shares in total acreage held by the top 10% and the top 5% of the farm size distribution respectively.

Unlike the fairly straightforward regional analysis of farm size distributions presented above, the comparison of local Gini coefficients offers a less straightforward image of regional differences in land inequality. Inequality does seem to have been considerably lower in the polder parish of Oostkerke (0.49), situated in coastal Flanders, as also attested in Dombrecht and Ryckbosch, 2017. This might seem surprising since coastal Flanders is usually thought to have followed the path towards a more capitalist, polarised social structure, while inland Flanders was deemed to remain a more egalitarian peasant society (Thoen and Soens, 2015; Soens, 2009). However, this becomes less surprising once we take into account that the penny levy sources only give us an indication of the inequality between households who lived in their own house or cultivated land, and thus excludes from view any landless labourers who did not live independently or locally. The relatively egalitarian distribution of land use among farmers in coastal Flanders does not preclude a more general inegalitarian social structure as the number of landless households was presumable larger there. Both the prevalence of seasonal labour and live-in farmhands potentially obscures important aspects of social inequality in the coastal area.

Table 8.3 also indicates that soil type is no clear predictor of land inequality. Unlike Oostkerke, the more recent polders in the north of Flanders (Waterland, Oudeman, Watervliet) and near Antwerp (Kieldrecht) indicate much higher levels of inequality (0.62-0.63). Lower levels of inequality are found in the sandy region of Flanders (Kaprijke and especially Desteldonk, 0.58-0.52), between the polders and the more inegalitarian regions to the south of Ghent. The highest levels of land inequality are found in Avelgem and Erpe and Mere in inland Flanders (0.67-0.68), which is also confirmed by the very high share of the total acreage in use there by the top 5% farms: 42% and 38% respectively. Although local Gini coefficients offer a less straightforward perspective than did the farm size distributions in the previous section, some regional patterns nevertheless transpire. Perhaps surprisingly so, land inequality seems to have been highest in peasant-dominated regions, and lower in more mixed regions and the capitalist, coastal village of Oostkerke.

IV.3 Elites and the characteristics of the farm size distribution

A closer look at some of the main characteristics behind these distributions might prove instructive in order to gain a better understanding of why Gini coefficients differ from place to place, and whether the same coefficient might in fact refer to a very different type of rural society. One way to do this is to look at the type of farm that dominated the landscape – in a very literal sense: which type of farm (defined in terms of size) held the largest acreage in each of these villages? Figure 8.7 offers a summary presentation of the prominence of each type of farm, by showing the share of total land held by each type, broken down into 6 categories: mini holdings (< 0.5 ha), small farms (0.5-2 ha), modest-sized farms (2-5 ha), middle-sized farms (5-10 ha), large (10-20 ha), and giant estates (>20 ha).

The most remarkable dominance of the largest category of farms was situated in the polder villages of Oostkerke (72%) and Watervliet (59%). The low level of Gini inequality in Oostkerke was clearly the result of a near absence of small and medium-sized farms, and a complete dominance of large land-holdings, compared to the other villages, which had a much more diverse landscape of farm sizes. In Pittem (43%) and Avelgem (28%), the largest farm size category also held the most estates in the village, but their dominance was clearly much less overwhelming. Moreover, in Avelgem – one of the villages with the highest levels of Gini inequality –this was the result of a very different type of rural society. Here the largest farms (>20ha) held

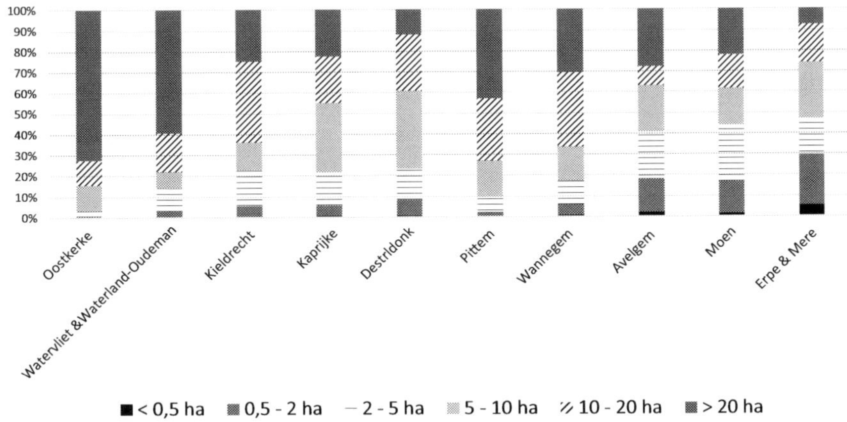

Figure 8.7. The share of total acreage per village held by each type of farm, 1571-1572

Sources: Municipal Archives Ghent, *Oud Archief Stad Gent*, series 28: 44/183, 58/237, 4/17, 78/325, 33/141, 32/137, 14/62, 47/197; series 28bis: 2/32 (courtesy of Tim Soens); State Archives Bruges, *Bundels Brugse Vrije*, 271 (courtesy of Kristof Dombrecht).

the most acreage (27%), but this was only marginally more than the total acreage held by the small (2-5 ha) and medium-sized (5-10 ha) farms: 23% and 22% respectively. In fact, the high level of inequality in Avelgem was the result of a numerical dominance of small and medium-sized farms, together with a handful of very large leasehold estates. These estates, the largest of which counted 93 ha, consisted of marshland next to the river Scheldt on which cattle and horses were kept, and which were mostly held in lease from Saint-Peters abbey in Ghent. Thus, the rural social structure of most of the village of Avelgem corresponded well to that of a traditional peasant society, and thus conformed to the larger social agro-system of which it was part. Yet, inequality was heightened remarkably by the local presence of the Scheldt grasslands – meadows used as pasturage or for growing hay, the long-standing ownership of large estates by Saint-Peter's Abbey of Ghent in the village, and thus the presence of a local elite with very large farms, who held these marshes in lease.

The farm size distribution in Avelgem was not dissimilar to that in Erpe-Mere, which had the highest Gini inequality of the villages included in our sample. In Erpe-Mere, most of the land was held by farms of medium (27%) acreage, small acreage (18%) and even very small size (24%). Inequality was high, precisely because this landscape of small farms was interspersed with some large (19%) and a few very large holdings (7%). Compared to the average farm size in the polders, Pieter Callebout's leasehold of 55 ha in Erpe, held from Franchoys de Schouteete, lord of Erpe, was nothing special, but among the modest farms surrounding him, his leasehold was extraordinarily large, thus adding considerably to inequality. Clearly, the typical rural social structure of the region as it has been described for the eighteenth century (Vermoesen, 2010) can already be discerned here, more than two centuries earlier: a dominance of (very) small-scale peasants, living next to the very large estates held in lease from the local aristocracy.

The situation in between the extremes of the polders (low inequality, large estates), and the southern parts of inland Flanders (high inequality, a majority of small estates with a minority of large estates) is exemplified by the cases of Kaprijke and Desteldonk. In both cases, the most prominent farm size category was the medium-sized farm (5-10 ha), with only a small share of the total acreage taken up by the very small (5-7%) and very large farms (12-22%). Again, this sixteenth-century rural configuration already prefigures the situation of the eighteenth century, as it has been described for the Land van Waas region (Ronsijn, 2013). At least in Desteldonk this situation seems to have been partly due to the absence of a local elite of large leaseholders. The largest farms in the village (the top 5 farms were between 18 and 35 ha) were largely – if not completely – owned in property, and usually assembled from a diversity of smaller parcels, rather than a single large estate with a homestead.

This superficial exploration of land (use) inequality in the sixteenth-century *penny levies* thus suggests at least four preliminary conclusions. First, statistical summary measures such as the Gini coefficient should not be interpreted as straightforward indications of overall social polarisation; regions characterised by a growing divide between landless labourers and farmers in fact demonstrated much lower levels of land inequality than the regions described as traditional peasant societies. Second, the regional differentiation noticeable for the eighteenth and nineteenth centuries can already be discerned in the sixteenth century – if in a somewhat embryonic form. Third, this regional differentiation is more adequately characterised as a continuum between capitalist agriculture in the coastal area, and peasant-dominated agriculture in the southern parts of inland Flanders. Rather than a stark split between both types of social agro-systems, we observe a gradual differentiation between both ideal types across Flanders – from the polders in the north, across the sandy soils in the middle, towards the sandy-loam soils in the south.

Finally, when abandoning the regional perspective, and focusing on case studies in more detail, it is worth observing that both very local and (supra-) regional processes determined the shape of local farm land distributions: ranging from the importance of local features of geography (woods, rivers or towns), to the long history and path-dependency of aristocratic and ecclesiastical ownership in the area. However, notwithstanding the differences in the features of local land distributions, there are also remarkable similarities. In almost all of the places examined, there was a small but clearly discernible local elite of large lease farmers holding estates of 40 ha or more. These people were invariably of non-noble status, but held their estates in lease from either large ecclesiastical landholders (such as the abbeys of Ghent or Rijssel) or from noble (usually absentee) landlords. On the other hand, the presence of a rural class of large freeholding farmers in Flanders, similar to the English *yeomen*, is much less evident from these sources. In some villages, such large farmers that hold their land in ownership emerge among the largest 5 or 10 estates, but only rarely so. The one exception here is the case of Desteldonk, where a tenant class seems to have been absent, and the local elite consisted of a group of relatively modest farmers who held their land in property.

IV.4 Ownership, leasehold and wealth

Although land use inequality is an important aspect of social and economic structures in rural societies, it is not the only dimension of economic inequality that matters. Examining property structures might be at least as instructive in order to gain insight into some of those other dimensions. Table 4 shows the prevalence of leasehold expressed as the percentage of total acreage in each parish. At first sight, the property structure of ownership in a village in the *penny levies* does not seem to correspond particularly well to either soil type, landscape or land inequality. Instead, it seems most of all to have been determined by institutional path dependency (van Bavel, van Cruyningen, and Thoen, 2010). The lasting influence of the reclamation history is clearly visible when one compares the polder of Watervliet, for instance, where leasehold was dominant (73%) to the polder of Kieldrecht, where it was not (39%).

Throughout most of inland Flanders, there seems to have been relatively little variance in the prominence of leasehold, which usually ranged between 45% and 65%. Moreover, a clear correlation with land inequality or rural social structures, as explored above, does not emerge at the local level. For instance, both places with high levels of leasehold such as Kaprijke (65% of ha in lease), and places with low levels of leasehold such as Desteldonk (46% of ha in lease) could enjoy low levels of farm size (land use) inequality. However, this means that the land ownership distribution in Desteldonk was considerably more egalitarian than in Kaprijke: the Gini of the land ownership distribution in Desteldonk is 0.59, compared to 0.74 in Kaprijke. However, what is typical of the very high levels of land inequality in the southern parts of inland Flanders (Avelgem and Erpe-Mere) is a relatively even spread between lease and ownership, with the large majority of small and medium-sized farms being held in property, and the minority of large estates being leaseholds. In fact, it is probably this mix of ownership and lease that shaped the rural structure of inland Flanders, and continued to keep it in place until the middle of the nineteenth century. The small farms held in property by the peasant population would keep them from migration and stimulated their engagement in proto-industrial activity for survival. In the longer term, it also spurred the continued fragmentation of estates, and thus the growth of rural inequality during subsequent centuries. At the other end of the spectrum, it is the ownership of large estates by mostly ecclesiastical,

Table 8.4. The prevalence of leasehold in selected case studies, 1571-1572

	% of ha in leasehold
Watervliet	73%
Kaprijke	65%
Wannegem	61%
Avelgem	53%
Erpe-Mere	51%
Pittem	49%
Moen	47%
Desteldonk	46%
Kieldrecht	39%

Sources: Municipal Archives Ghent, *Oud Archief Stad Gent*, series 28: 44/183, 58/237, 4/17, 78/325, 33/141, 32/137, 14/62, 47/197; series 28bis: 2/32 (courtesy of Tim Soens); State Archives Bruges, *Bundels Brugse Vrije*, 271 (courtesy of Kristof Dombrecht).

Table 8.5. The identity of landowners in selected villages, 1571-1572

Place	**% of ha owned by aristocracy**	**% of ha owned by religious institutions**	**% of ha owned by urban landowners**
Wannegem	24%	9%	
Kaprijke	3%	29%	24%
Avelgem	6%	22%	12%
Mere	3%	19%	
Erpe	14%	6%	
Moen	15%	1%	24%
Kieldrecht	10%	4%	
Desteldonk	0	7%	22%

Sources: Municipal Archives Ghent, *Oud Archief Stad Gent*, series 28: 44/183, 58/237, 4/17, 78/325, 33/141, 32/137, 14/62, 47/197; series 28bis: 2/32 (courtesy of Tim Soens); State Archives Bruges, *Bundels Brugse Vrije*, 271 (courtesy of Kristof Dombrecht).

aristocratic and urban landowners that shaped the top end of the land distribution, and social hierarchy, of these villages.

In the places where land inequality was the highest, such as Avelgem, Erpe and Mere, noble or ecclesiastical landlords typically held 20% or more of the total acreage all together – a small, but significant share of the total land of the village which they then leased out in large estates. Tellingly, the case of Desteldonk, where the lowest level of land use and ownership inequality was observed, had the smallest share of absentee landownership, with more than 70% of its acreage owned locally, only 7% by religious institutions, and no land owned by noble landlords. The historical absence of manorial and ecclesiastical power in this area clearly affected local levels of inequality, as it prevented a sizeable local elite of large leaseholders from emerging. However, it should be noted that this strong degree of local ownership was not indefinitely fixed by path-dependence. As the centuries wore on, its proximity to the city of Ghent would become increasingly clear in its property structure. By the middle of the nineteenth century, 57% of the land in Desteldonk was held by absentee landlords, most of it by the Ghent bourgeoisie (34%).[3] However, the interplay between the ownership by absentee landowners and local social structures is not necessarily straightforward. In the Kieldrecht polder, for instance, absentee landownership was rare yet inequality was high, whereas in Kaprijke, the high number of absentee landowners did not lead to higher levels of inequality.

V. The relationship between inequality and economic development

How did the rural social structures studied thus far relate to local levels of economic development? Naturally, economic development can be measured in any number of ways, many of which are highly contested and problematic, and most are hard to apply to the sixteenth-century countryside due to a lack of suitable sources. Nevertheless, I have attempted to gain some insight into the economic surplus created per locality by using wealth as a rough approximation for development. The total revenue from the Duke of Alva's 100th penny levy again serves as the basis for this analysis. Peter Stabel and Filip Vermeylen have conducted a comparative survey of the total revenues from this tax, where the levy on real estate was combined with the tax on movable wealth above 100 fl. They generally interpreted the fiscal revenue as a measure of de-urbanisation, an indication of the economic development of Antwerp, of the decline of Bruges, and of the rise of rural proto-industry in Western Flanders (Stabel and Vermeylen, 1997). The fiscal revenue of rural localities was determined primarily by a combination of human and natural capital: the fertility of the soil, cultivation, yield, cottage industry, livestock or dairy farming, the production of cash crops, or resources for the textile industry. In other words, the total fiscal revenue produced by a village, can be seen as a rough proxy for its economic development.

In order to make this proxy more fit for the purpose at hand, I have converted the fiscal revenues per locality to a measure that takes the human and natural capital into account, in order to single out the surplus capital produced by agrarian productivity. In order to do so, a formula similar to

3 Calculated from P.C. Popp, Atlas Cadastrale Parcelaire de la Belgique, Commune de Desteldonck (Brugge, 1860).

Table 8.6. Estimates of agrarian development in the selected case studies, 1569-1571

	Wealth tax revenue (in fl)	Households (n)	Surface (ha)	Productivity proxy
Brugse Vrije (polder)				
Oostkerke	63.719	77	1.517	251
Waterland-Oudeman& Watervliet	128.953	341	2.845	162
Land van Waas (polder)				
Kieldrecht	21.161	130	1.489	61
Brugse Vrije (sand)				
Kaprijke	57.520	291	1.429	105
Oudburg (sand)				
Desteldonk	18.659	101	575	92
Kasselrij Kortrijk (sand-loam)				
Pittem	60.222	278	2.455	91
Kass. Oudenaarde (sand-loam)				
Wannegem	9.922	53	365	86
Avelgem	44.758	281	976	97
Moen (loam)	28.205	174	776	89
Land van Aalst (sand-loam)				
Erpe & Mere	44.232	272	437	134

Sources: Municipal Archives Ghent, *Oud Archief Stad Gent*, series 28: 44/183, 58/237, 4/17, 78/325, 33/141, 32/137, 14/62, 47/197; series 28bis: 2/32 (courtesy of Tim Soens); State Archives Bruges, *Bundels Brugse Vrije*, 271 (courtesy of Kristof Dombrecht).

that for calculating Total Factor Productivity (TFP) is adapted to the wealth proxy from the 100th penny levy,

$$Rural\ Productivity\ proxy = \frac{Wealth}{\left(Land^{0.4} * Labour^{0.6}\right)}$$

whereby for 'Wealth' I use the total revenue from the 100th penny, for 'Land', I rely on the total acreage under cultivation as it can be calculated from the registers of the penny levies, and for 'Labour', I use the number of households residing within the village boundaries, as indicated by the same penny levies as a proxy.

A cursory glance at the results for the estimated total factor productivity in table 6, and a comparison with table 3, does not suggest a straightforward link between land inequality and economic development. The highest levels of rural productivity were present in the polder villages Oostkerke and Waterland-Oudeman, which could partly be due to an overestimation as a result of the fact that a part of the labour inputs in these areas probably does not show up in our sources. Yet, also Erpe and Mere, the most typical example of a peasant economy, seems to have had a relatively high level of productivity. As a result, both the places with the highest and those with the lowest levels of inequality scored best in terms of economic productivity. This suggests that in terms of productivity, agrarian economic development was highest in *both* the sparsely populated polders of coastal Flanders and in the very densely populated regions of inland Flanders. This reflects two distinct paths towards higher productivity: one labour-intensive, the other land-intensive. Probably both were characterised by higher levels of inequality – although in different forms. In inland Flanders, inequality was produced by the contrast between a large number of very small peasants who owned their land, combined with the presence of a handful of very rich leasehold farmers. In the coastal areas, inequality came from the contrast between a large group of medium and large-sized farmers on the one hand, and the landless labours they hired for wages on the other. In between, the areas where polarisation was less stark and population density was neither particularly high nor low, productivity tended to be lower as well. However, within these other places, there does not seem to be a noticeable pattern to the productivity estimates, which generally vary little.

VI. Conclusions

This paper aims to be little more than a cursory exploration of a single source's potential in reconstructing rural inequality in sixteenth-century Flanders. Despite a number of drawbacks and complications raised above, the *penny levies* from 1569-1572 offer substantial possibilities for reconstructing the distribution of farm sizes, property structures, and the composition of local elites throughout a variety of sub-regions in the Flemish agrarian landscape. The exploration thus far has indicated that land inequality varied across Flanders, and in general showed a continuum in terms of social and economic structure from north to south. Yet, despite this regional pattern, local levels of inequality did not necessarily correspond to particular soil types, as polders, sandy, sand-loam and loam regions could all give rise to rather diverse levels of land inequality, and various underlying distributions of farm size. Rather, it has been suggested that the reclamation history and resulting property structures were crucial in shaping land distributions in most places. This factor of path dependency, and its relationship to relatively inflexible property structures helps to explain why many of the characteristics shaping the rural geography of eighteenth- and nineteenth-century Flanders can already be discerned in the analysis of these sixteenth-century sources.

The above analysis also suggests that the scale of analysis is an important issue when studying rural inequality, especially so in the case of sixteenth-century

Flanders. It is well known that the 'social agro-system' approach emphasises the importance of agricultural regions rather than nations in shaping social relations as well as the organisation of agricultural production. Within this approach, attention has often been paid to the interaction between power relations, often resulting from the path-dependent effects of a region's particular reclamation history, and soil type. Despite the obvious importance of this regional approach, it remains important to question how regional structures interacted with both local and supra-regional processes. The case studies sketched above suggest that to a high degree, local social structures were also determined by on the one hand very local factors (such as the presence of a river with bordering marshlands, the proximity of an urban centre, or the presence of a strong manorial lordship), and on the other hand supra-regional processes (such as the absentee landownership in the hands of aristocratic, ecclesiastical and urban elites, or the opportunities for international trade which spurred the growth of proto-industrial production). Even if the Flemish countryside can be very meaningfully divided into a number of more or less coherent agro-systems, ties of commerce and landownership nevertheless tied them firmly together in the hands of a stratum of aristocratic, ecclesiastical and mercantile elites that was usually supra-regional in orientation.

Finally, a very preliminary comparison has been carried out between inequality levels on the one hand, and a rough approximation of total factor productivity per locality on the other hand. This, very tentatively, suggests that both capital- and labour-intensive agrarian development in the sixteenth century were associated with a growth in inequality (compare with Dombrecht and Ryckbosch, 2017; Ryckbosch, 2016; Alfani and Ryckbosch, 2016).

Bibliography

Abbeele, H. van den (1985) *De penningkohieren als sociaal-ekonomische en demografische bron. Het Land van Waas omstreeks 1571*, MA Thesis Ghent University, Ghent.

Alfani, G. and Ryckbosch, W. (2016) 'Growing apart in early modern Europe? A comparison of inequality trends in Italy and the Low Countries, 1500-1800', *Explorations in Economic History*, 62, pp. 143-153.

Allen, R. C. (1992) *Enclosure and the yeoman: the agricultural development of the South Midlands 1450-1850*, Oxford.

Arnould, M.-A. (1946) 'L'impôt sur le capital en Belgique au XVIe siècle', *Le Hainaut Économique*, 1, pp. 17-45.

Bavel, B. van, P. van Cruyningen and E. Thoen (2010) 'The Low Countries, 1000-1750' in: B. van Bavel and R. Hoyle, *Social Relations: Property and Power*, Turnhout, pp. 169-198.

Brenner, R. (1976) 'Agrarian class structure and economic development in pre-industrial Europe', *Past & Present*, 70, 1, pp. 30-75.

Cassiman, A. (1950) 'De XXe Penningkohieren, een bron voor zoekers en vorsers uit Oost- en West-Vlaanderen', *Cultureel Jaarboek Voor de Provincie Oost-Vlaanderen*, 2, pp. 70-88.

Craeybeckx, J. (1947) 'Aperçu sur l'histoire des impôts en Flandre et au Brabant au cours du XVIe siècle', *Revue Du Nord*, 29, 114, pp. 87-108.

Craeybeckx, J. (1948) *De Tiende Penning van Alva in Vlaanderen en Brabant*, MA Thesis, Ghent University, Ghent.

Curtis, D. R. (2013) 'Trends in rural social and economic history of the pre-industrial Low Countries: recent themes and ideas in journals and books of the past five years (2007-2013)', *BMGN. The Low Countries Historical Review*, 128, 3, pp. 60-95.

Deininger, K. and P. Olinto (1999) *Asset distribution, inequality, and growth*, The World Bank.

Deprez, P. (1956) 'Uitbatingen en grondbezit in Meigem (1571-1787). Een methodologisch artikel', *Handelingen van de Maatschappij voor Geschiedenis en Oudheidkunde te Gent*, 10, pp. 153-170.

Dombrecht, K. and W. Ryckbosch (2017) 'Wealth inequality in a time of transition: coastal Flanders in the sixteenth century', *Tijdschrift voor Sociale en Economische Geschiedenis*, 14, 2, pp. 63-84.

Engerman, S. L. and K. L. Sokoloff (2005) 'Colonialism, Inequality, and long-run paths of development', *National Bureau of Economic Research*.

Frankema, E. (2010) 'The colonial roots of land inequality: geography, factor endowments, or institutions?', *The Economic History Review*, 63, 2, pp. 418-451.

Hoffman, P. T. (2000) *Growth in a Traditional Society: The French Countryside, 1450-1815*, Princeton.

Kay, C. (2002) 'Why East Asia overtook Latin America: agrarian reform, industrialisation and development', *Third World Quarterly*, 23, 6, pp. 1073-1102.

Le Roy Ladurie, E. (1966). *Les Paysans de Languedoc*, Paris.

Maddens, N. (1972) 'Zestiende-eeuwse fiskale bronnen ter bestudering van de sociaal-ekonomische toestanden op het vlaamse platteland', in: *Economische Geschiedenis van België. Behandeling van de Bronnen en Status Quaestionis.* Colloquium, Brussels, pp. 21-29.

Neves, P. C., Ó. Afonso and S. T. Silva (2016) 'A meta-analytic reassessment of the effects of inequality on growth', *World Development*, 78, pp. 386-400.

Pée, L. (1971) *Agrarische en sociaal-ekonomische toestand en bevolkingsevolutie in het Land van Dendermonde tijdens de Tweede Helft der XVIe eeuw*, Gent.

Rammelaere, C. de (1962) 'Bijdrage tot de landbouwgeschiedenis in Zuid-Oostvlaanderen (1570-1790)', *Handelingen der Maatschappij voor Geschiedenis en Oudheidkunde te Gent*, XVI, pp. 21-40.

Ridder, C. de (1985) *De Penningkohieren als Sociaal-economische Bron. De Oudburg en het Meetjesland rond 1570*, MA Thesis Ghent University, Ghent.

Ronsijn, W. (2013) 'Mediated and Unmediated Market Dependence in the Flemish Countryside in the Nineteenth Century: Two Paths of Rural Development', *Continuity and Change*, 28, 1, pp. 89-120.

Ryckbosch, W. (2016) 'Economic inequality and growth before the industrial revolution: the case of the Low Countries (fourteenth to nineteenth centuries)', *European Review of Economic History*, 20, 1, pp. 1-22.

Soens, T. (2009) *De spade in de dijk?: waterbeheer en rurale samenleving in de vlaamse kustvlakte (1280-1580)*, Ghent.

Soens, T. and E. Thoen (2008) 'The origins of leasehold in the former County of Flanders', in: B. van Bavel and P. Schofield (eds), *The Development of Leasehold in Northwestern Europe, c. 1200-1600*, Turnhout, pp. 31-55.

Sokoloff, K.L and S. L. Engerman (2000) 'Institutions, factor endowments, and paths of development in the New World', *Journal of Economic Perspectives*, 14, 3, pp. 217-232.

Stabel, P. and F. Vermeylen (1997) *Het fiscale vermogen in Brabant, Vlaanderen en in de Heerlijkheid Mechelen: De Honderste Penning van de hertog van Alva (1569-1572)*, Brussels.

Thoen, E. (2001) 'A "Commercial survival economy" in evolution. The Flemish countryside and the transition to capitalism (Middle Ages–19th Century)', in: P. Hoppenbrouwers and J. L. van Zanden (eds), *Peasants into Farmers? The Transformation of Rural Economy and Society in the Low Countries (Middle Ages-19th Century) in Light of the Brenner Debate*, Turnhout, pp. 102-157.

Thoen, E. (2004) '"Social agrosystems' as an economic concept to explain regional differences. An essay taking the former County of Flanders as an example (Middle Ages-19th Century)', in: P. Hoppenbrouwers and B. van Bavel (eds), *Landholding and Land Transfer in the North Sea Area (Late Middle Ages-19th Century)*, Turnhout, pp. 47-66.

Thoen, E. and T. Soens (2015) 'The family or the farm: a Sophie's choice? The late medieval crisis in Flanders', in: J. Drendel (ed.), *Crisis in the Later Middle Ages: Beyond the Postan-Duby Paradigm*, Turnhout, pp. 195-224.

Van Twembeke, J. (1986) 'De Penningkohieren', *Jaarboek van de Heemkring Scheldevelde. Vereniging voor Lokale Geschiedenis van de Streek tussen Leie en Schelde*, XV, pp. 41-59.

Vandenbroeke, C. and H. van den Abbeele (1991), *Een exploratieve studie van vier Oostrozebeekse Penningkohieren*, Gent.

Verbeke, C. (1988). *De Penningcohieren als Sociaal-Economische en Demografische Bron. De Roede van Tielt rond 1571/72*, MA Thesis Ghent University, Ghent.

Vermoesen, R. (2010) 'Paardenboeren in Vlaanderen". *Tijdschrift voor Sociale en Economische Geschiedenis*, 7, 1, pp. 3-37.

THIJS LAMBRECHT

9 Economic inequality in late medieval and early modern rural Hainaut (*c.* 1420 – *c.* 1540)

This last decade, the increased interest in inequality has produced a wave of new empirical studies on wealth and income disparities during medieval and early modern times. The research team headed by Guido Alfani in particular has played a key role in putting pre-industrial inequality back on the agenda of political, social and economic historians (for an overview of their work see Alfani, 2020). Their research has produced precious and novel data on inequality in different parts of Italy. At present, two regions stand out in particular for the availability of their long-term data on economic inequality: (northern) Italy and the Low Countries. Although differences can be observed in inequality levels between these regions (Alfani and Ryckbosch, 2016), they also share a common trend. From the fifteenth to the nineteenth centuries there was a gradual growth of inequality. One of the structural characteristics of the early modern period turns out to be the deepening of inequality. After a short reversal following the demographic catastrophe of the Black Death, economic inequality started to rise again from the first half of the fifteenth century. The near general consensus emerging from this research has been that inequality tended to rise almost continuously and almost everywhere in Europe from the late middle ages until the 19th century (see also Alfani and Thoen, Introduction to this book).

The main aim of this chapter is to produce and discuss new empirical and quantitative data on economic inequality in the northern part of the former county of Hainaut during the fifteenth and sixteenth centuries. To this date, no data are available on economic inequality in Hainaut. The results of this study will facilitate comparative research on the determinants of inequality at a regional level within the Low Countries. Comparable data as those studied in this chapter, are available for a large number of urban centres in the Low Countries for late medieval and early modern times (see Ryckbosch, 2015 for an overview). Recently, however, a number of historians have done extensive research on rural economic inequality during the fifteenth and sixteenth centuries using fiscal sources and data from Flanders and Brabant (Dombrecht and Ryckbosch 2017; Van Onacker, 2017). For the northern Low Countries similar data are available for the Guelders area (Van Schaik, 1987).

Thijs Lambrecht • Ghent University

Inequality in rural Europe (Late Middle Ages – 18th century), ed. by Guido Alfani and Erik Thoen, CORN, 18 (Turnhout, 2020), pp. 169-190.

 DOI 10.1484/M.CORN-EB.5.121953

The first section of this chapter discusses and evaluates the fiscal sources for rural Hainaut. In the second section, I reconstruct and discuss economic inequality in different rural settlements. The third section, finally, takes a look at the data for Hainaut from a comparative perspective.

I. Sources and data

Research on rural inequality in Flanders, Brabant and Guelders has relied predominantly on fiscal sources. In particular, tax lists produced by rural communities to meet the rising fiscal demands of the central state have proved a useful starting point to reconstruct inequality in the past. Within the Low Countries, the richest data are available for the county of Flanders. For the fifteenth century some 30 tax lists have been preserved. Unfortunately, these lists suffer from a geographical bias as most of the surviving documentation concerns villages in the region of Bruges. Large parts of the county are not covered by these lists. Also, many of these lists relate to small settlements with very few taxpayers. The small number of observations (frequently fewer than 20 taxpayers) render these lists unsuitable for research on economic inequality. Finally, in the vast majority of cases, we only have one tax list which seriously hampers long-term reconstructions of the distribution of economic resources (Lambrecht and Ryckbosch, 2020). For the Duchy of Brabant we have fewer data and sources as for only one village tax lists have survived from the fifteenth century (Van Onacker, 2017: 70-77).

The patchy and random survival of late medieval fiscal documentation for the countryside is somehow to be expected. In contrast to other regions, no extensive surveys of land, wealth or income were produced before the middle of the sixteenth century that could serve as a base for taxation. Taxes were allocated between members of the rural communities taking into account the income enjoyed by these rural households (see also below). Taxation, moreover, varied from year to year. Therefore, tax lists were quickly outdated and there was no administrative or legal incentive to preserve them. In other words, the nature and frequency of rural taxation militated strongly against the long-term survival of these fiscal sources. Because they became obsolete quickly after they had been drafted, they did not constitute the object of extensive archival care of rural communities. In the context of Hainaut an additional factor comes into play. In 1940 a substantial part of the medieval and early modern records produced by rural communities was destroyed after the bombardment of the archival repositories of Mons and Tournai. Thousands of documents were lost forever. Fortunately, some of the medieval fiscal documentation had already attracted the attention of historians during the 1930's. After the destruction of these original records in 1940, historians like Maurice Arnould (1914-2001) published their transcriptions and notes on these sources. For example, the original tax lists for the village of Hoves were destroyed but all relevant data were published already in 1940 by Arnould (Arnould, 1940). These text editions and analyses are of sufficient quality to be used in quantitative historical research. However, as in Flanders, they suffer from a geographical bias. All available tax lists from the fifteenth and early sixteenth centuries originated in rural communities located in the north-eastern and northern part of the county. This is important as Hainaut was not a homogeneous economic region but a patchwork of regional systems with their own characteristics (Sivery, 1980: 80-96). The variation in economic geography that characterized late medieval Hainaut is not reflected in the surviving tax lists.

The earliest rural fiscal sources for Hainaut date from 1426 and concern communities under the jurisdiction of the Chapter of Saint-Vincent located in the city of Soignies. The context of this source is different compared to the other fiscal data we have for Hainaut as it does not concern a regular ducal tax. In 1426 the inhabitants of the city of Soignies and the Chapter of Saint-Vincent incurred a heavy fine of 3000 gold *écus* as punishment for their support and allegiance to a political opponent of the Duke of Burgundy. The fine was to be divided between the individual members of the Chapter, the inhabitants of the city of Soignies and the rural population over which the Chapter exercised jurisdiction (Lejeune, 1869: 170). The original account listing all taxpayers, their tax quotes and place of residence was destroyed in 1940. However, we dispose of a near complete transcription of this document (Destrait, 1943). Whereas the fiscal data for the city of Soignies has been subject to analysis (see Van Uytven en Blockmans, 1971: 279-280), the tax lists for the rural communities have not been used in historical research to this date. The account contains the names of the tenants of the Chapter in the villages of Horrues, Chaussée-Notre-Dame, Cambron Saint-Vincent, Cambron Casteau, Mesvin and of Erbaut. For some villages – such as Horrues – large numbers of tenants were recorded whereas in other villages the number of tenants was limited. We restricted our analysis of the data to villages with a minimum of 10 tenants. As the lists for Mesvin and Erbaut do not meet this criterion, they have been omitted from further analysis.

The data available for analysis are presented in Table 9.1 (based on Destrait, 1943: 223-230). The largest group of tenants lived in the village of Horrues where 109 households were listed as being subjects of the Chapter of Saint-Vincent. A substantial proportion of the tenants (28 out 109), however, were recorded as being temporarily absent from the village. In most cases, they were residing in the nearby town of Enghien or in the neighbouring county of Flanders. A small number of tenants was also absent from Chaussée Notre-Dame. As the account suggests, these tenants emigrated temporarily from their villages to nearby cities as a reaction to the wartime situation that characterized this period. In addition to the absentee tenants in two villages, the tax list also mentions a number of people who were tax exempted. Two of them were clerics and were probably exempted based on their fiscal privileges. Three out of the 8 households that were exempted were headed by a widow. Probably, they were exempted based on social grounds as was the case with two inhabitants of Erbaut who were not taxed because they

Table 9.1. Number of households and taxpayers in rural settlements where the Chapter of Saint-Vincent held judicial power, 1424-1426

	Households 1424	Tenants of the Chapter of Saint-Vincent 1426			
		Taxed	Exempt	Absent	Total
Horrues	150	79	2	28	109
Chaussée-Notre-Dame	93	72	2	2	76
Cambron Saint-Vincent	90	47	2	0	49
Cambron-Casteau	64	10	2	0	12
Total	**397**	**208**	**8**	**30**	**246**

Sources: see text.

had nothing (‘*pourtant que il n'ont rien*’, quotation from Destrait, 1943: 230). Overall, however, the number of tenants that enjoyed such legal or economic exemption was limited (only 8 out 246).

In addition to the number of tenants, Table 9.1 also contains the results of the hearth census executed in 1424 (Arnould, 1956: 264-266). A comparison between the number of households in 1424 and the tax lists of 1426 reveals some discrepancies. In all villages the number of resident households was larger than the number of taxed households. This substantial difference, however, is to be expected. Hearth censuses report all households resident in a parish whereas these tax lists only records households living within the jurisdiction of the Chapter. Due to the fragmentation of seigniorial power, most parishes in this part of Hainaut counted multiple seigniories within their territories (Arnould, 1987). Therefore, the number of households residing within a parish will almost never overlap with the number of seigniorial tenants.

The exceptional character of this fiscal source makes it difficult to evaluate its content and reliability. First, we have no information on the object of taxation. We do not know if tenants were assessed on their wealth, income, rent, landholding or other indicators. The absence of any indication as to how assessors proceeded in establishing individual tax contributions is an issue. Second, the large number of absentee tenants in Horrues is problematic as approximately one-quarter of the tax base was not assessed and taxed. How tax assessors dealt with the tax quotes of these absentees is not clear (were these redistributed among the resident tenants or not?). In any case, the data from this source – for Horrues in particular – needs to be treated with caution.

The other fiscal data we have for Hainaut was produced in the context of regular state taxes. Within the county, taxes were divided between villages based on the number of households or hearths. Each community, therefore, contributed to the fiscal burden taking into account the size of its resident population. Unlike Flanders, which was characterized by a more fine-grained system of fiscal allocation, rural communities in Hainaut paid taxes in proportion to their demographic weight. To this end, hearth censuses were executed by the comital administration between the fourteenth and sixteenth centuries (see Arnould 1956 for the text edition and critical comments on these sources). Once the tax quote of each village was established, local officials drafted lists to collect the ducal taxes. As in neighbouring regions, the criteria and methodology adopted by local tax officials to distribute the tax burden was not made explicit. There is no written evidence of an uniform set of guidelines on how local tax officials had to proceed to assess the tax quote of each household. We only dispose of some general guidelines adopted throughout the county. One of these principles stated that the rich should support the poor (*'le fort portait le faible'*). The community as a whole was responsible for payment of the taxes (Arnould 1956: 79-80). The share of each household was determined by their respective *'faculté et richesses'*. This can be translated as their 'wealth' and 'ability' to contribute to taxes. Additionally, local officials based their individual assessments on the *'chevance'* or the economic resources of each household that enabled them to gain an income (Arnould, 1956: 137). As in other regions, rural tax officials probably based their assessments primarily on the income generated by various economic activities that accrued to the household (Arnould, 1940: 197). Wealth and the ability to contribute to taxes was probably used as a secondary criterion (for Flanders see Zoete 1994: 57-66). As in other parts of the Low Countries, the direct taxes raised in the countryside of Hainaut were probably based on an assessment that closely approximated household income (Hanus 2014: 306).

One of the characteristics of the Hainaut tax system was inclusiveness. The vast majority of the population was taxed and few enjoyed exemption. This becomes apparent when we compare the number of households recorded in hearth censuses with the number of taxpayers recorded in fiscal sources. In 1469, for example, the hearth census ordered by the Duke of Burgundy recorded 182 resident households in the village of Hoves (Arnould, 1956: 258). The tax lists from 1465-1466 and 1470 are containing 187 and 198 taxpayers respectively (Arnould, 1940: 209-210). In other words, probably all households were taxed during the fifteenth century in Hoves. This fiscal inclusiveness is also confirmed when we look at the individual contributions of taxpayers. In 1465, for example, some 23 per cent of the taxpayers paid less than the value of a daily wage. Taxpayers assessed at the bottom of the fiscal distribution contributed in some cases no more than the value of a couple of hours of work. The low threshold to enter the tax lists and the close overlap with data from the hearth census suggests that everybody who was able to contribute anything to taxes was included in the lists. Rural communities such as Hoves clearly maximized their efforts to extend the tax base down the social scale. A similar pattern was established for rural settlements in the Campine region of the Duchy of Brabant. Here too there was a close overlap between the number of households recorded in hearth censuses and the number of taxable households (Van Onacker, 2017: 74-75). This situation stands in stark contrast to some other regions on the Low Countries. In parts of the county of Flanders, for example, a significant part of the population was excluded from taxation due to their poverty or legal-fiscal privileges. In some cases, up to half of the resident households were excluded from taxation on these grounds (Zoete, 1994: 200). In the Guelders area too, 40 to 50 per cent of the rural population did not contribute anything to taxes (Van Schaïk, 1987: 235).

Having established that tax lists in Hainaut probably cover the entire resident population, we can also check to what extent the tax lists capture the diversity in income variation. This can be achieved by comparing the number of taxpayers with the number of fiscal categories in which they were assessed. In 1470 for example, 198 taxpayers were assessed in 31 fiscal categories in Hoves. Out of these 198 taxpayers, 23 were assessed at 2 shillings (Arnould 1940: 210). As they were assessed at the same tax rate, this suggests that these 23 households in Hoves enjoyed a similar income. We may safely assume that actual variation in income was greater than the number of fiscal categories suggests. Therefore, a tax system that was characterized by a high ratio between the number of taxpayers and the number of fiscal categories was better suited to capture income differences between households. A high number of categories relative to the number of taxpayers generally points towards a more fine-grained fiscal technology. For the county of Flanders, for example, most communities used 20 to 25 categories in the fifteenth century. In large communities the ratio between taxpayers and tax categories was in most cases lower than in small settlements due to the workload in drafting tax lists (Lambrecht and Ryckbosch, 2020). The data for Hoves indicate that the situation was largely comparable to Flanders. Overall, the ratio was low (see Table 9.2). However, taking into account the high number of taxpayers, the ratio is comparable with that of Flemish communities. This suggests that the tax assessors in Hoves made some effort to construct a fiscal distribution that captured the income distribution. Moreover, the tax system in Hoves became more fine-grained over time. In 1517, on average 5 inhabitants were assessed in the same fiscal category compared to 8 in 1465.

As in the other principalities of the Burgundian Netherlands state taxation increased in course of the fifteenth century. During the second half of the fifteenth century ducal taxes were collected in Hainaut on an almost annual basis. In addition to the increased frequency, state taxes also tended to increase relative to the income of the population. This trend can be reconstructed in some detail from some (rare) village accounts (Arnould, 1962). Boussoit-sur-Haine was a small rural settlement located to the east of Mons with a population ranging between 25 and 30 households in the middle of the fifteenth century. During the first half of the sixteenth century population rose to 35-45 households (Arnould, 1962: 89). As in a number of other villages in this region, communal lands (pasture) were commercialized and leased to the highest bidder. The proceeds of the commercial rent of the village commons were used – among others – to redeem the ducal fiscal duties of the settlement. As the accounts are containing information on both ducal

Table 9.2. Fiscal categories and taxable households in Hoves, 1465-1517

	Tax categories (n)	Taxpayers (n)	Ratio
1465	23	187	0.12
1470	31	198	0.16
1504	25	192	0.13
1508	30	205	0.15
1514	35	186	0.19
1517	37	189	0.20

Sources: calculated from Arnould 1940.

taxes and the evolution of land rent, the accounts can be used to shed light on the evolution of the weight of state taxation between the 1440's and 1530's. Using the data published by Arnould we have constructed a tax/rent ratio by comparing the payment of taxes levied by the community to the commercial rents received for the village commons (See Figure 9.1).

Because not all accounts have been preserved the picture is incomplete. However, we have a sufficient number of years for which data are available to inform us about the trend of state taxation. During the 1440's and 1450's state taxation was relatively low. This changed during the last quarter of the fifteenth century when growing political tension and conflict resulted in warfare and higher taxes. The data presented in Figure 9.1 clearly show that surplus extraction increased during the first decades of the sixteenth century. If the evolution of short term leases can serve as a crude indicator of the overall trend of rural income in this region, the sixteenth century marked a clear break with the late medieval period in terms of the level of fiscal surplus extraction. Relative to the commercial rent of pasture land, state taxation increased almost fourfold between the 1450's and the 1530's. The growth in fiscal surplus extraction from the late fifteenth century onwards resulted in growing social tensions in this region. During the late fifteenth century, cities such as Ath, had to resort to loans to fund the growing fiscal demands of the state. The city was divided on how these loans should be repaid. The leading political class of wealthy rentiers were in favour of indirect excise taxes on popular foods and beverages, whereas the merchants and artisans preferred a wealth tax. This conflict lasted a number of years and the central authorities had to intervene to restore order in the city (Dugnoille, 2000). As in other cities of the Low Countries, this period witnessed growing concerns about the division and allocation of taxes and their effects on different social groups (Blondé, Hanus and Ryckbosch, 2018). For the countryside, such social conflicts have not been documented. The absence of such open conflicts between social groups about the allocation of fiscal burdens in rural settlements could indicate that rural dwellers perceived the direct tax system that operated within their communities as just and equitable. One of the factors that

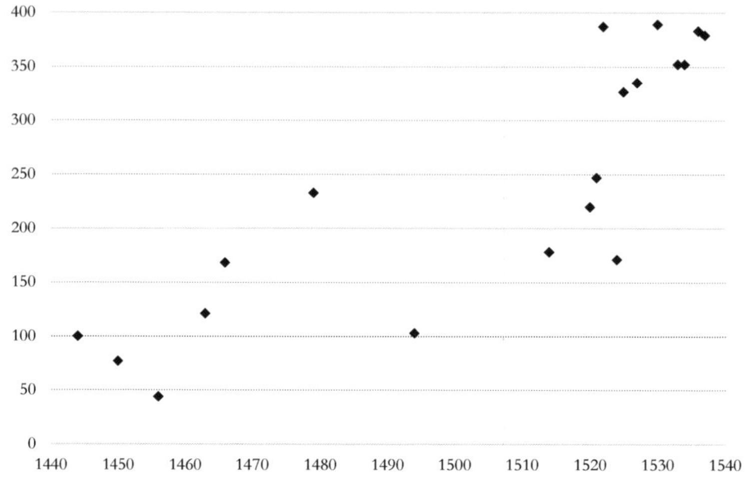

Figure 9.1. Tax/rent ratio in Boussoit-sur-Haine, 1444-1537 (1444 = index 100)

Sources: calculated from Arnould 1962.

could have contributed to this general acceptance of the fiscal methodology adopted by rural communities is the fact that there was a broad consensus within the community about direct taxation. The accounts of Hoves inform us that a large number of residents from different social groups were involved in drafting the tax lists (Arnould, 1941: 232).

II. Inequality in Hainaut

Having established that the ducal fiscal documentation available for Hainaut does not suffer from serious flaws, we can use these sources to reconstruct some aspects of economic inequality. Inspired by other research on inequality, the number of inequality measures and statistics has been limited to four (see Table 9.3). In addition to the widely used Gini coefficient, the share of the top 10 and bottom 50 per cent of the distribution have also been included. Finally, I also calculated the ratio between the third quartile (Q3) and first quartile (Q1) of the distribution. This Q3/Q1 ratio is a useful addition to the statistical toolkit because it informs us about variation within the fiscal middling groups. Low Q3/Q1 ratios are indicating that fiscal middling groups were fairly homogenous whereas high Q3/Q1 rations are suggesting substantial differences (Blondé, 2004: 52-53).

A glance at the Gini coefficients indicates that there were substantial differences in inequality levels within this group of rural settlements. Gini coefficients range between a low 0.28 in Kain to a high 0.77 in Horrues during the fifteenth century. In general, the highest levels of inequality can

Table 9.3. Inequality statistics for rural communities in Hainaut, 1426-1513

	Year	Gini	Top 10%	Bottom 50%	Q3/Q1	N
Horrues	1426	77,9	68,9	6,1	6	79
Chaussée Notre-Dame	1426	66,3	51.2	8.9	6.7	72
Cambron[1]	1426	69,4	56.1	8.6	5	57
Hoves	1465	43.4	28.9	20.4	3	187
Hoves	1470	52.4	34.7	14.4	4	197
Hoves	1504	52.9	37.9	14.9	5	191
Hoves	1508	51.8	36.4	15.8	4	205
Hoves	1514	56.2	42.7	14.3	3.6	186
Hoves	1517	59.8	42.7	11.9	5	189
Kain	1495	28.1	19.3	28.6	1.8	42

Sources: own calculations from Destrait 1943 (Horrues, Chaussé-Notre-Dame, Cambron), Arnould 1940 (Hoves) and Arnould 1941 (Kain).

be observed in the villages under the jurisdiction of the Chapter of Soignies in 1426. In all settlements, the top 10 per cent of the population held more than half of the wealth/income of their communities. At the bottom of the distribution we also observe some similarities: the bottom 50 per cent of the population held between 6 and 9 per cent of the wealth/income. Such high levels of inequality have also been recorded for the city of Soignies. Based on the tax data from 1426, Soignies was one of the most unequal late medieval urban settlements within the Low Countries (Van Uytven and Blockmans 1971: 279-280). Both city and countryside in this region of Hainaut, therefore, seem to have been characterized by high levels of economic inequality. These results, however, are surprising in light of recent international and national research on inequality. Hainaut was struck hard by the Black Death and the recurrent outbreaks of plague during the second half of the fourteenth century and early fifteenth century resulted in a substantial population decline (Sivery, 1965) As research for northern Italy has shown, the decades following the Black Death were characterized by declining inequality compared to the first half of the fourteenth century. In general, economic inequality tended to decline in the aftermath of the Black Death (Alfani and Ammannati 2017). The high level of economic inequality observed in these Hainaut villages – with Gini coefficients ranging between 0.66 and 0.77 – seems to contradict this trend.

1 In this table the fiscal data for the neighbouring villages of Cambron Saint-Vincent and Cambron Casteau has been grouped.

Second, inequality levels were also high compared to neighbouring regions. Indeed, such high inequality levels have not been record elsewhere in the Low Countries during this period. For example, evidence for the county of Flanders from the first quarter of the fifteenth century indicates that Gini coefficients ranged between circa 0.35 and 0.60. Only one Flemish rural community approached the skewed distribution of income as recorded in these Hainaut villages, but only at a much later stage (Lambrecht and Ryckbosch, 2020). The 1426 tax data probably suffers from a number of defects as it does not reflect the distribution of economic resources of the taxable population in a realistic way. Possibly, the tax assessors adopted a progressive scale when allocating the tax burden. A progressive tax scale, in which richer households paid more relative to their taxable assets than poorer sections of the community, could explain these high levels of inequality.

At the other end of the spectrum the village of Kain catches attention due to the low level of economic inequality recorded there. All inequality statistics point to a relatively egalitarian society and community. Unfortunately, we have no other data for this village that would enable us to reconstruct inequality during other periods. In any case, a comparison with data for the county of Flanders indicates that Kain was characterized by exceptionally low levels of inequality. Not a single Flemish rural settlement records Gini coefficients below 0.30 during the fifteenth century. All these Flemish settlements with low inequality were characterized by a specific set of local economic institutions that prevented the accumulation and concentration of economic assets (Lambrecht and Ryckbosch, 2020). Possibly this was also the case in Kain but in the absence of more detailed information about the distribution of economic resources (such as land) it is not possible to explain and contextualize this low economic inequality.

Hoves, for which we have a series of observations between 1465 and 1517, is better documented. Hoves was medium-sized rural settlement situated in the north-eastern part of the county. It was part of the district (*'bailliage'*) of Enghien which closely bordered the Duchy of Brabant and the County of Flanders. Demographic data indicate that the district of Enghien belonged to the economically most advanced regions within the county of Hainaut. As the data from the hearth censuses indicates, the region of Enghien was one of the most densely populated regions during the late middle ages. In 1444 the county of Hainaut registered on average 5.85 households per km^2. At that time, the district of Enghien registered almost twice as many households per km^2 (10,28). This leading demographic position within the county was maintained throughout the sixteenth century. Between 1444 and 1541 the district of Enghien recorded household densities that were consistently 30 to 45 per cent above the county average (Arnould, 1956: 298). Hoves consisted of different hamlets, each dominated by a large farm that once constituted the exploitation centre of a seigniorial demesne. These large farms were surrounded by a sea of mall peasant holdings that combined small-scale agricultural production with income from wage labour and rural industries (Arnould, 1940). The byelaws from 1416 contain additional information on economic activities in this village. There is a reference to communal land (*'warescaux'*) in the byelaws, but the exact extent and use of these communal lands remains unknown. As elsewhere in this region, these communal lands probably consisted of small patches of pasture. Importantly, there are also a number of references in the bylaws that hint at the local production of flax and the commercial production of linen (Verriest, 1946: 90-95). During the late middle ages Hoves was listed as one of the villages that supplied linen to the urban markets of Mons and Lessines (Sabbe, 1975: 99-100). Linen weaving thrived in this part of Hainaut during the second half of the fourteenth and fifteenth centuries and supplied a substantial part of the rural population with additional income. During the first decades of the sixteenth century, however, employment opportunities in this economic sector dwindled as the centre of proto-industrial linen production shifted to the rural villages of Flanders (Sabbe, 1975: 180-182). Occupational data from 1560 indicate that some 25 per cent of the households were still active in rural textile production in Hoves. In the region of Enghien in particular, rural households were active in the production of linen and tapestries (Arnould, 1985: 204-207). Economic structures and activities in the district of Enghien, therefore, closely resembled those found in the neighbouring southern part of the county of Flanders. As in inland Flanders, most rural households in the region of Enghien can be classified as peasants that combined small-scale subsistence farming with proto-industrial textile work and occasional agricultural wage labour. The economic elites of these communities consisted of commercial farmers that leased their land from urban dwellers and ecclesiastical institutions (see Thoen, 2001 and Thoen, 2004).

From the rich fiscal data available for Hoves we can calculate inequality statistics at six intervals. Overall, there was a tendency of rising economic inequality. In 1465 the Gini coefficient stood at 0.43. Half a century later the coefficient had risen to 0.59. The rise of inequality as reflected in the fiscal data on income was unequal over time. Economic inequality increased between 1465 and 1470 but then remained stable until circa 1510. During the 1510's inequality would increase again. A more detailed picture of changes in the distribution of rural taxable income in Hoves can be obtained from the division in deciles (see Table 9.4). The total number of taxpayers was divided into ten equal parts with every decile (D) containing 10 per cent of the taxable population. The lowest decile (D1) contains the poorest part of the population whereas the highest decile (D10) represents the richest 10 per cent.

As can be seen from the data in Table 9.4, the vast majority of the population in Hoves experienced a relative income decline between 1465 and 1517. Only the richest 20 per cent of the population was able to increase their relative income position. The rise of inequality in Hoves, therefore, was mainly the result of the elites getting richer. A small group of rural elite households experienced a substantial improvement of their relative position. The top 10 per cent of the households in Hoves witnessed an increase in their relative income of almost 50 per cent in the course of half a century (from 28,98 to 42,69 per

Table 9.4. Distribution of taxable income in Hoves, 1465-1470 (%)

	1465	1470	1504	1508	1514	1517
D1	1,75	0,91	1,53	1,80	1,47	0,87
D2	3,07	1,82	2,37	2,41	2,12	1,59
D3	4,36	2,62	2,59	3,13	3,00	2,19
D4	4,85	3,90	3,62	3,98	3,56	3,11
D5	6,69	5,44	4,87	5,07	4,59	4,19
D6	8,41	7,60	6,50	6,30	5,47	5,63
D7	10,44	10,37	8,68	8,38	7,47	7,78
D8	13,63	13,14	12,99	12,17	11,03	11,56
D9	17,81	19,51	18,86	20,41	18,62	20,38
D10	28,98	34,70	37,98	36,36	42,67	42,69
Total	100,00	100,00	100,00	100,00	100,00	100,00

Sources: calculated from Arnould 1940. D = decile.

cent). This clearly suggests that a small group of wealthy households was able to navigate successfully through the crisis years of the late fifteenth century and also succeeded in claiming a larger part of the rural income afterwards. The picture that emerges in Hoves is one of relative stability during the last quarter of the fifteenth and first decade of the sixteenth century followed by an upswing afterwards.

The period covered by the fiscal data encompasses the civil wars of the late fifteenth century following the death of Charles the Bold in 1477 and the subsequent struggle for power in the Burgundian Low Countries. This period resulted in a severe economic crisis characterized by high taxation, military destruction, harvest failure and rural emigration (for details on this period see Sivéry, 1980: 539-567). As has been shown for the neighbouring region of Flanders, the effect of the civil war and revolt against Maximilian of Austria was a restructuring of access to land. In contrast to medium-sized and small farms, large tenant farmers were better equipped to cope with the effects of short-term economic crisis. Their stronger position even allowed them to extend their landholding within their communities at the expense of medium-sized and small peasant holdings (Thoen, 1981). Large farmers were better equipped to deal with the adverse economic conditions of the 1480's and 1490's because they had access to capital. For other social groups, economic crisis as a result of warfare resulted in higher levels of indebtedness. This was also the case in Hainaut during the 1480's. In 1484 legal measures were taken to protect impoverished and indebted peasantries against the high fees that were associated with legal procedures to reclaim debts. According to the ordinance of 1484, many peasants had accumulated arrears in the (re) payment of their leases and loans and were subsequently threatened by the forced sale of their land and movables at the request of their creditors. The high fees demanded by legal practitioners to reclaim debts increased the financial burden of the peasants even more. In addition to capping legal fees, the ordinance also offered peasantries some protection against foreclosure. Creditors, for example, could not confiscate and sell the animals and tools that peasantries required to execute their work (Faider, 1871: 229-237). These measures indicate that during the 1480's and 1490's large numbers of peasantries were faced with high levels of indebtedness that threatened the survival of their holding. The difficulties experienced by peasantries to hold on to their land during this period are also reflected in the distribution of feudal properties (fiefs). Between 1474 and 1502 the elites of Hainaut were able to extend their feudal properties at the expense of peasantries. Landowners with large capital reserves – in most cases noble families – were able to acquire the indebted properties of small fief holders (Koenigsberger, 1956: 7-9). Changes in the distribution of land within Hoves, therefore, could be one of the factors that accounted for the rise in economic inequality during this period. In such a scenario, village elites – and large tenants in particular – were able to extend their landholdings at the direct expense of medium-sized and small holdings.

A second possible explanation for changes in economic inequality focuses on the evolution of factor prices and factor shares. This explanation considers the prices of different factors of production and not their distribution. In a rural context the evolution of land rent and wages can serve as a reliable proxy for the production factors land and labour. To this end I have reconstructed a rent/wage ratio for Hainaut based on the rental price of pasture land in Boussoit and the wages of an unskilled worker in the construction industries (for land prices see Arnould, 1962; for wages see Delatte, 1938: 114 and Sivéry, 1980: 561). As can be seen from Figure 9.2 changes in the distribution of rural income are also reflected in the evolution of factor prices. During the middle of the fifteenth century income from land and labour moved in tandem during a couple of decades. Before 1480 no substantial changes can be observed in the rent/wage ratio. This suggests that factor shares remained more or less stable during a large part of the fifteenth century. Both those making a living from land (either as owners and/or tenants) and labour did not experience a profound shift in their relative social and economic position as reflected in factor prices. The early sixteenth century, on the other hand, marked a fundamental break with the late medieval period. Factor shares changed profoundly as illustrated by the rapid rise of the rent/wage ratio. Wages remained more or less stable during this period whereas returns from land (as reflected in commercial rent) rose rapidly. This suggests that rural income from land that accrued to land owners and their tenants rose faster than earnings from rural wage labour. The available data are indicating that this region did not experience any profound labour shortages as nominal wage rates remained stationary throughout the late fifteenth and early sixteenth centuries. Although the population in the district of Enghien dropped by almost a third between 1479 and 1501 (from 2103 to 1427 households, see Arnould, 1956: 297) this decrease of the labour supply did not translate into

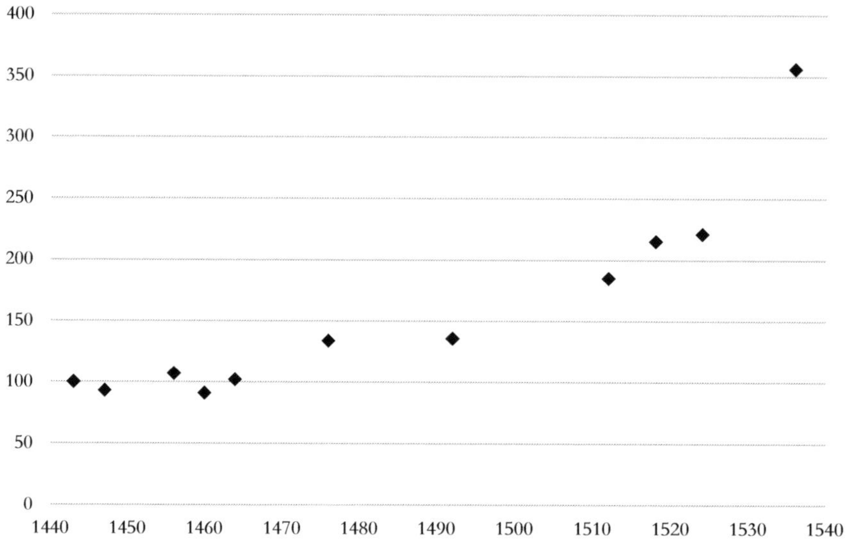

Figure 9.2. The land rent to wage ratio in Hainaut, 1443-1536 (1443 = 100)

Sources: see text.

an improved bargaining position for rural labourers. Commercial land rent, on the other hand, continued to rise during the first decades of the sixteenth century illustrating the swift recovery and subsequent growth of the agrarian economy of the Low Countries.

In addition to the relative deterioration of the production factor labour, there are also strong indications that a substantial part of the rural population gradually sunk into poverty during the first decades of the sixteenth century. There are some clear signs of growing pressure on poor relief resources during this period. For example, the small city of Enghien was one of the first urban settlements to restructure the management and distribution of poor relief in the Southern Low Countries (see Delannoy, 1975: 9-16). As in a number of other cities – Lille, Valenciennes and Ypres – city magistrates strengthened their grip and control over poor relief during the late 1520's and early 1530's. This process entailed the introduction of well-circumscribed definitions of the deserving poor, the prohibition of begging and the centralization of poor relief resources (van Nederveen Meerkerk and Vermeersch, 2009). This pattern can also be encountered in the measures adopted by the magistrates of Enghien in 1528. Significantly, part of these reforms were clearly inspired by growing pressure on poor relief resources resulting from the immigration of poor rural households. The reform programme of 1528 stipulated that newcomers to the city had to wait a minimum of two years before they were eligible for poor relief. Also, house owners in Enghien were not allowed to lease dwellings to poor immigrants (Delannoy, 1975: 13). The growing poverty in the countryside is also reflected in the hearth censuses of Hainaut. In 17 villages from the district of Enghien circa 31 per cent of the population (631 out of 2038 households) was classified as to poor to contribute anything to taxes in 1531 (calculated from Arnould, 1956: 258-260).

The growth of a rural proletariat in this region seems to indicate that the rise of economic inequality was the result of changes in the distribution of economic assets. In this section I have explored the hypothesis that the late fifteenth century witnessed a restructuring of access to land that favoured a small group of large tenant farmers. They were able to extend their farms by incorporating land that was abandoned by other social groups that were not able to successfully navigate this economic crisis. Such a process of land concentration can clearly also be witnessed in the case of feudal properties. Those with access to capital during the crisis years of the late fifteenth century were able to strengthen their position. Large farmers could not only extend their landholdings within their communities, but also profited from cheap labour. Indeed, as the rent/wage ratio indicates labour costs declined relative to the income generated by land during this period. These changes in both the distribution of land and factor prices benefited large tenant farmers who depended on wage labour. As shown for other regions, this crisis caused inequality to rise. Interestingly, rural elites were able to strengthen their economic position in a context of rising state taxation. Admittedly, this explanation of rising economic inequality in Hoves constitutes a working hypothesis at this stage. More research is required to test some of the hypotheses advanced in this section. In any case, the available data for Hainaut are indicating that – as in other parts of Europe – economic inequality was rising during the transition from medieval to early modern times.

III. Inequality in context

The last section of this chapter confronts the data on economic inequality in Hainaut –and in Hoves in particular – with identical data from other regions within the Low Countries. In particular, this section will compare inequality statistics of rural settlements in Flanders and Brabant during the fifteenth century. As a recent paper has illustrated, substantial differences in economic inequality can be encountered at the local and regional level. A quantitative analysis of fifteenth-century fiscal sources for rural settlements in the county of Flanders shows that Gini coefficients oscillated between a low 0.30 and a high 0.70. Even within a fairly limited geographical range, substantial differences could be encountered (Lambrecht and Ryckbosch, 2020).

In recent years, economic historians have focused on longitudinal reconstructions of economic inequality over the long-term in particular. Although such an approach is extremely valuable for the debate on the origins and drivers of economic inequality, a national or regional approach may hide from view the factors that shaped inequality at the local level. Why some communities were more equal than others was in many cases determined by local circumstances that have an impact on the distribution of economic resources. A cross-sectional analysis has the potential to expose and identify those factors that shaped local inequality. As shown in the analysis of Flemish fiscal data, local differences in economic inequality were clearly related to local economic structures. Although it is sometimes difficult to uncover these local determinants of high, medium or low inequality, such a comparative approach at the local level can expose some structural determinants of rural inequality. In the county of Flanders, for example, rural settlements with low inequality were characterized by a specific set of economic institutions that prevented the accumulation and monopolization of factors of production (see Lambrecht and Ryckbosch, 2020 for examples).

To contextualize the data for Hainaut I will compare the data for Hoves from 1465 with similar data for the village of Rijkevorsel and the rural district of Aardenburg (for Rijkevorsel (1464) see Van Onacker, 2017: 71; for the district of Aardenburg (1475) raw data was obtained from Zoete, 1990: appendix). Each of these settlements has been chosen because they represent a particular model of rural economic structures (Thoen, 2001). As has been argued above, the village of Hoves can be characterized as a typical peasant society. The vast majority of the population eked out a living from combining small-scale subsistence agriculture with proto-industrial linen production and occasional day labouring on the holdings of large tenants. Rijkevorsel, situated in the Campine are of the Duchy of Brabant, represents the communal model. Village communities in this region were characterized by extensive common lands. In many of the villages in this region, the vast majority of the land was held in common (De Keyzer, 2018: 36). All members of the community had access to the commons which were mainly used to pasture livestock. The majority of the population consisted of landowning peasants engaged in mixed farming. Income from mixed farming was supplemented with commercial sheep breeding and the sale of raw wool. In addition to this dominant group of independent peasantries, Campine communities also counted a number of large tenants among their ranks (Van Onacker, 2017: chapter 4 & 5). Lastly, the district of Aardenburg was selected to represent the commercial regions of the Low Countries. Aardenburg was situated in the coastal region of Flanders and was characterized by heavy clay soil. As many other villages in that area, the district of Aardenburg experienced a long-term transition from a peasant society to agrarian capitalism. Owner-occupied farms gradually disappeared and were replaced by larger leasehold farms. What we observe then is a region in transition characterized by a growing concentration of land into the hands of large tenants. By the end of the sixteenth century these large tenant farms would become the dominant political, social and economic force of these coastal communities. These large farms typically specialized in commercial cattle breeding and relied heavily on living-in servants. The number of labourers in these villages was low as employment opportunities for casual day labouring were limited (see Soens 2009; Thoen and Soens,

2015). The three villages display substantial differences in terms of property structure, farm size, economic activity and social structure. Therefore, we would expect that these different social and economic characteristics are also reflected in inequality statistics.

What do the statistical measures teach us about economic inequality in these three rural model villages? The lowest level of economic inequality was recorded in Hoves with a Gini index of 0.43 (see Table 9.3). Rijkevorsel recorded the highest level of inequality with an index of 0.60 (Van Onacker, 2017: 71). Aardenburg is situated between Hoves and Rijkevorsel with an index of 0.51 (Lambrecht and Ryckbosch, 2020: in press). Somewhat counterintuitively, the highest levels of inequality are encountered in the communal model. More details about the distribution of income can be obtained from Figures 9.3 and 9.4 where the fiscal data is presented in deciles. Figure 9.3 clearly shows that high levels of economic inequality in Rijkevorsel were the result of the share of the top 10 per cent of the population. In 1464, they claimed some 46 per cent of the taxable income (Van Onacker, 2017: 71). In both Aardenburg and Hoves the share of the top 10 per cent was markedly lower with 36.9 and 28.9 per cent respectively. The differences between these villages are particularly marked when looking at the share of the top ten per cent. In the ninth decile, for example, there are hardly substantial differences between the three villages. There are also some noteworthy differences at the bottom part of the distribution. In Rijkevorsel, the bottom 50 per cent of the households held only 8.7 per cent of the income (Van Onacker, 2017: 71). With 16.1 per cent, the share of the bottom 50 per cent in Aardenburg was twice as large compared to Rijkevorsel (see Figure 9.4). Comparatively, the bottom 50 per cent of the households in Hoves held most of the income with circa 21 per cent. Both at the top and bottom of the income distribution, therefore, some considerable differences can be observed. Finally, we can also look at the Q3/Q1 ratio to gain more insight into the position of the middling groups. Again, Rijkevorsel records the highest values with a Q3/Q1 ratio of 8 in 1464 (Van Onacker, 2017: 71). Hoves and Aardenburg record an identical Q3/Q1 ratio of 4. This indicates that middling groups (those dispersed around 50 per cent of the median) were far less homogenous in Rijkevorsel compared to Hoves and Graty. Based on late medieval fiscal data, we could conclude that the Campine economy produced rather unequal villages where a small elite managed to claim a large part of the rural income. Also, the comparatively high Q3/Q1 ratio indicates that the middling groups were far from homogenous. Finally, the poorest sections of the population enjoyed a comparatively low share of the rural income. To some extent, this pattern can also be observed in commercial rural societies, albeit less pronounced. In commercial regions there was no distinct rural elite as in the Campine region. Probably, the lower level of elite income combined with the low Q3/Q1 can be taken as evidence of a typical yeoman society. The most equal income distribution was encountered in a peasant village. Each of the quantitative measures indicates that late medieval peasant

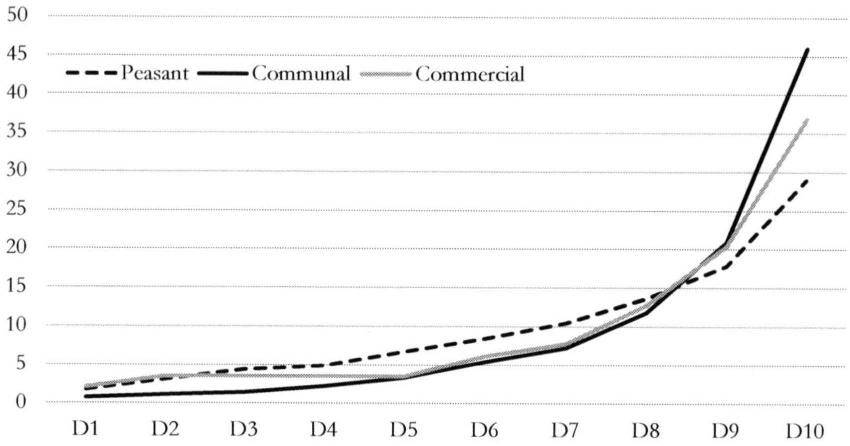

Figure 9.3. Distribution of taxable income in peasant (Hoves), commercial (Aardenburg) and communal (Rijkevorsel) rural settlements in the Low Countries, 1465-1475 (deciles)

Sources: see text.

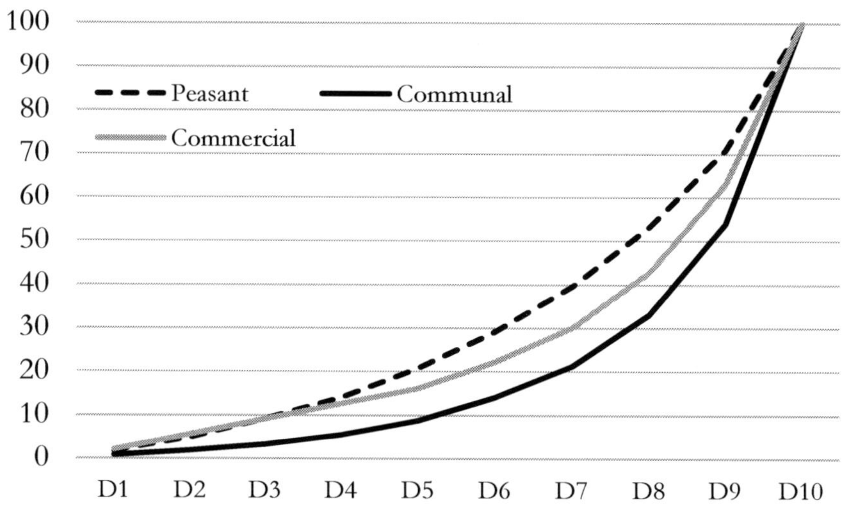

Figure 9.4. Distribution of taxable income in peasant (Hoves), commercial (Aardenburg) and communal (Rijkevorsel) rural settlements in the Low Countries, 1465-1475 (deciles cumulative)

Sources: see text.

communities produced the least unequal rural societies in this particular geographical and temporal context. Probably, the possibilities of peasants to combine agricultural activities with proto-industrial work strengthened their position in the income distribution and enabled them to close the income gap with large tenant farmers who relied predominantly on income generated by agricultural activities.

IV. Conclusion

In this chapter new evidence was presented on economic inequality in Hainaut during the fifteenth and sixteenth centuries. As in other regions of the Low Countries, the lack of sources impedes any long-term analysis of economic inequality. For rural societies in particular, there is a dearth of quantifiable long-term data on economic inequality (see also Yante, 2006). The available data, therefore, should be used and interpreted with caution as they only provide us with a snap-shot of economic inequality at random intervals. Based on the analysis of the Hainaut data, however, a number of tentative conclusions can be formulated. The data series for Hoves in particular suggest that this region in Hainaut followed a typical European trajectory in terms of economic inequality. From the fifteenth century onwards, economic inequality was rising in many parts of Europe (see Alfani 2020 for an overview of the available data and studies). Combined with the data for fifteenth and sixteenth-century coastal Flanders (Dombrecht and Ryckbosch, 2017), we can now safely conclude that the transition from medieval to early modern times was characterized by a deepening of economic inequality in the Low Countries. Importantly, this trend can be observed in different types of societies. The rise of inequality was geographically pervasive as in both town and countryside income distributions became more skewed (for urban settlements see Ryckbosch, 2016). Interestingly, different types of rural societies experienced the same tendencies. In both commercial and peasant regions inequality was rising during the late medieval period. As we have suggested, the late fifteenth-century wars and crisis that characterized the Burgundian Low Countries could have acted as a catalyst of rising inequality. While such a hypothesis makes sense in this particular local and regional context, the deepening of inequality throughout Europe in this period suggests that other factors were at play too. One of the important challenges of future research on economic inequality consists of identifying the common processes and mechanics that can account for this rising inequality throughout Europe. The comparative (albeit tentative) analysis of economic inequality in agrarian and rural regions within the Low Countries has revealed substantial differences. The analysis of fiscal data from the 1460's and 1470's indicates that there were indeed different geographies of inequality operating within the Low Countries. Somewhat unexpectedly, these patterns do not conform to our existing knowledge about the differences in social and economic organisation of these rural communities. Commercial rural societies were less unequal than expected whereas communal landholding did not translate into equality. Within a comparative perspective, the most equal rural societies in the late medieval Low Countries were those characterized by peasant agriculture. Admittedly, such findings require more research and further data analysis to expose and identify the forces that shaped economic inequality at the local level.

Bibliography

Alfani G. (2020), 'Economic inequality in preindustrial Europe, 1300-1800: methods and results from the EINITE project', *Economic inequality in pre-industrial societies: causes and effects.* Florence, in press.

Alfani G. and Ammannati F. (2017), 'Long-term trends in economic inequality: the case of the Florentine state, *c.* 1300-1800', *Economic History Review*, 70, pp. 1072-1102.

Alfani G. and Ryckbosch W. (2016), 'Growing apart in early modern Europe? A comparison of inequality trends in Italy and the Low Countries', *Explorations in Economic History*, 62, pp. 143-153.

Arnould, M.-A. (1940), 'Les cahiers de taille de Hoves-Graty (1465-1517). Les finances et la population d'un village hennuyer à l'aube des temps modernes', *Annales du Cercle Archéologique de Mons*, 57, pp. 185-238.

Arnould, M.-A. (1941), *Acquits ou documents justificatifs, rendues par le receveur des aides de Hainaut à l'appui de ses comptes (1496-1540)*, Brussels.

Arnould, M.-A (1956), *Les dénombrements de foyers dans le Comté de Hainaut (XIVe-XVIe siècle)*, Brussels.

Arnould, M.-A. (1962), 'L'incidence de l'impôt sur les finances d'un village à l'époque bourguignonne. Boissoit-sur-Haine, 1400-1555', *Contributions à l'histoire économique et sociale*, 1, pp. 41-105.

Arnould, M.-A. (1985), 'Les tapissiers champêtres de la région d'Enghien en 1560-1561. Contribution à l'histoire de l'industrie et de la société rurale', in: J.-L. Delattre et. al. eds, *La Belgique rurale du moyen âge à nos jours. Mélanges offerts à Jean-Jacques Hoebanx.* Brussels, pp. 195-214.

Arnould, M.-A. (1987), 'Les communautés rurales en Hainaut', in: *Les communautés rurales.* Paris, volume 5, pp. 281-315.

Blondé B. (2004), 'Bossche bouwvakkers en belastingen. Nadenken over economische groei, levensstandaard en sociale ongelijkheid in de zestiende eeuw', in B. Blondé, B. De Munck and F. Vermeylen eds, *Doodgewoon. Mensen en hun dagelijks leven in de geschiedenis. Liber amicorum Alfons K. L. Thijs.* Antwerp, pp. 45-62.

Blondé B., J. Hanus and W. Ryckbosch (2018), 'The predatory state? Urban finances, politics and social inequality in sixteenth-century 's-Hertogenbosch', in: B. Dewilde and J. Poukens eds, *Entrepreneurs, institutions and government intervention in Europe (13th-20th centuries). Essays in honour of Erik Aerts.* Brussels, pp. 101-115.

Delannoy Y. (1975), 'Ordonnances sur le faict des commungs povres de la ville d'Enghien, 23 octobre 1528', *Annales du Cercle Archéologique d'Enghien*, 17, pp. 2-16.

Delatte I. (1938), 'Prix et salaires en Hainaut au XVIe siècle', *Annales du Cercle Archéologique de Mons*, 55, pp. 97-114.

Destrait, L. (1943), 'La taille de 1426 dans la ville et terre de Soignies', *Annales du Cercle Archéologique de Soignies*, 9, pp. 212-231.

De Keyzer M. (2018). *Inclusive commons and the sustainability of peasant communities in the medieval Low Countries.* New York.

Dombrecht K. and Ryckbosch W. (2017), 'Wealth inequality in a time of transition: Coastal Flanders in the sixteenth century', *The Low Countries Journal of Social and Economic History*, 14, pp. 63-84.

Dugnoille, J. (2000), 'Fiscalité et tension sociale à Ath au tournant des XVe et XVIe siècles', in C. Billen, J.-M. Duvosquel & A. Vanrie eds, *Hainaut et Tournaisis. Regards sur dix siècles d'histoire.* Brussels, pp. 293-311.

Faider C. (1871), *Coutumes du pays et comté de Hainaut. Sources et origines de la charte générale de 1619.* Brussels.

Hanus J. (2014), *Affluence and inequality in the Low Countries. The city of 's-Hertogenbosch in the lang sixteenth century, 1500-1650.* Brussels.

Koenigsberger H. G. (1956), 'Property and the price revolution (Hainault, 1474-1573)', *Economic History Review*, 9, pp. 1-15.

Lambrecht, T. and Ryckbosch, W. (2020), 'Economic inequality in the rural Southern Low Countries during the fifteenth century: sources, data and reflections', in: *Economic inequality in pre-industrial societies: causes and effects.* Florence, in press.

Lejeune, T. (1869), *Histoire civile et ecclésiastique de la ville de Soignies.* Mons-Brussels.

Ryckbosch W. (2016), 'Economic inequality and growth before the industrial revolution: the case of the Low Countries (fourteenth to nineteenth Centuries)', *European Review of Economic History*, 20, pp. 1-22.

Sabbe, E. (1975), *De Belgische vlasnijverheid. Deel I: de Zuidnederlandse vlasnijverheid tot het Verdrag van Utrecht (1713).* Kortrijk.

Sivery, G. (1965), 'Le Hainaut et la Peste Noire', *Mémoires et Publications de la Société des Sciences, des Arts et des Lettres du Hainaut*, 79, pp. 431-447.

Sivery, G. (1977), *Structures agraires et vie rurale dans le Hainaut à la fin du moyen-âge.* Lille.

Soens T. (2009), *De spade in de dijk? Waterbeheer en rurale samenleving in de Vlaamse kustvlake (1280-1580).* Ghent.

Thoen, E. (1981), 'Warfare and the countryside: social and economic aspects of the military destruction in Flanders during the late middle ages and the early modern period', *Acta Historiae Neerlandicae*, 13, pp. 25-38.

Thoen E. (2001), 'A commercial survival economy in evolution. The Flemish countryside and the transition to capitalism (middle ages-19th century)', in: P. Hoppenbrouwers and J.-L. Van Zanden eds, *Peasants into farmers? The transformation of rural economy and society in the Low Countries (middle ages-19th century) in light of the Brenner debate.* Turnhout, pp. 102-158.

Thoen E. (2004), 'Social agrosystems' as an economic concept to explain regional differences. An essay taking the former county of Flanders as an example (Middle Ages-19th century)', in: B. J. P. van Bavel and P. Hoppenbrouwers, eds, *Landholding and land transfer in the North Sea Area (late Middle Ages – 19th century)*, Turnhout, pp. 47-66.

Thoen, E. and Soens T. (2015), 'The family or the farm: a Sophie's choice? The late medieval crisis in Flanders' in: J. Drendel ed., *Crisis in the Later Middle Ages. Beyond the Postan-Duby paradigm.* Turnhout, pp. 195-224.

van Nederveen E. and Vermeersch G. (2009), 'Reforming outdoor relief. Changes in urban provisions for the poor in the Northern and Southern Low Countries (*c.* 1500-1800)', in: M. van der Heijden, E. van Nederveen Meerkerk, G. Vermeersch and M. van der Burg eds, *Serving the urban community: the rise of public facilities in the Low Countries.* Amsterdam, pp. 135-154.

Van Onacker, E. (2017), *Village elites and social structures in the late medieval Campine region.* Turnhout.

Van Schaïk, R. (1987), *Belasting, bevolking en bezit in Gelre en Zutphen (1350-1550).* Hilversum.

Van Uytven R. and W. Blockmans (1971), 'De noodzaak van een geïntegreerde sociale geschiedenis', *Tijdschrift voor Geschiedenis*, 84, pp. 276-290.

Verriest, L. (1946), *Corpus des records de coutumes et des chefs-lieux de l'ancien Comté de Hainaut.* Mons.

Yante, J.-M (2006), 'Estimation et enregistrement des capacités individuelles dans les Pays-Bas méridionaux. À propos de documents des XIIIe-XVe siècles', in: A. Rigaudière ed., *De l'estime au cadastre en Europe: le Moyen Âge.* Paris, pp. 363-381.

Zoete A. (1990), *Organisatie en betekenis van de beden in het graafschap Vlaanderen onder de hertogen Jan zonder Vrees en Filips de Goede, 1405-1467.* Ghent, unpublished PhD.

Zoete A. (1994), *De beden in het graafschap Vlaanderen onder de hertogen Jan zonder Vrees en Filips de Goede (1405-1467).* Brussels.